Anastasia Krupnik

Anastasia Again

Anastasia At Your Service

Three favourite stories about the crackle-brained, fizzle-headed, freckle-faced dynamo who thinks for herself!

The Anastasia *Series*

Anastasia Krupnik
Anastasia Again!
Anastasia at your Service
Anastasia ask your Analyst
Anastasia on her Own
Anastasia has the Answers
Anastasia's Chosen Career
Anastasia at this Address

Lois Lowry

Anastasia Krupnik

Anastasia Again!

Anastasia
At Your Service

Lions
An Imprint of Harper Collins*Publishers*

Anastasia Krupnik, Anastasia Again,
Anastasia At Your Service first published in the USA by
Houghton Mifflin Co. 1979, 1981, 1982

First published in one volume in Lions 1993
3 5 7 9 8 6 4 2

Lions is an imprint of HarperCollins Children's Books,
a division of HarperCollins Publishers Ltd,
77–85 Fulham Palace Road,
Hammersmith, London W6 8JB

Printed and bound in Great Britain by
HarperCollins Manufacturing, Glasgow

Contents

Anastasia Krupnik

For Kip

1

Anastasia Krupnik was ten. She had hair the colour of straw, fourteen freckles across her nose (and seven others in places that she preferred people not to know about), and glasses with large owl-eyed rims, which she had chosen herself at the optician's.

Once she had thought that she might like to be a professional ice skater. But after two years of trying, she still skated on the insides of her ankles.

Once she had thought that she might like to be a ballerina, but after a year of Saturday morning ballet lessons, she still couldn't get the fifth position exactly right.

Her parents said, very kindly, that perhaps she should choose a profession that didn't involve her feet. She thought that probably they were right, and she was still trying to think of one.

Anastasia had a small pink wart in the middle of her left thumb. She found her wart very pleasing. It had appeared quite by surprise, shortly after her tenth birthday, on a morning when nothing else interesting was happening, and it was the first wart she had ever had, or even seen.

"It's the loveliest colour I've ever seen in a wart," her mother, who had seen others, said with admiration.

"Warts, you know," her father had told her, "have a kind of magic to them. They come and go without any reason at all, rather like elves."

Anastasia's father, Dr Myron Krupnik, was a professor of literature and had read just about every book in the world, which may have been why he knew so much about warts. He had a beard the colour of straw, though not much hair on his head, and he wore glasses for astigmatism, as Anastasia did, although his were not quite as owly. He was also a poet. Sometimes he read his poems to Anastasia by candlelight, and let her take an occasional (very small) sip of his wine.

Katherine Krupnik, her mother, was a painter. Very often there was a smudge of purple on her cheek, or a daub of green on one wrist or elbow. Sometimes she smelled of turpentine, which painters use; sometimes she smelled of vanilla and brown sugar, which mothers use; and sometimes, not very often, she smelled of *Je Reviens* perfume.

In the bookcases of their flat were four volumes of poetry which had been written by Myron Krupnik. The first one was called *Laughter Behind the Mask*, and on the back of the book was a photograph of Myron Krupnik, much younger, when he had a lot of hair, holding his glasses in one hand and half smiling as if he knew a secret. Anastasia's father hated that book, or said that he did. Anastasia sometimes wondered why he kept it in the bookcase if he hated it so much. She thought it must be a little like the feeling she had had when she was eight, when she hated a boy named Michael McGuire so much that she walked past his house every day, just to stick out her tongue.

The second book of poetry by her father had a photograph of him with slightly less hair and a moustache; it was called *Mystery of Myth*. Her father liked it. But her mother didn't like it at all. The reason her mother didn't like it at all was because on one of the inside front pages it said, "For Annie". Anastasia didn't know who Annie was. She suspected that her mother did.

The third book was her mother's favourite, probably because *it* said, inside, "For Katherine". It was called *Come Morning, Come Night* and was filled with love poems that Anastasia found very embarrassing.

But the fourth book was her favourite. Her father's photograph showed him bald and bearded, the way she had always known him. The poems were soft sounding and quiet, when he read them to her. The book was called *Bittersweet*; and it said, inside, "To someone special: Anastasia".

Sometimes, when no one was in the room, Anastasia took *Bittersweet* down from the shelf, just to look at that page. Looking at it made her feel awed, unique, and proud.

Awed, unique, and *proud* were three words that she had written on page seven of her green notebook. She kept lists of her favourite words; she kept important private information; and she kept things that she thought might be the beginnings of poems, in her green notebook. No one had ever looked inside the green notebook except Anastasia.

On page one, the green notebook said, "My name is Anastasia Krupnik. This is the year that I am ten".

On page two, it said, "These are the most important things that happened the year that I was ten:".

So far, there were only two things on the list. One was, "I got a small pink wart". And the other was, "My teacher's name is Mrs Westvessel".

Mrs Westvessel wore stockings with seams up the back, and shoes that laced on the sides. Sometimes, while she sat at her desk, she unlaced her shoes when she thought no one was watching, and rubbed her feet against each other. Under the stockings, on the tops of her toes, were tiny round things like small doughnuts.

Anastasia described the toe doughnuts to her mother, and her mother nodded and explained that those were called corn pads.

Anastasia wrote "corn pads" on page twenty-seven of her notebook.

Mrs Westvessel also had interesting brown spots on the backs of her hands, very large and lopsided bosoms, and a faint grey moustache.

"I think Mrs Westvessel is probably over one hundred years old," Anastasia told her parents at supper. "Probably about one hundred and twenty."

"Nobody lives to be one hundred and twenty," said her mother as she poured some mushroom gravy over Anastasia's meat loaf. "Unless they're in Tibet."

Her father wrinkled his forehead. "Perhaps Mrs Westvessel is a mutant," he said.

"Yes," agreed Anastasia. "Mrs Westvessel is a mutant, I believe."

Later she wrote "mutant" on page twenty-seven, under "corn pads". Anastasia was a very good speller; she sounded out the syllables of "mutant" correctly on the first try.

Anastasia didn't like Mrs Westvessel very much. That made her feel funny, because she had always liked – sometimes even loved – her teachers before.

So she wrote in her green notebook, "Why don't I like Mrs Westvessel?" and began to make a list of reasons. Making lists of reasons was sometimes a good way to work things out.

"*Reason one:*", wrote Anastasia, "because she isn't a good teacher".

But then she crossed out reason one, because it was a lie. Anastasia wasn't crazy about telling lies, even to herself; she did it, sometimes, but it always gave her a stomach-ache.

Mrs Westvessel, she knew, was really a pretty good teacher. At any rate, she had taught Anastasia to remember the difference between minuends and subtrahends, which was not a particularly interesting thing to know; and also how to say "I love you" in both French and German, which was not only very interesting but might come in handy some day.

"*Reason two:*", wrote Anastasia, after she had crossed out reason *one*, "because she is so old".

That wasn't a lie, so it didn't give her a stomach-ache; but it was a reason that Anastasia felt a little strange about. Anastasia felt a little strange about old people in general. Probably it was because of her grandmother, who was the oldest person she knew. Her grandmother was so old that she lived in a nursing home; and Anastasia didn't like to visit her there. The nursing home smelled of medicine and antiseptic, a bad combination of smells.

But Mrs Westvessel smelled of chalk dust and glue, which was not a bad combination at all. And Mrs Westvessel, although she was old, never *acted* old. When they were studying Ireland in geography, Mrs Westvessel had done an Irish jig in her laced-up shoes, with her bosoms bouncing. *That*, thought Anastasia, wasn't an *old* thing to do.

So she slowly crossed out reason *two*. Then she couldn't think of any others.

Finally she wrote, "*Reason three:* because I am stupid".

Not stupid in school. Anastasia, particularly after she had finally mastered the difference between minuends and subtrahends, was actually a very good pupil.

"I'm stupid," said Anastasia sadly to herself,

"because sometimes – too many times – I don't feel the same way about things that everybody else feels.

"I was the only one at Jennifer MacCauley's birthday party," she remembered gloomily, "who thought green ice cream was nauseating. Everyone even *said* I was stupid, for that.

"I'm the only person in the world," she reminded herself, " – the whole entire world – who likes cold spinach sandwiches. That's really stupid.

"And now," she thought, "I'm the only kid in class four who doesn't like Mrs Westvessel."

So reason *three* seemed to be the reason. "Because I'm stupid." She left it there, frowned, and closed her green notebook. "Sometimes," she thought, "maybe it isn't a good idea after all to make a list and find out the answer to a question."

But when Mrs Westvessel announced one day in the autumn that the class would begin writing poetry, Anastasia was the happiest she had ever been in school.

Somewhere, off in a place beyond her own thoughts, Anastasia could hear Mrs Westvessel's voice. She was reading some poems to the class; she was talking about poetry and how it was made. But Anastasia wasn't really listening. She was listening instead to the words that were appearing in her own head, floating there and arranging themselves into groups, into lines, into poems.

There were so many poems being born in Anastasia's head that she ran all the way home from school to find a private place to write them down, the way her cat had once found a very private place – the pile of ironing in the pantry – in which to create kittens.

But she discovered that it wasn't easy. She hung the Do Not Disturb sign from the Parker House Hotel on the doorknob of her bedroom door. She thought that might make it easier.

She got herself a glass of orange juice with ice in it, to sip while she worked. She thought that might make it easier.

She put on her Red Sox cap. She thought that might make it easier.

But it still wasn't easy at all. Sometimes the words she wrote down were the wrong words, and didn't say what she wanted them to say, didn't make the sounds that she wanted them to make. Soon her Snoopy wastebasket was filled with crumpled pages, crumpled beginnings of poems.

Her mother knocked on her bedroom door and called, "Anastasia? Are you all right?"

"Yes," she called back, taking her pencil rubber out of her mouth for a minute. "I'm writing a poem."

Her mother understood that, because very often Anastasia's father would close the door to his study when he was writing a poem, and wouldn't come out even for supper. "Okay, love," her mother said, the way she said it to Anastasia's father.

It took her eight evenings to write one poem. Even then, she was surprised when she realized that it was finished. She read it aloud, alone in her room, behind the Do Not Disturb sign from the Parker House Hotel;

and then she read it aloud again, and smiled.

Then she read it aloud one more time, put it into the top drawer of her desk, took out her green notebook, and added to the list on page two under "These are the most important things that happened the year that I was ten", as item three: "I wrote a wonderful poem".

Then she flipped the Do Not Disturb sign on her doorknob to its opposite side, the side her mother didn't like. "Maid," said the opposite side, "please make up this room as soon as possible."

Her poem was finished just in time for Creativity Week.

Mrs Westvessel was very, very fond of Weeks. In their class, already this year, they had had Be Kind to Animals Week, when the notice board had been filled with newspaper clippings about dogs who had found lost children in deep woods, cats that had travelled three hundred miles home after being left behind in strange cities, and a cow in New Hampshire that had been spray-painted red during hunting season so that she would not be mistaken for a deer.

During My Neighbourhood Week, one entire classroom wall had been covered with paper on which they had made a mural: each child had drawn a building to create My Neighbourhood. There were three Luigi's Pizzas; two movie theatres, both showing Superman; one Red Sox Stadium; a split-level house with a horse tied to a tree in the backyard; two Aquariums; two Science Museums; one Airport control tower; three prisons; and a condemned block of flats with a large rat on the front steps. Mrs Westvessel said that it was not what she had had in mind, and that next time she would give better instructions.

Creativity Week was the week that class four was to bring their poems to school. On Monday morning Mrs Westvessel took them on a field trip to Longfellow's home on Brattle Street. On Tuesday afternoon, a lady poet – poetess, she should be called, according to Mrs Westvessel; but the lady poet frowned and said she preferred poet, please – came to visit the class and read some of her poems. The lady poet wore dark glasses and had crimson fingernails. Anastasia didn't think that Longfellow would have liked the lady poet at all, *or* her poems.

Wednesday was the day that the members of the class were to read their own poems, aloud.

Robert Giannini stood in front of the class and read:

I have a dog whose name is Spot.
He likes to eat and drink a lot.
When I put water in his dish,
He laps it up just like a fish.

Anastasia hated Robert Giannini's poem. Also, she thought it was a lie. Robert Giannini's dog was named Sputnik; everyone in the neighbourhood knew that; and Sputnik had bitten two kids during the summer and if he bit one more person the police said the Gianninis would have to get rid of him.

But Mrs Westvessel cried, "Wonderful!" She gave

Robert Giannini an A and hung his poem on the wall. Anastasia imagined that Longfellow was eyeing it with distaste.

Traci Beckwith got up from her desk, straightened her tights carefully, and read:

In autumn when the trees are brown,
I like to walk all through the town.
I like to see the birds fly south.
Some have worms, still, in their mouths.

Traci Beckwith blushed, and said, "It doesn't rhyme exactly."

"Well," said Mrs Westvessel, in a kind voice, "your next one will be better, I'm sure." She gave Traci Beckwith a B plus, and hung the poem on the wall next to Robert's.

Anastasia had begun to feel a little funny, as if she had ginger ale inside her knees. But it was her turn. She stood up in front of the class and read her poem. Her voice was very small, because she was nervous.

hush   hush   the sea-soft night is aswim
with wrinklesquirm creatures
listen(!)
to them   move   smooth   in the moistly dark
here in the   whisperwarm   wet

That was Anastasia's poem.

"Read that again, please, Anastasia, in a bigger

voice," said Mrs Westvessel.

So Anastasia took a deep breath and read her poem again. She used the same kind of voice that her father did when he read poetry to her, drawing some of the words out as long as liquorice sticks, and making some others thumpingly short.

The class laughed.

Mrs Westvessel looked puzzled. "Let me see that, Anastasia," she said. Anastasia gave her the poem.

Mrs Westvessel's ordinary, everyday face had about one hundred wrinkles in it. When she looked at Anastasia's poem, her forehead and nose folded up so that she had two hundred new wrinkles all of a sudden.

"Where are your capital letters, Anastasia?" asked Mrs Westvessel.

Anastasia didn't say anything.

"Where is the rhyme?" asked Mrs Westvessel. "It doesn't rhyme at *all.*"

Anastasia didn't say anything.

"What kind of poem *is* this, Anastasia?" asked Mrs Westvessel. "Can you explain it, please?"

Anastasia's voice had become very small again, the way voices do, sometimes. "It's a poem of sounds," she said. "It's about little things that live in tidepools, after dark, when they move around. It doesn't have sentences or capital letters because I wanted it to look on the page like small creatures moving in the dark."

"I don't know why it doesn't rhyme," she said, miserably. "It didn't seem important."

"Anastasia, weren't you *listening* in class when we

talked about writing poems?"

Anastasia looked at the floor. "No," she whispered, finally.

Mrs Westvessel frowned, and rubbed her jiggly bosom thoughtfully. "Well," she said, at last.

"Well. Anastasia, when we talked about poetry in this class we simply were not talking about worms and snails crawling on a piece of paper. I'm afraid I will have to give you an F."

An F. Antastasia had never had an F in her entire life. She kept looking at the floor. Someone had stepped on a red crayon once; the colour was smeared into the wood for ever.

"Iworkedveryhardonthatpoem," whispered Anastasia to the floor.

"Speak up, Anastasia."

Anastasia lifted her head and looked Mrs Westvessel in the eye. "I worked very, very hard on that poem," she said, in a loud, clear voice.

Mrs Westvessel looked terribly sad. "I can tell that you did, Anastasia," she said. "But the trouble is that you didn't listen to the instructions. I gave very, very careful instructions to the class about the kind of poems you were to write. And you were here that day; I remember that you were.

"Now if, in geography, I explained to the class just how to draw a map, and someone didn't listen, and drew his own kind of map" (everyone glanced at Robert Giannini, who blushed – he had drawn a beautiful map of Ireland, with cartoon figures of people throwing bombs all over it, and had got an F), "even though it was a very *beautiful* map, I would have to give that person a failing mark because he didn't follow the instructions. So I'm afraid I will have to do the same in this case, Anastasia.

"I'm sorry," said Mrs Westvessel.

"I just bet you are," thought Anastasia.

"If you work hard on another, perhaps it will be better. I'm *sure* it will be better," said Mrs Westvessel. She wrote a large F on the page of poetry, gave it back to Anastasia, and called on the next pupil.

At home, that evening, Anastasia got her green notebook out of her desk drawer. Solemnly, under "These are the most important things that happened the year that I was ten", in item three, she crossed out the word *wonderful* and replaced it with the word *terrible.*

"I wrote a terrible poem," she read sadly. Her goldfish, Frank, came to the side of his bowl and moved his mouth. Anastasia read his lips and said, "Blurp blurp blurp to you too, Frank."

Then she turned the pages of her notebook until she came to a blank one, page fourteen, and printed carefully at the top of the right-hand side: THINGS I HATE.

She thought very hard because she wanted it to be an honest list.

Finally she wrote down: "Mr Belden at the chemist's." Anastasia honestly hated Mr Belden, because he called her "girlie", and because once, in front of a whole group of class five boys who were buying baseball cards, he had said the rottenest, rudest thing she could imagine anyone saying ever, and especially in front of a whole group of class five boys. Mr Belden had said, "You want some Kover-up Kreme for those freckles, girlie?" And she had not been anywhere *near* the Kover-up Freckle Kreme, which was $1.39 and right between the Cuticura Soap and the talcum powder.

Next, without any hesitation, Anastasia wrote down "Boys". She honestly hated boys. All of the class five boys buying baseball cards that day had laughed.

"Liver" was also an honest thing. Everybody in the world hated liver except her parents.

And she wrote down "pumpkin pie", after some thought. She had *tried* to like pumpkin pie, but she honestly hated it.

And finally, Anastasia wrote, at the end of her THINGS I HATE list: "Mrs Westvessel". That was the most honest thing of all.

Then, to even off the page, she made a list on the left-hand side: THINGS I LOVE. For some reason it was an easier list to make.

Her parents were having coffee in the living room. "They're going to find out about the F when they go for a parent-teacher meeting," thought Anastasia. "So I might as well show them." She took her poem to the living room. She held it casually behind her back.

"You guys know", she said, "how sometimes maybe someone is a great musician or something – well, maybe he plays the trumpet or something really well – and then maybe he has a kid, and it turns out the kid isn't any good at *all* at playing the trumpet?" Her parents looked puzzled.

"No," said her father. "What on earth are you talking about?"

She tried again. "Well, suppose a guy is a terrific basketball player. Maybe he plays for the Celtics and he's almost seven feet tall. Then maybe he has a kid, a little boy, and maybe the little boy *wants* to be a great basketball player. But he only grows to be five feet tall. So he can't be any good at basketball, right?"

"Is it a riddle, Anastasia?" her mother asked. "It seems very complicated."

"What if a man is a really good poet and his daughter tries to write a poem – I mean tries *really hard* – and the only poem she writes is a *terrible* poem?"

"Oh," said her father. "Let's see the poem, Anastasia."

Anastasia handed the poem to her father.

He read it once to himself. Then he read it aloud. He read it the way Anastasia had tried to, in class, so that some of the words sounded long and shuddery. When he came to the word "night" he said it in a voice as quiet as sleep. When he had finished, they were all silent for a moment. Her parents looked at each other.

"You know, Anastasia," her father said, finally. "Some people – actually, a *lot* of people – just don't understand poetry."

"It doesn't make them bad people," said her mother hastily.

"Just *stupid*?" suggested Anastasia. If she could change, under "Why don't I like Mrs Westvessel?" the answer "Because I'm stupid" to "Because *she's* stupid", maybe it wouldn't be such a discouraging question and answer after all.

But her father disagreed. "Not stupid," he said. "Maybe they just haven't been educated to understand poetry."

He took his red pen from his pocket. "I myself", he said grandly, "have been *very* well educated to understand poetry." With his red pen he added some letters to the F, so that the word *Fabulous* appeared across the top of the page.

Anastasia decided that when she went back to her room she would get her green notebook out again, and change page two once more. "I wrote a fabulous poem," it would say. She smiled.

"Daddy, do you think maybe some day I could be a poet?" she asked.

"Don't know why not," he said. "If you work hard at it."

"How long does it take to make a whole book of poems?"

"Well, let's see. That last book of mine took me about nine months."

Anastasia groaned. "That's a long time. You could get a *baby* in nine months, for pete's sake.

Her parents both laughed. Then they looked at each other and laughed harder. Suddenly Anastasia had a very strange feeling that she knew why they were laughing. She had a very strange feeling that her list of THINGS I HATE was going to be getting even longer.

Things I Love!	Things I Hate!
Making Lists	Mr Belden (at the chemist's)
Mars Bars	Boys
Writing Poems	Liver
My Room	Pumpkin Pie
My Wart	Mrs Westvessel
Frank (my goldfish)	

2

The rats. So they were going to have a baby.

Anastasia had been angry a lot of times.

She had been angry the day that she came down with the flu and had a temperature of 103° and had to miss the special Children's Concert that the Boston Symphony was doing, and her parents gave the tickets to the terrible Truesdales who lived in the upstairs flat.

She had been angry at the paperhanger who insisted on wallpapering her bedroom with the wallpaper right-side up, when Anastasia preferred the way it looked upside down.

She had been very, very angry at the person who stole her new bike when she forgot to chain it to the fence outside the J. Henry Bosler Primary School.

But she had never in her life been as angry as she was the evening that her parents told her that they were going to have a baby.

"What are you trying to do, be in the *Guinness Book of World Records?*" she asked her mother. "You're too *old* to have a baby!"

"Thirty-five?" her mother asked, with raised eyebrows. "Thirty-five is too old? Thirty-five is going to put me in The *Guinness Book of World Records?* Come on, Anastasia. Thirty-five is the prime of life!"

"Ten is," muttered Anastasia. "Ten is the prime of life."

"Wrong, both of you," said Anastasia's father. "The prime of life is forty-five. *I'm* in the prime of life."

"Anyway," added Anastasia, "you don't need a baby. You have *me.*"

"Stupid, stupid, *stupid,*" she thought immediately. "I'm being stupid, again. I'm the only one in the whole world, for pete's sake – the whole world including even my parents – who thinks that I'm important enough to be the only kid in the family."

Her mother sat glumly, examining some burnt umber paint on the back of her hand. Her father rolled his eyes the way he did every time the Patriots missed a first down.

"Yes," he said. "We certainly do have you."

There was a long silence.

"So," said Anastasia, finally. "You're not going to change your minds?"

Her mother rubbed her middle softly with her paint-smeared hand. "It's too late for that, Anastasia."

"It's a *fait accompli,*" said her father.

"You know I can't understand Greek, Daddy."

"French."

"Well, French, then. I can't understand French either. What's a *fait accompli:* another word for baby?"

"In this instance, I guess it is. A baby boy."

Anastasia hooted. "You guys may think I don't know anything, but I *do* know that you can't tell what kind of baby it is until it's born. What do you mean, a baby boy? Did you consult a fortune teller?"

"Actually," said her mother, brightening a little and pouring herself another cup of coffee, "it's really pretty interesting, Anastasia. They have this special test they do, on certain women . . ."

"What do you mean, *certain women?*"

Her mother blushed. "On women who are thirty-five or older, if they're pregnant."

"See?" said Anastasia. "*See?*"

"And", her mother went on, ignoring her, "they did this test on me, and it showed that the baby is healthy. A healthy boy."

Anastasia kicked the rung of her chair with one plimsoll. She was quiet, thinking. Her parents both stirred their coffee at the same time, and sipped, at the same time, as if they'd been rehearsing: one, two, three, stir, and one, two, three, sip.

"You have probably been thinking a lot about where you're going to put this, ah, baby boy, in this *extremely* small, extremely crowded flat," Anastasia said.

"Yes," said her father with interest. "We have been thinking about that. Any ideas?"

"Simple," said Anastasia, standing up. "Very simple. It can have my room. Because I'm moving out. Excuse me. I have to go and pack."

She stomped down the hall to her bedroom. In the darkest corner of her wardrobe she found the heavy canvas bag that was left over from her father's days in the Navy; it had KRUPNIK M A stencilled on the side. Once, when she was smaller, her father had put her into it, pulled the drawstring close, and carried her around the flat while she giggled.

Anastasia took the orang-utan poster from her wall, rolled it up, and put it into the canvas bag. Then she added three pairs of underpants and a box of crayons. Carefully she put in her green notebook and a sweat shirt with a picture of Amelia Earhart. Sadly, she realized that she couldn't pack her goldfish. But her comic books went in, and a box of Kleenex, and a folded programme from a performance of *Peter Pan*. Reluctantly, she added her arithmetic book. Then she cleaned her water-colour brushes in the glass of muddy water that had been on her desk for a week, put the brushes into her box of paints, and tucked that into the bag. Under her chest of drawers was a rather stale chocolate biscuit. She added that.

Then she went back to the kitchen. Her parents were still drinking coffee, looking distressed, and talking to each other quietly.

"Excuse me for interrupting. But I would like to have my silver cup, the one with my name on it, that my grandmother gave me when I was born. You don't have to polish it or anything."

Her mother went to the cupboard to look for the cup.

"You know, Anastasia," said her father, "the baby won't be born until March. So there's no need to hurry in making a decision about moving out. I would think that you'd like to stay for Christmas at least."

Anastasia didn't say anything. But she began to think. It would be nice to be around for Christmas.

Her mother was holding the little blackened cup.

"I really should polish this," she said. "You can barely see the name."

"That's *another* thing," said Anastasia. "What are you going to *name* this baby?"

"Goodness," said her mother. "We haven't even thought about that. Maybe you have some suggestions. . ."

"As a matter of fact," said her father, "I think we should give Anastasia the full responsibility for naming the baby. It will be her brother, after all."

"Of course, I won't be here," said Anastasia.

"That's right," said her father. "I forgot that for a minute. Tell you what, though. If by some chance you should decide to stick around, you may name the baby."

"Anything I want?"

"Well," said her mother, "maybe we should . . ."

"Anything you want," said her father decisively.

Anastasia stood there, thinking.

"Okay," she said, finally. "I'll stick around, and I'll

name the baby. You can put the cup back."

She retured to her room and unpacked. Chocolate biscuit, paints, arithmetic book, *Peter Pan* programme, Kleenex, sweat shirt, green notebook, crayons, underpants, and orang-utan. She put the KRUPNIK M A canvas bag back on the floor of her wardrobe. She had been thinking the entire time she was unpacking.

Then she sat down on her bed, picked up a pencil from the floor, and opened the green notebook to one of the very last pages where nothing was written at all.

In a secret corner, very small, she wrote the name she had chosen for her parents' baby boy. It was the most terrible name she could think of. When she had written it, she smiled and closed the notebook.

Things I Love!	Things I Hate!
Making Lists	Mr Belden (at the chemist's)
Mars Bars	Boys
Writing Poems	Liver
My Room	Pumpkin Pie
My Wart	Mrs Westvessel
Frank (my goldfish)	My Parents
	Babies

3

"Reasons for maybe becoming a Catholic," wrote Anastasia in her green notebook.

1. There are fourteen Catholics in class four, and four Jews, and everybody else is something else – I don't know what – but whatever it is is not very interesting. So I would make the fifteenth Catholic. And if ever they start a club or something, I would automatically be in it. That would be nice.

2. And I would get a new name. Maybe at about the same time I get a new brother.

Anastasia thought vaguely that probably there were other good reasons for becoming a Catholic. But she didn't know what the other reasons might be; and the ones she had listed seemed good enough.

"I think I might become a Catholic," she said to Jennifer MacCauley, who she hoped was going to be her very best friend in class four. Jennifer had a lot of things going for her: she had naturally curly reddish-brown hair, a broken-off front tooth from falling down the basement stairs, and more Barbie doll clothes than any other girl in the class.

She also, she had told Anastasia, was before long going to have a new and very impressive name. Right now her name was Jennifer Elizabeth MacCauley. But one of these days, she said, she was changing her name to Jennifer Elizabeth Theresa MacCauley. That was because she was Catholic.

Catholics, Jennifer told Anastasia, were allowed to give themselves an extra name when they were old enough. They were even allowed to choose the name themselves; Jennifer had already chosen Theresa.

That appealed to Anastasia, who had never liked her own name very much, and who had no middle name at all. When her brother was born, she knew, *his* new name was going to cause – well, maybe not trouble, but talk. It was certainly going to cause talk. It would be rather nice to get a new name herself at the same time.

"It has to be a saint's name," Jennifer pointed out.

Anastasia wasn't exactly sure what a saint was. But their names seemed okay. Some even seemed spectacular, for pete's sake. She looked at the list that Jennifer showed her.

"Perpetua," she said, reading from the list. "Anastasia Perpetua Krupnik. I like that. I definitely think I might become a Catholic."

"You can't," said Jennifer apologetically. "You're too

old."

"What do you mean, too old?" asked Anastasia. "I'm only ten."

"Look," said Jennifer. She opened the top drawer of her desk – they were in Jennifer's bedroom – and searched through the broken crayons, crumpled spelling papers, and half a pack of cards. She found a snapshot and handed it to Anastasia.

"Big deal," Anastasia said, looking at it. "That's just you in a bride's outfit." Secretly, she looked a little harder and was envious. She had wondered, often, what it would feel like to wear a bridal gown. Not that she ever wanted to get married. Or to have a *baby*, for pete's sake.

"Ha," said Jennifer. "Bride's outfit, my foot. That's my First Holy Communion dress. I was seven. Everyone is around seven when they make their First Holy Communion. After that you're a real Catholic."

"Liar," said Anastasia.

"No, honest," Jennifer said. "Really. You can't be a Catholic unless you do that."

"Is there a law that you have to be seven?"

"I guess so."

Anastasia thought it over carefully. "There can't be," she said, finally. "What if you were on a trip around the world the whole time you were seven?"

Jennifer shrugged. "I don't know," she admitted.

"What if you had leprosy when you were seven?"

Jennifer looked confused.

"What if you were *Jewish* when you were seven?"

Finally Jennifer said, "Well, sometimes there's

something they do in the Catholic Church. They give a disp — , they give a dispen — , a dispensation. That's what they give."

"What's that?"

"It means that you can do something against the Catholic rules."

"So. I'll get a dispensation, then. What do I have to do?"

"I don't know. You have to go to the church, I guess, and talk to the priest."

"Couldn't you do it, Jennifer? Couldn't you talk to the priest and bring my dispensation home for me? Like picking up the homework from Mrs Westvessel if I'm absent?"

"I don't know, Anastasia."

"For a Catholic, you sure don't know much, Jennifer."

Jennifer looked uncomfortable.

Anastasia sighed. "When do you go to church next?" she asked.

"Saturday."

"I'll come with you then, on Saturday. I'll talk to them about getting the dispensation. Probably I can bring it home with me. Then how long will it take to be a Catholic?"

"A while. You'll have to go to catechism classes."

"Well, that's okay. I want my mother to have time to order new name tapes for my camp clothes, since my name will be different."

"You don't have to put your whole name on things. I don't have my whole name on my camp clothes."

"Listen, Jennifer, do you think I'm going to become a Catholic and get a name like Anastasia Perpetua Krupnik and not let people *know* about it?"

Anastasia went home. She wanted to tell her parents about her decision to become a Catholic, but she knew that she had to tell them at the right moment, in the right way, because it would be something of a surprise. They might even be a little upset, she suspected, that she was changing her name.

So she waited until they were seated at the kitchen table for supper, waited until her mother had served the stewed chicken, and then she stood up and said, "Look." She began to sign herself with the sign of the cross, the way Jennifer MacCauley had showed her. She got mixed up and realized she was doing it backwards.

"Wait a minute," she said. Then she said aloud, thinking, "Forehead. Belly button. Left nipple. Right nipple." She did it again, correctly.

Her parents looked at her, puzzled.

"That's terrific, Anastasia," her father said, finally. "Look at mine." He stood up and said, "Nose. Stomach. Left ear. Right ear." He touched them in that order and sat back down. Her mother shook her head as if she thought they were both crazy.

"*Daddy*," said Anastasia angrily, "don't make fun of me. I was doing the sign of the cross. I'm going to become a Catholic."

"You're *what*?" said her mother.

"That is both interesting and preposterous," said her father, and began eating his chicken.

"I am too," said Anastasia. "First, I'm going to the church on Saturday with Jennifer to talk to the guy there about picking up my dispensation."

"Oh?" said her mother, with interest.

"And then I'm going to catechism classes. I'm not sure how many I have to go to."

"Oh?" said her father.

"And then I have to get a wedding dress, and then I make my First Holy Communion."

"A wedding dress?" asked her mother.

"Yes. They make them in small sizes for Catholics."

"And then?"

"Well, you may not like this part much. But then I change my name. I will be Anastasia Perpetua Krupnik."

Her parents looked at each other thoughtfully, and then they both looked at Anastasia.

"And that's it?" asked her father.

"Yes. Then I'm a Catholic."

"You know," said Anastasia's mother, "most people, making an important decision like that, would discuss it first with their parents."

Anastasia looked pointedly at her mother's middle, which was beginning to bulge slightly so that she had left the button at the top of her jeans undone. "Most people", she said to her mother, "making an important decision like *that* would discuss it first with their child."

They each took a bite of chicken. Finally Anastasia's father said, "You're going to church Saturday, you said? To pick something up?"

"Yes, my dispensation. I'll show it to you when I get

home."

"Fine. I suggest that we don't really need to discuss this any more now. We'll wait till Anastasia has been to the church and talked to the, ah, the guy there, about everything."

They all nodded. Anastasia's mother passed the peas around again, and they began to talk about names, in general. Dr Krupnik said that the funniest name he knew of was that of a new Harvard instructor in Economics: Weatherly Scarf.

Mrs Krupnik said that Weatherly Scarf wasn't as funny as the name of a model who had once posed for Life classes when she was an art student. The model had been named Felicity Brest.

Anastasia thought that neither of those names was as funny as the name that she was going to name their new baby in March. But she didn't say that.

And no one said anything at all about the name Anastasia Perpetua Krupnik.

It was raining on Saturday, but Anastasia wore her best dress anyway, underneath her yellow raincoat, and carried a large Lord and Taylor's shopping bag, just in case she needed it for carrying the dispensation home.

She and Jennifer MacCauley walked along Brattle Street toward St Cecilia's Catholic Church.

"I never knew before that Catholics went to church on Saturday," Anastasia said. "I thought only Jewish people did that."

"Oh," said Jennifer, "we're not really going to church today. We go to church tomorrow, on Sunday. But on

Saturday we go to confession. That's where we're going now, to confession."

Anastasia looked at Jennifer and giggled. "*Confession?* That's just for criminals, like when they're in the police station and the cops talk to them for a long time, and maybe beat them up a little; then they finally confess."

"Well, this is sort of the same thing, only there's no police or anything, and they don't put you in jail. You just go to the church and confess your sins."

"I won't have to do that part. Because I don't have any sins."

"You do, too. Everybody does. They don't have to be *big* sins, like murdering anybody."

"I don't have any little sins, either."

"Liar. You told me you stole Mary Ellen Bailey's cupcake out of her lunchbox last week."

"A cupcake? That's a *sin?*"

"Yeah."

"If I'm a Catholic I have to confess about a cupcake?"

Jennifer nodded. "And also if you think bad thoughts about anyone."

Anastasia stood very still for a moment on Brattle Street. "What if in bed at night I wish that Mrs Westvessel would get a disease that would make pimples grow all over her face?"

Jennifer thought about that. "Yes," she stated, finally. "That would be a sin, to wish that."

"So I'd have to confess it?"

Jennifer nodded. They had started to walk again, and

had almost reached St Cecilia's Church. It took up the entire next block, and had stained glass windows of people looking terribly sad, some of them with arrows sticking out of their stomachs.

"And", said Jennifer, "you would have to say that you were sorry."

"*Sorry?*"

Jennifer nodded primly. "Most heartily sorry," she said.

"Even if I'm *not?*"

"Jennifer looked a little embarrassed. "Well," she said, "if you're a good Catholic, you really will be sorry."

Anastasia stopped where she was, on the pavement near the corner. She looked at her Lord and Taylor's shopping bag.

"Jennifer," she said, "my bag has a rip in the bottom. I don't think it'll hold the dispensation well."

Jennifer looked into the bag, at the small rip in the bottom. "Yeah," she said doubtfully.

"So I think I'll go on home."

"Yeah," said Jennifer. "I understand."

"Mom?" called Anastasia, when she let herself into the flat.

Her mother was in the room where she painted, standing in front of the easel with a long smear of pale yellow paint across the front of her shirt, right where the baby was beginning to make a small mound.

"Mmmmm?" answered her mother.

"Have you bought my wedding dress yet?"

"Nope. Not yet." Mrs Krupnik looked at her canvas carefully, and changed a tiny stroke of yellow with a narrow brush.

"Well, forget it," said Anastasia. "I've changed my mind."

Things I Love!	Things I Hate!
Making Lists	Mr Belden (at the chemist's)
Mars Bars	
Writing Poems	Boys
My Room	Liver
My Wart	Pumpkin Pie
Frank (my goldfish)	Mrs Westvessel
Secret Bad Thoughts	My Parents
Wedding Gowns	Babies

4

"I have fallen in love," Anastasia told her parents one morning at breakfast. It made her feel a little shy to talk about it. But she felt that her parents ought to know.

Her father blew a ripple into his coffee thoughtfully. "You seem a little young for that," he said.

"No, Myron," said Anastasia's mother. "She isn't too young at all. I myself fell in love for the first time when I was ten." She blushed a little.

"You *did?* With whom?" Anastasia's father always knew the right time to say whom. Anastasia had not yet mastered that.

"His name was Edward Mark." She blushed a little more.

"Edward Mark what?" asked Anastasia's father. Both of them seemed to have forgotten Anastasia altogether.

"That was all. Mark was his last name."

"Well, that's ridiculous. How on earth could you have become involved with someone who had two first names?"

"Myron, I was not, as you so crudely put it, 'involved'. I was simply in love. It was Platonic. Edward Mark and I played Monopoly together."

That interested Anastasia. She happened to know that her mother was not a very good Monopoly player. "Did Edward Mark get into building hotels?" she asked.

"If you were going to get involved with a hotel magnate," said Anastasia's father, "why didn't you make it Conrad Hilton?"

"I'm not going to talk about it any more," said Mrs Krupnik primly. "This is an unproductive conversation." She began clearing the table.

Myron Krupnik sipped his coffee and looked at his watch.

"Well," said Anastasia finally, "wouldn't you like to know whom it is that I'm in love with?"

"Who," said her father. "Use the nominative in that instance."

"Who it is," Anastasia corrected herself. "Who it is, is Washburn Cummings."

"How on earth could you have become involved with someone who has two last names?" asked her mother grouchily. But she was talking to Anastasia's father.

"*Will you people please listen to me for a change?* I

am in love with Washburn Cummings. That's important. Washburn Cummings is in class six. Washburn Cummings is black. Is it going to bother you guys if I get involved with someone who is black? And who is older than me?"

"Older than I," corrected her father automatically.

"Older than I."

Anastasia's mother was standing by the sink. She very often made speeches while standing by the sink. "I don't care if you get involved with someone who is black, or in class six. I just don't want you to get involved with someone who is insensitive, or who is wont to trespass on the inviolate memories of childhood in a way that is completely lacking in charity or compassion."

"I don't know what you're talking about," said Anastasia. "Washburn Cummings doesn't trespass on anything as far as I know. Once he got kicked out of the movies, though, for being loud and obnoxious."

Neither of her parents said anything. They were glaring at each other.

"Well, listen, you guys," said Anastasia. "Maybe we could talk about it later. I have to go to school now."

She went to get her jacket. As she buttoned it up, she went back to the doorway of the kitchen. "Washburn Cummings", she said, "is the same height as me. I mean, as I. But his hair is about two feet higher than that. So altogether, counting his hair, he is about as tall as you, Daddy."

"That's interesting," said her father, who hadn't

really been listening.

"Edward Mark", said her mother loudly, measuring out the words very carefully, "had the most beautiful head of golden curls I have ever seen in my life."

"Well, that's just terrific," said Myron Krupnik, rubbing his hand over his own head which had not had very much hair for a very long time. "I hope he's had a wonderful career modelling for Breck shampoo."

Anastasia walked to school, not at all certain that her parents had grasped the significance of being in love for the first time.

Washburn Cummings, in all honesty, did not even know that Anastasia existed.

But everyone at the J. Henry Bosler Primary School knew about Washburn Cummings. On the day that he came to school wearing a tee shirt with an obscene saying printed across the front, and was sent home by the head to change, Washburn Cummings made a quick trip around the J. Henry Bosler Primary School, appearing briefly at the door of each classroom and opening his jacket to flash the tee shirt at the class. By the time that the head heard he was doing it, Washburn Cummings had flashed every classroom down to class two and was already heading down the front steps, bouncing an imaginary basketball and wiggling his hips.

"Who was *that?*" asked Mrs Westvessel with a puzzled look on her face, after Washburn Cummings had appeared at the door.

"That was Washburn Cummings," said the whole class.

"And what was written on his shirt?" she asked.

No one answered. A few people giggled.

"Who are my speed readers here?" asked Mrs Westvessel. "Mary Ellen Bailey? Robert Giannini? Someone *must* have been able to read that tee shirt."

Mary Ellen Bailey blushed. Robert Giannini, who always carried a briefcase to school, went up to Mrs Westvessel's desk and whispered into her ear.

Mrs Westvessel blushed. "Well," she said. "Well. My *goodness*. Let's take out our arithmetic books, class."

On the way home from school, walking with Jennifer MacCauley, Anastasia wiggled her hips and bounced an invisible basketball.

"*Anastasia*," said Jennifer. "That's disgusting."

"No, it isn't. It's just a thing you do to be cool. Anyway, I'll tell you a secret. I'm in love with Washburn Cummings."

Jennifer groaned. "How do you know? How can you *tell* when you're in love?"

That was something that Anastasia had thought about a great deal. She had stood in the corner shop, reading a questionnaire called "Is it really love?" in *Cosmopolitan* until the pharmacist, Mr Belden, had said, "Pay for it or close it up, girlie". Short of money, overdrawn on her pocket money, she had had to close it up; but she remembered some of the questions.

"You think about him all the time. You stop wanting to see other men. You . . ."

"You never see any other men anyway," Jennifer interrupted.

"Quiet. He appears in your dreams, usually as a hero. You . . ."

Jennifer interrupted again. "Washburn Cummings appears in your dreams? As a hero?"

"Yeah. I dreamed the other night that I was lost. I was walking on Huron Avenue, and I couldn't find my house anywhere. Then Washburn Cummings appeared, coming out from behind a tree, and offered to show me the way home."

"Ha. Was he wiggling his rear?"

"No. He was being very kind. And he was wearing a cowboy hat."

"Washburn Cumming's hair wouldn't *fit* under a cowboy hat."

"Well, in my dream it did. Maybe he'd had a haircut. Let me finish about being in love. You find yourself wanting to fulfil his fantasies . . ."

"What are fantasies?"

"Imaginations."

"Oh, great. What are Washburn Cumming's imaginations, do you think?"

"Well, one time I saw him in the playground with a transistor radio, and he was just sitting there listening, with a happy look on his face."

"To what? A Red Sox game?"

"No. It was Roberta Flack. I think maybe he really likes Roberta Flack. I find myself wanting to fulfil his fantasy about Roberta Flack. I'm practising singing."

"You can't sing. You didn't even make Glee Club."

"Only because she put me in the alto section, and in 'This Land Is My Land' we had to sing a different tune from the rest of you. I can't do that. But I can sing a tune okay. Listen."

They stopped on the corner, and softly, in her Roberta Flack voice, Anastasia sang, "'The first time ever I kissed your lips . . .'."

Jennifer made a face. "The singing's all right. But the thought of kissing Washburn Cummings is absolutely revolting."

"That's because you're not in love with him. You wait, Jennifer. When you're in love with someone, everything will seem different. You'll *want* to kiss someone."

"Not someone who acts as revolting as Washburn Cummings," said Jennifer, and turned to go up her street. Anastasia bounced her invisible basketball all the way home, wondering how she could make Washburn Cummings notice her. Maybe *Je Reviens* perfume.

Hair. That's what would do it, Anastasia decided. Obviously Washburn Cummings was interested in hair styles. He kept a comb tucked into his own hairdo all the time; in the playground, sometimes, she could see him take the comb out of its perch and rake it upwards through his hair.

"I'm going to take a shower and wash my hair before I go to bed," she called to her mother at 8.30 that night.

She used all the shampoo, squeezing the last bright

green globs from the bottom of the tube. Then she combed her wet hair flat, down to the tops of her shoulders, looked at it in the mirror, wished that there were *more* of it, and plaited it into as many skinny pigtails as she could. Fourteen soggy plaits. When she went to bed it was like sleeping with her head on a complicated pile of twisted rope.

But it worked. In the morning she unplaited all the pigtails, combed it up instead of down, and looked into the mirror in amazement. It was as much like Washburn Cumming's hair as shoulder-length bright yellow hair could possibly be. She squashed it into her blue knitted ski cap before she went in for breakfast.

"One might ask", said her mother, "why you are wearing a ski hat to breakfast in November."

"One might ask that," said Anastasia, with her mouth full.

"One might also ask", said her father, "why I am wearing socks that don't match." He held up his feet, carefully keeping his balance on the kitchen chair. One sock was dark blue; the other was dark brown. "It's because I have no clean matching socks."

"Gotta go," said Anastasia, grabbing her jacket from the doorknob where it usually hung.

Outside, around the corner, she took the ski hat off. She found the comb that she had put in the pocket of her jeans, combed her hair up into the air again, and headed towards school – the long way so that she would pass Washburn Cummings's house.

The timing was just right. Washburn Cummings

came dribbling through his front door just as Anastasia was walking past.

"Hello," she said, twitching her hips a little. She had practised both the hello and the hips for quite a long time the night before.

Washburn Cummings stopped mid-dribble, stood still for a moment, and then tossed his invisible basketball with an absent-minded hook shot into a nearby tree.

"You stick your finger in a socket?" Washburn Cummings asked.

"What do you mean?"

"Your hair, girl. You look like you electrocuted yourself." He started to laugh. Often Anastasia's parents had told her that there is laughing *with* someone, and there is laughing *at* someone, and one is okay but the other is not. Washburn Cummings was definitely, she realized, laughing *at* her, and it was not okay, and she began to have a very serious stomach-ache.

"Halloween was all over last month," laughed Washburn Cummings. "It's not cool, baby, to wear your monster costume after Halloween's all finished. Nooooot coooool." He retrieved the basketball from the air somewhere, bounced it a few times on the pavement, wiggled his hips, and began to dribble his way towards school.

Anastasia decided that she could not go to school that day. Her stomach hurt too much. She stuffed her hairdo back into the ski hat and stopped at the chemist's on her way home to buy a new tube of shampoo. It cost her entire week's pocket money. As she was leaving Belden's Pharmacy, the new issue of *Cosmopolitan* caught her eye. "*Love – or Hate? Sometimes It's Hard to Tell*", it said on the cover.

"You open it, you buy it, girlie," called Mr Belden. He was watching her from the place where he measured out penicillin pills.

"Bug off, Mr Belden," muttered Anastasia. She took her shampoo and her stomach-ache home, took a shower, washed her hair, and went to bed for the rest of the day.

"Call me if you throw up," said her mother. "I'll be doing the washing."

But Anastasia didn't feel like throwing up. She sat on her bed and wrote, "I hate Washburn Cummings" in her notebook forty-three times until her stomach-ache went away. Then she read the *Boston Globe*, and found an article that told of a government research project which had found the average life span of a love affair to be five months.

"Mine was only three weeks," she thought. "But I'm young yet. And stupid. Stupid, stupid, *stupid* again."

Things I Love!	Things I Hate!
Making Lists	Mr Belden (at the
Mars Bars	chemist's)
Writing Poems	~~Boys~~
My Room	Liver
My Wart	Pumpkin Pie
Frank(my goldfish)	Mrs Westvessel
Secret Bad Thoughts	~~My Parents~~
Wedding Gowns	Babies
~~Washburn Cummings~~	Boys
	Washburn Cummings

5

"Why did you have to give me the name Anastasia? None of the other kids can spell it, so when they have to vote for somebody by secret ballot, nobody ever votes for me. Like when I was nominated for Class Secretary, only four people voted for me, and the other twenty-two voted for Mary Ellen Bailey."

"The reason they didn't vote for you is because the Class Secretary has to have good handwriting. And your handwriting looks like hieroglyphics," said her father, looking up from the newspaper. "That time you tried to forge an absence excuse, you got caught right away, remember, because no parent – no adult, in fact – would get caught dead with handwriting like that."

"No adult would get caught dead with a name like Anastasia," Anastasia muttered, changing the subject back again, quickly, away from the handwriting and the absence excuse. "Why did you guys name me that?"

"Interesting question," said her father. "Choosing names is a fascinating procedure. Have you picked a name for the baby yet, Anastasia? What thought process did you go through to choose one?"

Anastasia pretended she hadn't heard his question. "If I didn't have such a stupid name, maybe Washburn Cummings would have liked me better," she said, even though the thought had not really occurred to her till that moment. But there was a possibility that it was true.

Her mother frowned and counted the stitches on her knitting needles. She was starting to make a baby sweater. "What's wrong with it, really? I think it's a lovely name."

"You have to pay *extra*, for pete's sake, to have it stencilled on a tee shirt. There are too many letters. That's *one* thing wrong with it.

"And *another* thing is that you can't make a nickname out of it. A nickname that ends in *i*." Anastasia glowered and picked some fuzz out of her belly button. She was sitting on the living room rug wearing last summer's bikini. She had been practising standing on her head, until she fell and knocked over a lamp. Now she had a serious headache.

Her father scrunched his nose. "A nickname that ends in *i*? What on earth are you talking about?"

Anastasia sighed, lay on her back, and began

raising her legs slowly one at a time. It was an exercise that ballet dancers did. It hurt a lot.

"The girls in my class started a club," she explained gloomily. "It's called the '*i* Club' and your name has to end in *i*. Everybody's in it but me. Jenni and Becki and Traci and Cindi and Suzi and Luci and . . ."

"Good grief," said her mother, and rolled her eyes upwards. "Why would you want to belong to a club like that?"

"One. Because everybody's in it but me. Two. Because they're all getting tee shirts with their names on them."

"Well, look," said her father as he started in on the crossword puzzle, "if the tee shirt's that important, I'd be willing to fork out the extra money that a long name costs."

"Daddy," said Anastasia, sighing so hard that the shoulders lifted up and down. She stood up. "Look at me. I mean look at my body."

He looked. "Not bad for ten years old," he said. "The legs are a little skinny, but I've seen worse."

"I mean look at my *chest*," said Anastasia. "And picture my name across it."

He looked for a long time. Finally he said. "You know, Anastasia, my mind works *verbally*. Your mother is the one with the visual imagination. Why don't you ask her to look at your chest?

"Does anyone know a four-letter word for ruler?" he asked, going back to the crossword puzzle.

"King," said Anastasia. "That's ridiculously easy."

"*The New York Times* wouldn't use *king*," her father grumbled, but he wrote it in lightly.

Anastasia went and stood in front of her mother. "Picture my name across my chest," she ordered.

"Wait till I finish this row." She knitted for a minute. "Okay. Let me look."

Her mother looked at her chest for a long moment. Then she sighed. "Yes," she said. "I see what you mean."

"Into the *armpits*, right? The letters would go right into my armpits!"

Her mother nodded. "By the time you're sixteen you'll have a bigger chest," she said.

"Terrific. That's just terrific," said Anastasia. "By the time I'm sixteen I ..."

Tsar!" interrupted her father. "I knew it couldn't be *king*. Not in *The New York Times*." He rubbed out *king* and wrote in tsar.

"As a matter of fact," he said, looking up. "Let me tell you something about your name. Anastasia was the youngest daughter of the tsar of Russia, Tsar Nicholas."

"Big deal," said Anastasia. "Did she have a tee shirt with her name on it?"

"And she was murdered."

"No kidding?"

"No kidding. The whole family was wiped out by the Bolsheviks, kids and all."

"Was she just a little kid?"

"I don't remember how old. A teenager. And they all got shot."

"Hey, that's cool."

Her father raised his eyebrows. "Well, I'm not sure I would call it cool. I don't suppose *they* thought it was cool at all. But here's an interesting thing: years later, some lady popped up out of nowhere and said she was Anastasia, that she hadn't been killed, really, just shot; and that later she escaped and grew up in hiding."

"Better than growing up in Hoboken, ha ha," said Anastasia, doing her Groucho Marx imitation, which her father ignored. He hated her Groucho Marx imitation. He thought his was better.

"I'm sorry," she said politely, apologizing for the Groucho Marx. "Was she really Anastasia?"

"I'm not sure that anyone ever really knew. Some people thought she was, some people thought she wasn't."

"But there was a *chance* that the tsar kid didn't die?"

"Sure. There was that possibility."

Anastasia thought. She thought for a long time. She assumed the lotus position, which was supposed to be good for thinking, even though you practically had to throw your hips out of joint to do it.

"Mom," she said slowly, "you didn't do natural childbirth when you had me, right?"

"Right."

"They knocked you out cold, right? Whonk. Out

cold."

"Well, that's overstating it. They gave me an injection of something and I went to sleep briefly."

"So it's fair to say that you didn't actually *see* me being born?"

"You sound like a lawyer."

"Well, this is important. You didn't see me being born?"

"I felt you about to be born. I was put to sleep. I woke up a short time later and saw you being cleaned up. You looked very repulsive and you were screaming and you peed all over the nurse's hand."

"But for those few moments when you were asleep, there was *time* actually for them to switch babies on you."

Her mother groaned. "No way."

"You said that there were a few minutes . . ."

"Okay, so there were a few minutes when I was zonked out. Why would they switch babies? The only other baby born that day anyway, at that hospital, was Chinese. The parents had a restaurant over on Tyler Street in Boston. The father was terrifically handsome, I remember."

"But they could have switched babies! I might not even be yours!"

"The Chinese baby was a boy, come to think of it. They named him Stanley. I always wondered why they named him Stanley."

"*I could be the real Anastasia!*"

Her father stood up. "I need a drink suddenly," he

said. "I need a cold beer."

Before he went to the kitchen, he said, "Anastasia, it was 1918 when she was shot. If you are she, you are remarkably well preserved."

"Rats," said Anastasia.

"Know what?" said her father, when he came back with his beer and let her slurp the foam. "When your grandmother's here at Thanksgiving, you can ask her about the tsar, and about Anastasia. I wasn't born then. But she was a young woman. She'd remember."

"Daddy," Anastasia pointed out, using the kindliest voice she had, because she was talking about his mother, "Grandmother doesn't remember *anything*.

"She doesn't even remember *me*, for pete's sake," she muttered, forgetting the kindly voice. And she got that strange feeling again, the feeling she always had when she smelled medicine and other nursing home smells. It was a feeling of being scared and sad at the same time.

Things I Love!	Things I Hate!
Making Lists	Mr Belden (at the chemist's)
Mars Bars	
Writing Poems	~~Boys~~
My Room	Liver
My Wart	Pumpkin Pie
Frank (my goldfish)	Mrs Westvessel
Secret Bad Thoughts	~~My Parents~~
Wedding Gowns	Babies
~~Washburn Cummings~~	Boys
My Name	Washburn Cummings
	All My Friends
	~~My Name~~

6

"The Macy's parade is the most boring thing I have ever seen," said Anastasia gloomily, "and I hate Thanksgiving."

Her mother opened the oven door, poked a fork into the turkey skin so that juice ran out and made a hissing noise. "You like turkey," she said.

"Yeah. But we could have turkey any time. I hate the Macy's parade, and after that I hate the football games, and also I hate pumpkin pie. Why do you have to make pumpkin pie at Thanksgiving? Is there a *rule* somewhere that you have to make pumpkin pie at Thanksgiving? If you want to know the truth, pumpkin pie smells like throw-up. It's gross."

"Anastasia Krupnik, *you* are being gross, and if you don't get out of this kitchen I'm going to throw something at you, maybe a pumpkin pie. Go. Go and talk to your grandmother."

Anastasia muttered something as she left the kitchen.

"What did you say?" her mother called.

"Nothing," she called back. What she had muttered was, "I hate my grandmother".

Anastasia's grandmother was ninety-two. Nobody else's grandmother was ninety-two. Robert Giannini's grandmother was fifty; she played the Hammond Organ in a bar and lounge. She wore false eyelashes, Robert said, and called out "All *riiiight*", when the TV showed close-ups of the cheer leaders during Thanksgiving football games.

Jennifer MacCauley's grandmother was fat, worked in a bakery, and brought home all the unsold cakes at the end of each day. "Weight Watchers here I come", Jennifer MacCauley's grandmother always said, and laughed.

But Anastasia's grandmother was ninety-two and lived in a nursing home. The wrinkles on the side of her mouth were scabby. She talked with her mouth full, and what she said usually didn't make any sense, and there were food spots on the front of her dress.

She made Anastasia feel sad, and scared. Who needed *that?*

Anastasia wandered into the living room where her father was asleep on the couch with the *Boston Globe* open across his chest. In the corner by the window, her grandmother sat in a big chair, smoothing her dress across her lap over and over again with her thin hands. There were veins like cat's cradles pulled tight on the backs of her hands.

Anastasia sighed, sat down on the floor beside her grandmother, and said "Hello, Grandmother", politely. She had already said hello four times since her father had brought her from the nursing home. But her grandmother forgot things.

The scary, claw-like hands smoothed her hair. Funny how soft and nice that felt. If she didn't look at the hands it was okay. If she just looked at her grandmother's moist, kind eyes, everything seemed almost okay.

"What's your name? You have such pretty hair."

"Anastasia." She had already told her that, again and again. Most people remembered their grandchildren's names, she thought angrily, and also their birthdays.

"My boy's hair is this colour. His name is Myron," said the old woman.

For pete's sake, thought Anastasia. Myron is forty-five years old, asleep on the couch, and he's bald.

"Myron is a good boy," her grandmother said dreamily. "Better than his brothers. Myron always does his homework. Do you do your homework, little girl?"

"Mostly I do. But I don't like arithmetic much."

"Myron is the youngest, so I spoil him a little. His brothers are all so much older and they like to tease."

Anastasia glanced at her father and tried to imagine him little, being teased by big brothers. It was hard. His mouth was open, and he was snoring a little; his glasses were pushed up on his forehead, scrunching his eyebrows. His feet stuck out beyond the end of the couch, almost touching the Swedish ivy that grew in the deep blue pot. Dr Myron Krupnik was six feet four inches tall.

"Your little boy Myron is my father," she said politely to her grandmother, hoping that her grandmother would understand.

But her grandmother just stroked her hair some more with the skinny hands, and stared out through the window. "Do you have a brother, little girl?"

Anastasia sighed. "Not yet," she said. "But in March I will. My mother and father said that I could name him. What names do you like, Grandmother?"

Not that it mattered. Anastasia still had the name that she had chosen, written in the secret place in the back of her green notebook. She hadn't changed her mind about the name. It would serve the baby right. Also her parents.

"Sam," said her grandmother. "Sam is a good name."

Yuck, thought Anastasia. Sam.

The old woman leaned forward suddenly and whispered. "Sam's hands fit around my waist," she said, "and do you know, he can pick me right up and swing me around in the air? Sometimes he tickles me on the back of the neck with his moustache.

"But he doesn't come back any more. I wonder where Sam is," she said. "Do you know where he went?" She sat back stiffly, and looked around. "Is he invited? Is he coming today?"

"No," said Anastasia. "I guess he couldn't come."

Her grandmother looked back out through the window, leaning forwards to see down the street. Her eyes were curious and almost happy. "He might come," she said. "Sometimes he surprises me."

She began to talk to herself, words that Anastasia didn't understand, and to smooth the lap of her dress once more. Anastasia got up and went back to the kitchen. Her mother was stirring gravy.

"Did you invite someone named Sam for dinner?" she asked her mother. "Grandmother says someone named Sam might come. There aren't enough places set."

Her mother tasted the gravy and added a little salt. "She's daydreaming," she told Anastasia. "Sam was your grandfather. He died before you were born. She forgets that."

"I forget it, too. Maybe I'm as bad as she is," said Anastasia, though she didn't believe it. "You want me to carry in the plates and put them on the table?"

"Sure. Put the one with the blue flowers at Grandmother's place. That's always been her favourite."

The plate with the blue flowers had a crack in it that was turning brown along its length. It had lasted a lot of Thanksgivings. But it was going to break one of these days.

"Are you going to have to mash up her turkey and then we all have to watch her mushing it around, like last year?"

"Your eating habits aren't that terrific either, my

friend," her mother said.

"She dribbles cranberry sauce on her dress, and she talks with her mouth full. I hate that."

Her mother didn't say anything.

"And she forgets my name. I hate that, too."

Her mother didn't say anything. She put mashed potatoes into a yellow bowl. Anastasia started to cry. A salt-flavoured tear came down the side of her face and into the corner of her mouth; she tasted it with the tip of her tongue, and waited for the next one.

"I don't hate Grandmother," she said in a voice that had to find its way out lopsided, around the tears. "But I hate it that she's so old.

"It makes my heart hurt."

Her mother took a paper napkin from the kitchen table, knelt on the floor beside Anastasia, daubed at her wet cheeks with the napkin and put her arms around her.

"All of our hearts hurt," she said. They went together to wake up Anastasia's father, and the three of them helped the grandmother to the table, where they sat her in the best chair, the one with arms. They all smiled when the old woman recognized her favourite plate, touched the blue flowers fondly, and said, "Forget-me-nots."

Things I Love!	Things I Hate!
Making Lists	Mr Belden (at the chemist's)
Mars Bars	
Writing Poems	~~Boys~~
My Room	Liver
My Wart	Pumpkin Pie
Frank (my goldfish)	Mrs Westvessel
Secret Bad Thoughts	~~My Parents~~
Wedding Gowns	Babies
~~Washburn Cummings~~	Boys
My Name	Washburn Cummings
My Grandmother	~~All My Friends~~
My Friends	~~My Name~~

7

"Hey sport, you're on holiday, right?" Dr Myron Krupnik asked Anastasia one morning.

"Right. Christmas holiday. Goes till the third of January," said Anastasia, stuffing her jeans into a pair of heavy socks so that she could pull on her boots.

"Got any plans for this morning?"

"Well, I made a list." Anastasia pulled a crumpled piece of paper from her pocket and read it aloud. "Thursday morning: make a snowman if there is enough snow. Start making Christmas presents. See if Mom will let me make some cakes." She wrinkled her nose. "Mom said no to that. She's out of flour. Actually, I used up the flour myself, making paste the other day. We had five pounds of flour. Now we have about fourteen pounds of paste, and it's beginning to smell bad."

"Well," said her father, "*my* holiday doesn't start until the day after tomorrow. But I only have to teach one class this morning. Do you want to come along?"

"Will it be boring?"

Her father adjusted his glasses so that he could look down his nose at her. "*Boring*? Dr Krupnik's English 202, required for English majors, eighteenth- and nineteenth-century poetry, three prelims, four papers, and a final exam, *boring*?" He sighed. "Yes. It will probably be boring."

"Okay," said Anastasia, "I'll come. But wait while I change into my poetry outfit."

Anastasia's poetry outfit was quite simple. She put a black turtleneck shirt on with her jeans, replaced her owl's eye-shaped glasses with dark glasses, and undid her pony tail. She combed her hair straight and flat. If she had had time, she would have painted her fingernails crimson.

That was what the visiting lady poet who had come to their class had worn. She had also worn a cape. But Anastasia had no cape; she covered her poetry outfit with her green ski jacket, and walked with her father to the university.

She had never gone to one of her father's classes before. She had been to his office, in the same brick building, where his name – Dr Krupnik – was impressively etched in a brass nameplate attached to the door. She had run her fingers over the letters, liking the way they felt, thought briefly about asking for an A. Krupnick nameplate for her own bedroom door at home, decided it would be ostentatious (a word she had written on page seven of her green notebook) age ten, and discarded the idea. She would have a nameplate when her name was more important, she decided: maybe by the time she was twelve.

The classroom was not much different from class four's classroom of the J. Henry Bosler Primary School. There was no cage of smelly gerbils, no portrait of George Washington, no alphabet marching across the top of the blackboard, and no fire-resistant Christmas wreath. But it had the same large windows, the same blackboards, the same metal wastebasket, the same clock with nervous, jumpy hands, and the same smell of chalk dust and overflowing pencil sharpeners.

Someone had written "I work very hard for my Marx" on the board, but her father rubbed that out with the side of his hand when they entered the room.

"We have about five minutes", her father said, "before it is feeding time at the zoo. Here, read this while we wait." He gave her a mimeographed poem called "I Wandered Lonely as a Cloud".

Anastasia sat down in one of the front-row desks and read the poem. It was not a difficult poem. It was easier to understand than some of the ones that her father wrote. There were only two words that she didn't understand: *jocund* and *pensive*, and she underlined them carefully the way Mrs Westvessel had taught her to do. She could look them up when she got home. If they were any good, she could put them on the word list in her notebook.

The students began to enter the classroom. Anastasia was startled at their loudness – at the J. Henry Bosler Primary School pupils were not allowed to shove the desks around, or talk to each other when lessons were starting; and although the issue hadn't been raised in class four, she suspected they would not be allowed to smoke cigarettes, which some of her father's students were doing – but she was pleasantly surprised that they were all wearing variations of poetry outfits, so she felt she would blend in nicely. She wished that she had Frye boots, though.

"Who's the midget, Dr K?" asked one of the students, a boy. She thought it was a boy, at least; it was a little hard to tell, but the voice was rather deep for a girl.

Her father stood up. "Before we start, class, I would like you to meet my daughter, Anastasia, who is visiting today."

"All riiiggghht," said the girl in the desk next to Anastasia's, and smiled at her.

Dr Krupnik lit his pipe. "Today we will continue with Wordsworth. Since the Christmas holiday is upon us and we are busy, I gave you quite a simple assignment. Is it fair, or safe, to assume that you have all read and given some thought to an analysis of 'I Wandered Lonely as a Cloud'?"

Anastasia nodded gravely and said, "Yes." The rest of the class hooted and laughed. Mrs Westvessel would have sent them all to the head's office. Her father only grinned a little, and sighed.

"McAllister?" he said. "Let's hear from you. Tell us what you think of the poem."

The boy who had asked who the midget was groaned. "Frankly, Dr K," he said, "I think it's a crock of shit." Then he sat up straighter, looked embarrassed, glanced at Anastasia, and mumbled, "I'm sorry."

Her father puffed on his pipe for a moment. "I'm sure my daughter has heard the word *shit* before," he said, "although I expect she is as surprised as I am to hear it in a classroom."

Anastasia giggled. Actually, she had heard it that very morning, from her own father, when he realized that his pen had leaked ink on the pocket of his favourite shirt.

"Would you explain why you find the poem offensive, McAllister?" her father asked.

The boy looked at his mimeographed sheet. "Well, like, look at lines fifteen and sixteen. I mean, like, it's not enough that he has to write about all those flowers fluttering around, but then he has to come out and tell us 'A poet could not but be gay'? Come on. And *jocund*. What does *that* mean?"

"Jocund means cheerful, McAllister," said Anastasia's father. "Surely you have access to a dictionary? Would you *use* it occasionally, please?" Dr Krupnik sounded annoyed.

McAllister slumped back in his desk. He cracked his knuckles. Anastasia winced. So did her father.

"Miss Eisenstein? Would you tell us, please, which line or lines convey to you the theme of the poem, and what that theme might be?"

A fat girl dressed entirely in black – a super-poetry-outfit – adjusted her glasses.

"Well, I couldn't pick out any one or two lines, you know? You have to look at it in its entirety. And then you see the dichotomy . . ."

Anastasia's father interrupted. "Remember, Miss Eisenstein, we sort of had a friendly agreement that you wouldn't use the word dichotomy in this class any more? Because it has become a bit of a victim of over use?"

The fat girl frowned. "Well, look at it this way, you know? Wordswoth is talking about two different things: like solitude, and also community? I mean, see how the flowers are all in a group, dancing, but in the last stanza the poet is lying on his couch all alone?"

That was interesting, Anastasia thought. Her father wrote "Solitude – Community" on the board.

"That is interesting, Miss Eisenstein," said her father. But he said it with the same voice that he used when Anastasia described in detail the plot of a television programme. It meant that he didn't find it terribly interesting at all.

"Anyone else want to give it a try?" asked her father. "Miss Cameron?"

Anastasia turned around to look at the back of the classroom. A girl in the rear corner desk was at least six feet tall, dressed in a black leotard with a denim wraparound skirt tied loosely around her waist. Her hair was red and very, very long; it hung below the beginning of the skirt.

She yawned, unwrapped her thin leotarded legs from the legs of the desk, stretched her arms, and said, "To me the salient lines appear throughout the poem. 'Fluttering and dancing in the breeze'. 'Tossing their heads in sprightly dance'. 'The waves beside them dance'. 'And dances with the daffodils'. The whole thing flows, you know? Can you get with the flow? I'd say the theme is like movement as joy. Do you feel what I mean: 'movement as joy'?" The girl moved one of her thin arms across the air. The whole class watched her, puzzled.

"Ah, yes, Miss Cameron," said Anastasia's father. He wrote "Movement as joy" on the blackboard. "That's interesting. I'm not sure that Wordsworth would have known what you meant, or have gone with the flow, but it's, ah, interesting.

"Anyone else?" he asked. "Wilder? How about you?"

A heavy-set boy with very curly hair had his head down on his desk. He raised his head and looked around with half-open eyes.

"Futility of life," he said.

There was a long silence. Finally Dr Krupnik said, "Do you want to add anything to that, Wilder?"

"No."

"I find it fascinating, Wilder, that you have selected 'futility of life' to be the theme of the work of, so far, Pope, Gray, Cowper, Blake, and Burns. Now – Wordsworth, too?"

"Yeah," said Wilder.

Anastasia's father wrote "futility of life" on the board.

"Others?" he asked.

The boy named McAllister called out, "Why don't you ask your daughter?"

Dr Krupnik puffed on his pipe. Anastasia recognized it as a beginning-to-get-very-irritated style of puff.

"Because my daughter is not a registered member of this class," he said.

He paused for a long time and puffed again. "As a matter of fact," he said, finally, "let's call it a day. Go home, everybody, and have a good Christmas. *Read* over the holidays, please. Read *anything*."

That seemed an odd thing to say, thought Anastasia. At home he was always saying to her, "Are you reading again? Don't you ever do anything but read?"

The students all shuffled to their feet and out of the classroom. Some of them said "Merry Christmas". Someone called "Merry Christmas, Wilder!" Wilder was the only one who hadn't left. He had his head back down on the desk and appeared to be sound asleep. Maybe dead.

Anastasia held her father's hand as they walked home for lunch. She liked the feeling of his leather glove around her mitten. In a funny way that she didn't really understand, she felt bad for him.

"Daddy," she said shyly, "I think I understood a little bit of the poem. At least, I *liked* some parts of it."

He smiled and squeezed her hand. "What did you

like?"

"'The inward eye'," she confessed. "I liked where it said about 'the inward eye'."

He quoted the line as if it were an old friend. "'The inward eye which is the bliss of solitude'."

"Tell me what it means," said Anastasia. Inside, she pictured a head with a spooky eye.

"Well," said her father thoughtfully, "'the inward eye' can mean memory. Solitude means being alone. And bliss means happiness. So what do you think the whole line means?"

She put it together like a puzzle. "Memory is the happiness of being alone?" she asked.

"Not a bad thought, is it?" asked her father, in a soft voice.

"No," said Anastasia, a little puzzled. "But my trouble is that I don't have very many memories yet. And I'm not alone very much. So I guess I don't need 'the inward eye' yet, to be happy."

He smiled at her.

"But probably I *will*, someday," she said. "Probably everybody does some time, right, Daddy?"

"Right," he said. She could tell he was thinking.

"Daddy," she said, "I didn't understand some other things in your class. Like the boy named Wilder who was asleep. What did he mean when he said 'futility of life'?"

Her father thought about that. "Some people think that there's nothing to look forward to in life. Nothing important. Nothing that has any meaning for them.

"Feeling that way makes them bored and grouchy and lonely. Then they want to put a label on why they feel that way. Wilder's label is 'futility of life'. And he sleeps all the time in class because he stays up all night drinking beer and talking about how life has no meaning."

"That's stupid."

"Of course it's stupid." He squeezed her hand.

"You want to know something sad that I've just thought of, though?" Anastasia asked.

"Sure."

"Grandmother. She doesn't have anything left to look forward to. *Grandmother* has 'futility of life'. Maybe she should go out and drink beer all night.

"Her father looked thoughtful for a minute. Then he said, "No. Because your grandmother has something else that keeps her from being bored and grouchy and lonely. Can you guess what it is?"

Anastasia thought for a long time, about what her grandmother had. "Arthritis", she said finally, "and varicose veins. A pot of geraniums beside her bed at the nursing home, and twelve different kinds of pills. I don't think any of that's so terrific, for pete's sake."

"Nope," said her father. "None of that is terrific at all. But your grandmother has what we've just talked about. She has memories. The people at the nursing home tell me that she lives in the past, and that she's happy."

"'The inward eye'!" said Anastasia, understanding suddenly. "Grandmother has 'the inward eye'!"

"'Which is the bliss of solitude'," quoted her father, and tucked her hand into his coat pocket beside his own.

They were almost home. They walked along without saying anything for a moment.

"Daddy?"

"What?"

"I thought your class was kind of boring," Anastasia confessed.

"It was." He laughed. "It was hideously, horribly, *horrendously* boring."

"But Wordsworth was okay."

"Yeah," he said. "Good old Wordsworth. He's definitely okay."

Things I Love!	Things I Hate!
Making Lists	Mr Belden (at the chemist's)
Mars Bars	
Writing Poems	~~Boys~~
My Room	Liver
My Wart	Pumpkin Pie
Frank (my goldfish)	Mrs Westvessel
Secret Bad Thoughts	~~My Parents~~
Wedding Gowns	Babies
~~Washburn Cummings~~	Boys
My Name	Washburn Cummings
My Grandmother	~~All My Friends~~
My Friends	~~My Name~~
Wordsworth	
Christmas	

8

"Nothing interesting ever, *ever* happens to me," said Anastasia gloomily. "No *wonder* I don't have any memories yet."

"What on earth do you mean? I can think of lots of interesting things that have happened to you," said her mother.

"Name three."

"When you were two years old you ate ant poison and had to have your stomach pumped."

"That's one. And I don't even remember it."

"Well, when you were four you wandered off when we were in Harvard Square. And finally I called the police, and when they finally found you, you were at the bottom of Green Street, walking with an old lady who was wearing army boots and had a Tupperware bowl on her head."

"Yeah, that was neat. She said she always wore that bowl when she went out because it kept radio-activity from getting into her brain. She was going to take me home and we were going to live together and she said she would teach me to avoid all the filth and danger in the world. She needed me to help her wash the doorknobs in her flat. She had to do them all three times a day."

"Well, *that* sure was an interesting thing that happened to you."

"It's only two. Name a third."

Her mother thought and thought. "The second class field trip to the Franklin Park Zoo?"

"Yuck."

"Well, what sort of thing did you have in mind?"

"I was reading this newspaper at the shop. Just on the first page – the first page *alone* – I read about a man and his son in South America who were transported to another planet by a UFO; and a five-year-old girl in Idaho who had four kidneys, all of them working; and a pair of eight-year-old twins in New York who had lived all alone in a flat for four months after their mother ran away with a guy who sold cosmetics door-to-door. And I didn't even get to read the second page because Mr Belden told me that if I even *flicked* that newspaper open I had to pay for it."

"For that kind of reading I think I would have paid and flicked."

"I couldn't. I didn't have any money. Not only do I not have interesting things happen to me, but also I never have any money."

"Go and ask your dad for your pocket money. He's in the study looking through the wardrobe for the Christmas tree decorations."

"I will in a minute. But tell me something, first: has anything interesting ever happened to *you?*"

"Like being taken to another planet? Nope."

"No, I don't mean like that. But how about – well, for example, did you ever have a love affair? After you were grown up?"

"Not since I married your dad."

"But before? Did you *before* you got married?"

Her mother blushed. "Anastasia, that is a very *personal* question."

"Well, you're my mother, for pete's sake. You're supposed to be able to ask your mother personal questions."

"Yes."

"Yes *what?*"

"Yes, I once had a love affair. Before I even met your father."

"With who? I mean with whom?"

"Oh, goodness, Anastasia, no one you know. His name was John. He was a lawyer in New York when I was an art student."

"Was he married so that you had to meet secretly and maybe there would be a detective watching?"

"Good heavens, of course not. He was just a young lawyer, not married, and I . . ."

"Handsome? Was he terrifically handsome?"

Her mother blushed again. "Yeah," she said, laughing a little. "He was terrifically handsome."

"And did you do wildly romantic, crazy things?"

"Sure."

"Like what?"

Her mother grinned. "Well, one time we drove all the way out to Montauk Point in the middle of the winter and found a place to spend the weekend, and we walked on the beach in a raging snowstorm. After that we had dinner and drank a lot of wine and listened to Beethoven on a little radio that had a lot of static. And we hugged and kissed a lot. Is that the kind of thing you want to know about, Anastasia?"

"Just romance. Just the romantic parts are what I want to know about."

"Well, here's a romantic part. Once he had to go to Charleston, South Carolina, on business. Some kind of legal thing he was doing. And he asked me, on the spur of the moment, to go along. So we flew to Charleston – it was spring, by then – and the whole city smelled like azaleas and gardenias. We stayed at a hotel where there were fresh flowers everywhere, so that every time, even now, when I smell those Southern spring flowers, I still think of that time. And that night, we had dinner in the hotel, and there was candlelight, and after dinner we had tea, and we were happy and laughing and we read each other's fortunes in the tea leaves."

"Yeah. That's romantic. What fortune did he give you?"

"He looked in my teacup and told me that I would be

a good painter, and that he could see me ten years in the future, and I would be barefoot, with a smudge of paint on my ankle and another on my nose, and I would be laughing."

"That was nice. You liked that fortune, didn't you?"

"Yes. I liked it."

"And what was his?"

"Well, then I looked in his teacup and told him that I could see *him* in ten years, and he was a very successful lawyer, carrying a briefcase filled with important papers, and he was wearing a three-piece suit and being considered for a judgeship, and he had a big house in Scarsdale."

"And he liked that."

"He liked that."

"Then what?"

"Then we looked at each other and I started to cry." Anastasia was puzzled. Why would her mother *cry?* Then suddenly she understood.

"I know why. Because your fortunes didn't match."

"Right."

"And he cried, too."

"Nope. He was very sweet. Very sad. Very kind. And he said all the right things. But he didn't cry."

"Because men don't cry much."

"No. Men don't cry much."

"Daddy does, sometimes. He *always* cries when he hears that Sibelius violin concerto."

"Sweetie, that's one of the reasons I married your dad."

Anastasia understood that. "Yeah," she said. She looked at her mother. Her mother wasn't barefoot, because it was December; but she was wearing one green knee sock and one white knee sock, and there was a bit of orange paint on the white one; and there was another bit of orange paint on her chin. She was smiling, and she looked very, very beautiful to Anastasia. For a moment it didn't matter too much that in the middle, somewhere between the knee socks and the smile, was the baby.

"Daddy, I think love is one of the hardest things in the world to understand."

"Wait till you encounter calculus." Her father did his Groucho Marx eyebrow thing.

"Don't joke, Daddy. I really mean it. I need to start worrying about making myself some memories. I have to understand stuff."

"I'm sorry. You're right, Anastasia. Love is just about the hardest thing to understand. Maybe that's why there are painters and musicians and poets."

"And obstetricians," giggled Anastasia. "Can I have my pocket money? And have you found the Christmas tree decorations? And did you ever have love affairs?"

"Yes. No. Yes." He gave her 75 cents.

"What kind of box are they in? Do you remember?"

"A Jordan Marsh box, kind of smashed in on one corner. Tell me about your love affairs."

"Good grief. I had lots. Poets always do. They read poetry to women, usually young, wide-eyed women, and then the women get all misty-eyed and lick their lips a lot and next thing you know they say, 'I love you'. Happens all the time, to poets."

"There's the box, under that old sweat shirt." Anastasia pointed. "Did you really love any of them?"

"Nope. Pretended, though. Well, maybe I really loved one."

"Annie?"

"*How did you know about Annie?*"

"Your book. It says, 'To Annie'."

"Yeah," said her father. "I'd forgotten that. Annie was pretty wonderful. But she ran off to some place, Guatemala, I think, and broke my heart."

"What does a broken heart feel like when you're a grown up?"

"Stomach-ache. Lasts about six months. If you're a poet, you get some good poetry out of a broken heart, though."

"Did you ever have a love affair after you and Mom got married?"

"Sure. With your mom. It's still going on."

"Come on, Daddy. Be honest. With anybody else?"

"Nope. Because I've never had any clean underwear. Come on, kiddo, let's put up the Christmas tree."

"Grandmother, would you like to tell me about Sam?"

Anastasia was sitting beside her grandmother on the living room couch after Christmas dinner. She had tried and tried and tried to think of things to talk about. She had talked about the lights on the tree; she had talked about her best present, a record player, and had tried to show her grandmother some of her favourite albums; she had tried to talk about the tsar; and she had tried to talk about school. But her grandmother had only seemed puzzled and confused, nodding her head up and down with a questioning look. She held Anastasia's hand tightly, as if she were frightened.

"Maybe you would like to tell me about you and Sam when you were young," suggested Anastasia again.

Her grandmother smiled suddenly. "Is Sam here?" she asked, looking around.

"No," said Anastasia gently. "But tell me about him."

"He calls me Ruthie. 'Ruthie with the red, red hair.' Isn't that silly?"

Anastasia looked at her grandmother's white hair. She felt sad, even though it was Christmas. "No," she said. "It isn't silly."

"I made him a shirt for his birthday. It was a secret. I never sewed it when he was around. I kept it hidden away. I did every seam twice, by hand – such a soft, blue shirt. And when his birthday came, I made a special dinner, but I told him that I had no gift. I pretended to be very sorry, and of course he knew that we didn't have any money. It costs so much to feed the boys – goodness, how the boys eat! Are they here? Have they had dinner?"

Anastasia wasn't sure what to say. "Yes," she answered finally, "they've had dinner."

"Well, then I brought out the shirt! And my

goodness, wasn't Sam surprised! He put it right on, and gave me a hug even though I was so big because the baby was about to be born, and do you know what?"

"What?"

"That night, that very night, the baby came. Two weeks early. So Sam was wearing his birthday shirt when the littlest one, Myron, was born, right on his father's birthday! I looked up and saw Sam holding the baby against the blue shirt, and he told me we had another boy. That was such a happy time!

"What a happy, happy time," the old woman said softly, stroking Anastasia's hand.

"'The inward eye'," thought Anastasia, "that makes you feel happy, and not so all alone. Good old Wordsworth."

Suddenly her grandmother sat up straight, looked around, and said politely, "Little girl, I would like to go home now. I would like to be with Sam."

"Grandmother, I wish you could go and be with him," said Anastasia, and then felt frightened by what she had said. She looked across the room to where her mother and father were sitting and listening, and she knew that it had been all right to say it. She knew that they were wishing it, too.

"Merry Christmas, Grandmother," she called softly after the car as her father took her grandmother back to the nursing home. Funny, how it had never felt sad to say Merry Christmas before.

Things I Love!	Things I Hate!
Making Lists	Mr Belden (at the chemist's)
Mars Bars	
Writing Poems	~~Boys~~
My Room	Liver
My Wart	~~Pumpkin Pie~~
Frank (my goldfish)	Mrs Westvessel
Secret Bad Thoughts	~~My Parents~~
Wedding Gowns	Babies
~~Washburn Cummings~~	Boys
My Name	Washburn Cummings
My Grandmother	~~All My Friends~~
My Friends	~~My Name~~
Wordsworth	
Christmas	
My Parents	
Memories	

9

"Daddy, I need to know a word."

"Mmmmmmm?"

"What's a word that means, well, someone who changes his mind all the time?"

"How many letters?"

"Daddy, I'm not doing a crossword puzzle, for pete's sake. I just want to know a word to describe that. Someone who thinks one thing one day and another thing the next day."

"Well, let me think. *Mercurial*'s a pretty good word. Someone like that has a mercurial temperament."

Anastasia said that to herself a few times. Mercurial temperament. Mercurial temperament. It sounded pretty good. She got out her green notebook and wrote, on page two, under "These are the most important things that happened the year that I was ten," "I began to have a mercurial temperament."

She put the green notebook away and wandered into the little pantry between the kitchen and the dining room. Her mother was there, trying to put a curtain rod up over the little window. They had already taken all the dishes out of the pantry and painted the walls pale blue. It was going to be the baby's bedroom. Anastasia thought it a very peculiar sort of bedroom and she felt a little sorry for the baby, who could be lying in a little cot looking up at glass-doored cupboards that had once held cocktail glasses. But her mother had made some nice curtains for the little window; the curtains had blue and green cross-eyed unicorns on them.

Anastasia looked cross-eyed briefly at the curtains. She was pretty good at it, but it made her eyes hurt. Robert Gianinni could look cross-eyed all the time, just by taking off his glasses, and he said it didn't make his eyes hurt at all; but he couldn't *see* when he was cross-eyed.

"I have a mercurial temperament," Anastasia said to her mother.

"You also have a terribly dirty shirt on," her mother said. "Don't you have any clean clothes?"

"Yes, but I hate all my clean shirts. This is my favourite shirt. I'll save the clean ones for school. This is okay for Saturday."

Her mother hammered a nail into the window frame, said "ouch", and the bent nail fell onto the floor. Her mother put her thumb into her mouth.

"Don't you agree that I have a mercurial

temperament?"

"Tell me what it means," said her mother, sucking her thumb.

"It means someone who changes her mind a lot."

"What have you changed your mind about?"

Anastasia hoisted herself up on the counter top and sat with her legs dangling. What a strange bedroom, she thought again. With a sink and everything.

"Well, just for an example, do you remember that at Thanksgiving I told you I hated pumpkin pie?"

"Mmmmm."

"Did you notice at Christmas that I ate a whole lot of pumpkin pie?"

"Yes," said her mother thoughtfully. "As a matter of fact I *did* notice that. Christmas night, very late, I sneaked into the kitchen to get something to eat, and what I wanted was a piece of pumpkin pie. And it was all gone. You ate all the whipped cream, too."

"Yeah. Mercurial temperament."

Her mother took another nail from the package and began to line it up on the window frame.

"And remember I loved Washburn Cummings? And then after a while I *hated* Washburn Cummings? Guess what."

"What?"

"Now I'm starting to love him again."

Her mother took a whack with the hammer and another bent nail fell to the floor. "Damn," she said softly.

"And for a while I wanted to be a Catholic? And then

I didn't want to?"

"Do you want to be a Catholic again?"

"No," said Anastasia glumly. "But now I'm starting to think about being a Hare Krishna."

"A *what*?" Her mother took out another nail.

"Hare Krishna. You know those guys who wear yellow robes and have shaved heads and they dance around in Harvard Square saying 'Hare Krishna, Hare Krishna'?" Anastasia hopped down from the counter top and began to dance, shuffling her feet, around the little pantry. She bumped into the folded cot, which toppled against her mother, who was about to swing the hammer. Another nail fell on the floor.

"*Anastasia*," said her mother, angrily.

"Sorry," said Anastasia, and jumped up onto the counter top again. "And my name. Sometimes I hate my name and sometimes I think it's okay. Those Hare Krishna guys, they all take new names."

Her mother sighed, set the cot upright, and took out another nail.

Anastasia kicked her feet against the wooden drawers under the counter. What a weird bedroom, she thought, with drawers that used to hold tablecloths. Thunk thunk thunk. A little chip of white paint fell onto the floor beside the bent nails.

Her mother held the nail in her left hand, took a deep breath, and aimed the hammer with her right.

Thunk thunk. Anastasia kicked some more paint off the drawer, and said, "If you're not real careful you could hit the windowpane."

Her mother hit the windowpane with the hammer. The glass shattered and fell into the little sink.

Her mother stood very still for a moment. Then she said, very quietly, "If you don't get out of here, Anastasia, I am going to kill you."

Anastasia jumped down from the counter and shuffled away, doing her Hare Krishna dance. "I thought you liked me," she said. "You must have a mercuiral temperament, too."

She wandered into the kitchen where her father was slicing some garlic cloves. There were guests coming for dinner.

"Yuck," said Anastasia. "Those smell terrible."

Her father looked grouchy. "*Where* is your mother?" he asked. "Why do I seem to be preparing this dinner?"

"She's hammering, and she's very mad."

"Well, I'm not too cheerful myself. I don't know how to fix a leg of lamb. I'm an English professor. Go and tell her if she doesn't want to cook, we can call off the dinner party."

"I can't go and tell her. I'm not speaking to her, maybe not ever again. Can I eat with you guys tonight?"

"No." Her father poked the sliced garlic into the lamb a lot harder than it needed to be poked.

"Why not?"

"Because it's a grown-ups' party. Probably there won't be any food anyway. At least she made the *hors d'oeuvres* before she copped out. We can eat *hors d'oeuvres*. As a matter of fact, if you change out of that crummy shirt you can pass round the *hors d'oeuvres.*"

"I love this shirt. It has good memories attached to it. Bear in mind that I am someone who doesn't *have* a whole lot of memories yet."

"That shirt has the memory of a cheeseburger on the sleeve. Don't you have any decent clothes? Didn't your mother buy you a dress once?"

Anastasia ignored him. She lay down on the kitchen floor, on her back, and began breathing very loudly and quickly, huffing and puffing.

"Should I call an ambulance? Are you having an epileptic seizure?"

Anastasia stopped huffing, sat up, and looked at him with disdain. "Daddy, you of all people should recognize Lamaze breathing. I'm doing exactly what you and Mom do when you practise to have the baby. 'Transitional breathing'."

He patted some flour into the leg of lamb and looked at her with interest. "I'll be darned. I never realized it sounded so grotesque."

She lay down again and puffed for a while. "Do I have it right?"

"Sounds right to me. You've really been paying attention when your mother and I practise, haven't you?"

"Yeah," she admitted. "I only pretended I wasn't interested. Actually I was listening all the time. And I looked through the book, too."

"Hmmmmm," he said. He was scowling at the leg of lamb.

"Daddy, do you want to know *why* I'm doing the breathing?"

"Sure. Why?"

"Because I want to be there, the same as you, when the baby is born."

Her father went to the refrigerator, poured himself a beer, gave her a sip of the foam, and sat down at the kitchen table.

"You can't, sport," he said regretfully. "I wouldn't mind, and I'm sure your mom wouldn't mind. But the hospital has strict rules. No kids in the delivery room except the kid who is being delivered."

"*Why*?"

He sipped his beer and rubbed his beard. "Well, my guess is that it has to do with size. Everything is scaled to adult size. You're just not big enough, Anastasia. The hospital gown wouldn't fit you; it would drag on the floor. You're too short to stand by the delivery table; you'd bump your cute nose, sweetie."

"Daddy, that is the stupidest thing I have ever heard you say. *Ever*."

"Why is it stupid?"

"Have you ever heard of midgets?"

"Of course I've heard of midgets."

"Don't you think midgets have *babies*? For pete's sake, do you think they tell midgets, 'Sorry, but we can't let you in the delivery room even though you're having a baby because you'd bump your cute little *nose*', for pete's sake?"

He made a face, and touched her nose fondly.

"You're absolutely right. It was a stupid thing to say. It doesn't have anything to do with size. It's just a rule. And we have to go along with it."

"You mean you won't even try to talk them into letting me watch?"

"No, sport. You can see the baby after he's born. But not during."

"*Traitor.* I hope your dinner party turns out terrible."

Anastasia glowered at her father and stomped out of the kitchen. In the pantry, her mother was kneeling on the floor and touching up the chipped paint with a small brush.

"Don't you dare come stomping in here that way, Anastasia," said her mother. "I have just three weeks to get this room ready for the baby and I can't spend three weeks repairing your damage."

So Anastasia stood in the centre of the dining room, next to the table which was already set for the dinner, and called in her loudest voice, "Just for the record, everybody. I had *almost* changed my mind about that baby. I had *almost* begun to like that baby. I had *almost* begun to like the idea of having a brother living in the pantry, and I was even *about* to offer to maybe change his nappies occasionally. But just for the record for pete's sake, you guys shouldn't mess around with someone who has a mercurial temperament like mine, because just for the record I have absolutely changed my mind, and I do *not* like that baby at *all*."

Then she stomped noisily into her room, slammed

the door, and scowled at Frank, who came to the side of his bowl, stared at her solemnly, and moved his lips in a silent blurp.

"Shut up, Frank," said Anastasia.

She rummaged in her desk and found the green notebook. Then she leafed through the last pages until she found the secret page on which she had written the name for the baby. It was still as terrible a name as it had been the very first day that she heard it. That had been the day last September when she had walked past Washburn Cummings and his friends as they stood on the street corner near the J. Henry Bosler Primary School. They were singing. As Anastasia walked by, one of the boys had said "Shhhhh" and they had stopped singing. But they had started again when she was past, and she had stopped, knelt, pretended to tie her shoe, and listened to the song. It had a lot of verses, and she didn't understand all of them, but they were all about a man with a very peculiar, very terrible name.

Now she looked at the name where she had written it on the corner of the page in pencil. Carefully she went over the letters with a red marking pen.

The name was "One-Ball Reilly".

<u>Things I Love!</u>	<u>Things I Hate!</u>
Making Lists	Mr Belden (at the chemist's)
Mars Bars	
Writing Poems	~~Boys~~
My Room	Liver
My Wart	~~Pumpkin Pie~~
Frank (my goldfish)	Mrs Westvessel
Secret Bad Thoughts	~~My Parents~~
Wedding Gowns	<u>Babies</u>
~~Washburn Cummings~~	~~Boys~~
My Name	~~Washburn Cummings~~
My Grandmother	~~All My Friends~~
My Friends	~~My Name~~
Wordsworth	<u>My Parents</u>
Christmas	Hospital Rules
~~My Parents~~	
Memories	
Washburn Cummings (maybe!)	

10

Anastasia woke up, reached one arm out from her bed to her desk, and tapped some fish food into Frank's bowl.

Frank never slept, as far as she could tell; and he liked to eat all the time. On one page of her green notebook she had listed all the words that she could think of to describe Frank's appetite: the list began with *huge* and ended with her favourite, *indefatigable*, and it even included *humungus* although her father said that was not a real word.

Frank blurped silently at her, flipped his tail, and swam around the bowl catching the bits of food as they floated down.

Something felt very strange. Something was missing. Anastasia sat up in bed and looked around her room. Sometimes the Scotch tape dried out and her orang-utan poster fell off the wall; but it was still there. Her Red Sox cap was on the lampshade where it always was. Her arithmetic book was on the floor, where she had left it.

Something was so definitely missing that she took her legs out from under the covers and counted her toes. They were all there.

Then she began to count her fingers. When she got halfway through her fingers she realized what had happened.

"Mom! Daddy!" Anastasia yelled. "My wart is gone!"

She pulled back the covers of her bed and looked at the sheets. No small pink wart. It had simply disappeared as magically as it had come. Her left thumb felt naked.

She could hear her parents talking in the kitchen. She could smell coffee.

"Mom? Daddy?" she called. "Did you hear me? My wart is gone!"

Hastily she opened her green notebook to page two, and wrote, "I have no wart all of a sudden".

"Don't you guys even *listen* when I yell something important, for pete's sake?" Anastasia said, going into the kitchen where her parents were sitting at the table in their bathrobes. Her mother's stomach, she noticed suddenly, was huge. Humungus.

Both of her parents looked very sad.

"You don't have to feel bad for me or anything," said Anastasia. "It's not that big a deal. And probably some day I'll grow another one."

"Sweetie," said her father. "The nursing home has just called. Your grandmother died last night."

"'Ruthie with the red, red hair. Ruthie with the red, red hair'." Anastasia said that over and over again, to herself; and she started to cry.

"I remember her sitting there in the big chair at Christmas," Anastasia said, through her tears. "And the other weekend, remember? She liked those little cakes so much, when she was here that day? Remember that?"

Her parents nodded.

"And for pete's sake, she *wanted* to be with Sam, she said that, remember that she said that? And now I suppose she is, so I can't figure out why I feel like this. It's just that I remember how she used to touch my hair, and her hands felt soft; and I remember her eyes, how she looked at me sometimes, even though she couldn't even remember my name, for pete's sake; she still looked at me and rubbed my hair, and I remember how nice it felt . . ."

Anastasia cried and cried.

"I'm getting *memories*, all of a sudden!" she sobbed. "And they don't *feel* good!"

"And I wish I'd been nicer to her and not got so mad when she didn't know who I was." Anastasia wept.

She blew her nose on a paper napkin.

"It didn't hurt, did it, when she died?"

"No," said her father. "Her heart just stopped beating. She died of old age. Her time for living was simply over."

"Like my wart."

"Well," said her father, "maybe a little like your wart."

"You don't think I was stupid for crying, do you?"

"Goodness, Anastasia," her mother said. "Your dad and I both cried before you woke up. Look in the wastebasket. A whole batch of paper napkins crumpled up."

"I'll be back in a minute. I want to write something down."

In her green notebook, at the end of the list of important things that happened the year that she was ten, Anastasia wrote, "I have no grandmother all of a sudden".

Then she wrote, "But I have an inward eye, for the first time".

Late that morning, Anastasia went with her father to the Riverview Nursing Home.

"I don't want to see Grandmother dead," she said to him when he asked her to come along.

"No," he told her. "You won't. Grandmother's body has been taken away. But the people at the nursing home want us to come and get her things. I suppose they have someone waiting for her room."

So she went along. She had been to the nursing home before, to visit her grandmother, but she had never liked it much. The name Riverview was a lie. The Charles River was close by, but there was no view of it from the nursing home. From the window of her grandmother's room there was only a view of the underside of a fire escape, and one side of a Lutheran church.

"Grandmother must have hated looking at a fire escape all the time," Anastasia said when they went into the room and she saw the view again.

"I think", said her father, "that from her bed she could probably see the sky."

Anastasia lay down very straight and flat on the bare mattress of her grandmother's bed. She looked through the window and felt better.

"Yes," she said. "She could definitely see the sky."

"Would you help me, sweetie?" asked her father. "There are just these few things in the chest of drawers. Let's pack them into the suitcase."

So Anastasia helped her father fold the clothes that still smelled like her grandmother: like soap and powder and lilac cologne. It made them both feel sad.

"I remember that she was wearing this jumper at Christmas," said Anastasia, rubbing the wool of the grey jumper against her cheek.

"She was wearing this nightgown when I came to see her last Sunday," said her father, looking at a folded gown of yellow flannel.

"What's this?" asked Anastasia, taking a shoe box from the top drawer. She opened it and looked inside. "Look! The paperweight that I made for her in class one!"

She took out the little clay paperweight painted with tulips.

"And look! My school pictures!"

She took out the small photographs, three of them: first, second, and third class. In the first-class picture, her front teeth were missing. In the second-class picture, her hair was a mess and her new front teeth made her look like a chipmunk. The third-class picture wasn't too bad, she thought, looking at it. "Hello, little girl," she said, imitating her grandmother. "What's your name?"

Her father took a gold ring from the box. "This was her wedding ring," he said. Anastasia slipped it onto her finger; it almost fitted. Her grandmother had had small thin hands.

"Who's that? It looks like you, with funny clothes." She took a photograph from her father's hands.

"That was my father. That was Sam."

The man had her father's face, but without the beard; he had a neatly trimmed moustache, and a stiff collar. He had a nice, serious sort of smile.

"He was a good father, wasn't he, Daddy?"

"Yes," said her father. "He was a very good father."

"Grandmother sure loved him."

"She sure did."

"Boy," said Anastasia, "you know what I wish? I wish that everybody who loved each other would die at exactly the same time. Then nobody would have to miss anyone."

"Well," said her father slowly, "it just doesn't work that way. It just doesn't seem to work that way very often."

They packed the rest of her grandmother's things:

her glasses, the gold pin that she had worn on her dress at Thanksgiving and Christmas, her stockings, and a pair of soft woollen gloves. It didn't take very long.

Anastasia thought of her own room, and about the time when she had decided to leave home, and what she had packed into her father's US Navy bag. There were so many things in her room that she had had to leave most of them behind.

She wondered how it happened that when you were ninety-two you didn't have very many things left.

"When I'm old," she said, "I would like to keep my favourite things, like my orang-utan poster and Red Sox cap. And Frank, of course. If I have to go to a nursing home, would you make sure that I still have those things?"

"When you're old, sport," her father said, "I won't be around any more."

"Oh. I forgot. Well, I'll have to tell my children, I guess." Anastasia reminded herself to write that down in her green notebook: "Things That I Want To Take To The Nursing Home When I Am Old".

"Is there anything special that *you* want to have around when you're old? Because you should tell me, and I'll write it down," she said to her father.

"Just one," he said with a smile. "Your mother."

They snapped the suitcase closed and looked around the empty room. There was no sign of her grandmother left except the faint scent of powder and cologne. Anastasia lay down on the bed once more, flat on her back.

"Daddy, were there stars last night?"

"Yes. It was a very clear night. Millions of stars."

"Well, I feel absolutely sure that when Grandmother died she was looking at the sky and seeing millions of stars. Probably she was even smiling."

"And thinking of Sam," said her father.

"Yes. Thinking of Sam."

A nurse appeared at the door of the room and looked inside. Anastasia sat up quickly, feeling guilty because she had her shoes on the bed.

"Dr Krupnik?" said the nurse.

"Yes?"

The nurse smiled. "Your wife has just called. You'd better go right home. Your baby's on the way."

"For pete's sake," said Anastasia. "Everything's happening all at once. I think my wart must have caused it."

Things I Love!

- Making Lists
- Mars Bars
- Writing Poems
- My Room
- My Wart
- Frank (my goldfish)
- Secret Bad Thoughts
- Wedding Gowns
- ~~Washburn Cummings~~
- My Name
- ~~My Grandmother~~
- My Friends
- Wordsworth
- Christmas
- ~~My Parents~~
- Memories (esp. of my wart)
- Washburn Cummings (maybe!)
- My Late Grandmother
- My Parents

Things I Hate!

- Mr Belden (at the chemist's)
- ~~Boys~~
- Liver
- ~~Pumpkin Pie~~
- Mrs Westvessel
- ~~My Parents~~
- Babies
- ~~Boys~~
- ~~Washburn Cummings~~
- ~~All My Friends~~
- ~~My Name~~
- ~~My Parents~~
- Hospital Rules

11

The telephone rang late in the afternoon while Anastasia was alone in the flat.

Once she had made an anonymous phone call to Washburn Cummings, to ask him if his refrigerator was running. But Washburn Cummings had answered the phone in a fake deep voice, and said, "For whom does this bell toll?", which threw her timing off, so that she had hung up giggling in embarrassment.

She had always, since then, wanted to answer the phone by saying, "For whom does this bell toll?" but her nerve always failed at the last moment.

It did again. She picked up the receiver and said, "Hello."

It was Mrs Westvessel.

It made Anastasia feel very creepy to be talking to Mrs Westvessel on the telephone. For some reason she didn't like to think of Mrs Westvessel eating, or going shopping, or watching television, or being asleep. Teachers belonged only in front of a classroom, saying the spelling words in a loud, clear voice, or telling someone to turn around and sit up straight.

She also didn't like to think of Mrs Westvessel as having any first name except Mrs; so it felt very creepy to hear the voice say, "Anastasia, this is Dorothy Westvessel."

"Oh," said Anastasia. "Hello."

"Anastasia, when you were absent from school today, I thought it was just because you had a cold. Yesterday you were sniffling a little."

Anastasia couldn't think of anything to say, except, "Oh" again.

"But the evening paper just came, dear, and I saw that your grandmother had passed away. I called to tell you how sorry I am about that."

"Well," said Anastasia in a small voice, "she was very, very old."

"Yes, I know. But last year my mother died, and *she* was almost as old as your grandmother. And it made me feel very sad anyway, because I loved her. I know you must be feeling sad."

"Yes," Anastasia said. "I am."

"Well, I'll let you go, dear. But don't worry about your schoolwork. We all missed you in school today, but nothing very important happened. We had a film about Eskimos."

"Mrs Westvessel?"

"Yes, dear?"

"My mother's at the hospital because she's having a baby today."

"Well, Anastasia! My goodness! You are certainly having a day of important events, and when you get back to school we will have lots to talk about!"

Anastasia said goodbye politely, and Mrs Westvessel said goodbye politely; and Anastasia went to her room, found her green notebook, and crossed Mrs Westvessel off the list of THINGS I HATE.

"I am most heartily sorry that I wished Mrs Westvessel would get pimples," Anastasia confessed aloud to the empty flat. She really *felt* sorry, too, and thought briefly that she might have been an okay Catholic after all.

She flipped the pages of her notebook and looked at the baby's name. Good old One-Ball Reilly Krupnik; Anastasia hoped that he was coming along all right, getting born.

Maybe, after all, it wouldn't be too bad, having a brother. Anastasia wandered into the little pantry room. Her mother had replaced the broken pane of glass, carefully puttying the edges; and the unicorn curtains were in place. The cot was set up, and there was a folded blue blanket in it. In the drawers that had once held tablecloths, the little clothes were folded and stacked. She picked up a tiny undershirt, unfolded it, and wondered how anybody could possibly be so small.

"For pete's sake, One-Ball," Anastasia said aloud to the empty room, "you are going to be revoltingly helpless if you are that little."

"I suppose", she said, looking at the baby carriage that stood in a corner of the dining room, "that I would be willing to take you for walks, maybe past Washburn Cummings's house. But I am absolutely not under any circumstances *ever* going to change your nappies."

"Anastasia!" Her father came through the front door of the flat. "It's a boy!"

"Daddy," said Anastasia very patiently, "I *know* that."

Her father looked at her for a moment, and grinned. "Of course you do. I forgot. I need coffee. No, I need a beer. It was terrific. Your mother was terrific, and the baby is terrific. He weighs eight pounds and four ounces. Or maybe it's four pounds and eight ounces. No, I guess it's the way I said it first. I really need a beer."

Anastasia got him a beer and sipped the foam before she gave him the glass.

"Relax," she said, "and tell me about it. Did Mom do the breathing right?"

"Exactly right. And I didn't faint. For a minute I thought I was going to faint. But I didn't."

"Daddy, why would you *faint*? That's ridiculous."

"Of course it's ridiculous. Why would a grown man faint? The baby looks like you, Anastasia."

"Was he repulsive and screaming and did he pee on the nurse's hand?"

"That's exactly what he looked like and what he did. But then later, when he was all cleaned up and asleep, he looked terrific and he looked just like you. Same colour hair."

"Freckles? Does he have freckles?"

Her father thought. "No," he said. "I didn't notice any freckles."

"He didn't get my *wart*, did he?"

"No. No wart."

"Good. Maybe when he's older he'll get his own wart."

"Come on. I came home to get you and take you back to the hospital so you can see Mom and the baby."

They stopped at the shop on the way to the hospital.

"I need a box of your best cigars," Anastasia's father said to Mr Belden. "My wife has just had a baby boy."

Mr Belden leaned across the counter and shook his hand. "Congratulations," he said. Then he reached down to shake Anastasia's hand. "Congratulations to you, too, little girl. That's quite an accomplishment, to have a new brother." He took a foil-wrapped chocolate cigar from the sweets counter and gave it to her.

"I happen to know that you like Mars bars best," Mr Belden said to Anastasia, "but today you'll have to make do with a chocolate cigar, because of the baby. Compliments of Belden's Pharmacy."

"Thank you," said Anastasia in surprise.

Back in the car, Anastasia took her green notebook from the glove compartment, turned to THINGS I HATE, and crossed out Mr Belden's name.

Then she turned to the very last page, which was blank, and wrote something very carefully, very private, as a surprise. It made her feel good to write it.

In the hospital room, her mother was sitting up in bed, smiling. In a little cot beside her bed, the baby lay on his back with his eyes closed tight. Anastasia looked at him carefully. Yellow hair. No freckles. No warts. He didn't smell bad; he smelled clean and powdery. He wasn't crying.

"He's not a bad baby, for pete's sake," said Anastasia. She touched his curled-up hand; in his sleep, the baby opened his fist and wrapped his fingers around her thumb.

"Hey," said Anastasia in surprise. "I really like him!"

Her parents were smiling.

"Does he wet his nappies a whole lot?" Anastasia asked suspiciously.

"He's only five hours old," said her mother, "so I haven't had time to conduct an exhaustive study. But in all honesty, Anastasia, I have to tell you that I think he will probably wet his nappies a lot."

Anastasia sighed. "Well," she said, finally. "I can tell that this baby is going to be a lot of work. So probably I will be willing to change his nappies occasionally.

"Only *wet* ones, though. Nothing else."

"Fair enough," said her mother.

"Have you picked out his name?" asked her father.

"Have I picked out his name?" said Anastasia. "What kind of stupid question is that? Of *course* I've picked out his name. But wait a minute; I want to write something down.

"Give me back my hand, please," she said politely to

her brother, and took her thumb gently out of his fist. In her green notebook, under THINGS I HATE, she crossed out "BABIES".

Then she turned to the last page of her notebook, to what she had written in the car, and tore it out carefully. She laid the sheet of paper on the baby, on top of the white blanket that covered the little mound of his body and curled-up legs. She watched as the paper moved a tiny bit, up and down.

"Look," Anastasia whispered, awed. "Look how he breathes."

The paper said: "Someone Special: Sam".

"Hi, Sam," she said.

"Hi, Sam," said her mother.

"Hi, Sam," said her father.

"You know what?" said Anastasia, after a moment. "There's absolutely nothing left on my 'Things I Hate' list except liver, for pete's sake. I guess I'll always hate liver."

"Gee, Anastasia," said her father solemnly, "that's too bad, because that's what I was planning to give you for supper tonight."

Anastasia took her foil-wrapped cigar out of her pocket. Very slowly she removed all of the foil. Then she put the cigar into her mouth and chewed on it, frowning, briefly. Finally, she took it out of her mouth, wiggled her eyebrows up and down, Groucho Marx style, flicked an imaginary ash from her cigar, and said, "Say the secret word and you win a hundred bucks."

"And the secret word is not *liver*?" asked her father,

wiggling his own eyebrows.

"Nope."

"*Steak?*"

Anastasia grinned. "With mushrooms," she said.

Things I Love!	Things I Hate!
Making Lists	~~Mr Belden (at the chemist's)~~
Mars Bars	
Writing Poems	~~Boys~~
My Room	Liver
My Wart	~~Pumpkin Pie~~
Frank (my goldfish)	~~Mrs Westvessel~~
Secret Bad Thoughts	~~My Parents~~
Wedding Gowns	~~Babies~~
~~Washburn Cummings~~	~~Boys~~
My Name	~~Washburn Cummings~~
~~My Grandmother~~	~~All My Friends~~
My Friends	~~My Name~~
Wordsworth	~~My Parents~~
Christmas	~~Hospital Rules~~
~~My Parents~~	
Memories (esp. of my wart)	
Washburn Cummings (maybe!)	
My Late Grandmother	
My Parents	
Babies (esp. Sam)	

Anastasia Again!

To Laura Beard

1

"The suburbs!" said Anastasia. "We're moving to the *suburbs*? I can't believe it. I can't believe that you would actually do such a thing to me. I'm going to kill myself. As soon as I finish this chocolate pudding, I'm going to jump out of the window."

"We live on the first floor," her mother reminded her. "You've been jumping out of your window for years. The first time you jumped out of your window was when you were three years old and didn't want to take a nap any more."

"Yes," said Anastasia, remembering. "You thought I'd been kidnapped, when you came to my room to wake me up and I was gone. Actually I was outside picking all your tulips."

"I could have killed you for that. It was the first time I'd ever grown really terrific tulips."

"I wish you *had* killed me for that. Because there isn't any point in living if you have to live in the suburbs."

Her father put down the magazine he was reading, *The New York Review of Books*. He was reading an article called 'Morality and Mythology'. Anastasia didn't have any idea what that meant; but she liked reading about it, and she was absolutely certain that there wasn't a single person in the entire suburbs of the United States who would ever in their life read an article called 'Morality and Mythology'.

"How on earth," asked her father, "can you be so sure you would hate the suburbs when you have never lived anywhere but in this flat?"

"Daddy," Anastasia pointed out. "I *read*. You know that. You yourself taught me to read when I was four years old. I read books about the suburbs. I know what people who live there are like."

"Oh? And what are they like?"

"Not like us, that's for sure. One, they live in split-level houses with sets of matching furniture. Can you *imagine* that? Rooms of cute matching furniture? Good grief. I mean, think for a minute about our living room here in this flat. Think of all the neat stuff we have in it."

They thought. "Books," said her mother.

"Right. Millions of books. There aren't any bookcases in split-level houses. Right where the bookcases should be, people in the suburbs have a huge colour TV instead."

"We have a TV," said her father. "In fact, I'm about to miss the first inning of the Red Sox game."

"Daddy, we have an ancient, small black-and-white TV. And there are books on top of it, books behind it, books in front of it. That's not the same. I'm talking about a monster colour TV, and on top of it is a bowl of fake fruit."

"Fake fruit? Are you sure of that, Anastasia?"

"Absolutely. Just look in the houses to let ads in the paper. But forget that for a minute. Think some more about our own living room."

"Paintings," said her mother. "I think people in the suburbs have paintings on their walls."

"Wrong,'" said Anastasia. "The paintings on our walls are real. We have some of your paintings, Mum. And we have that one that I did of a cockerel, when I was five. And we have that really neat one by your friend Annie, Dad . . ."

"I wish you'd get rid of that, Myron," said Anastasia's mother.

"Annie was a fine painter," muttered her father. "And a fine person. You would have liked her. You will like her if she ever comes back from Central America. We'll have her for dinner."

"Over my dead body we'll have her for dinner," said Anastasia's mother.

"Mum. Daddy. You're missing the point. The point is that we have meaningful paintings on our walls."

"And people in the suburbs do not?"

"No they definitely don't. They have pictures of the Sierra Nevadas, painted-by-number. Or else pictures of kittens with big eyes, playing with balls of wool. It goes with the matched set of furniture."

"Actually," said her mother, "our furniture is pretty awful, some of it."

"No, it isn't! We're the only people in the whole world who have a white couch with a big sunflower embroidered on it!"

"Anastasia, the only reason for the sunflower is because I had to do something to cover up the spot where Sam threw up."

"But that's okay! I mean it's okay in the *city*. But if we lived in a split-level house in some development, people wouldn't understand it."

"ANASTASIA," said her father, in the booming voice that he used only when he was beginning to be quite annoyed with something, "YOU'RE MAKING ASSUMPTIONS."

"I am not. I never make anything. I didn't make the school basketball team, even."

"You are making assumptions."

"I don't even know what assumptions are. I can't even make decent brownies."

"*Premature* assumptions!"

"I didn't make the finals in the class seven's spelling bee. I can't make *anything*."

"YOU ARE MAKING HASTY JUDGEMENTS! IDIOTIC PREMATURE ASSUMPTIONS! AND YOU ARE ALSO MAKING ME MISS THE RED SOX GAME ON TV!"

Now Anastasia knew that he was really getting angry. She scowled. "I hardly ever even make my bed," she muttered. "The last thing I ever made in my life was a stupid potholer, in class four. I *never* made a premature assumption. If I did, it would come out crooked."

Her mother sighed. "I'll tell you what you make, Anastasia. You make life very difficult sometimes." She began to pick up the chocolate pudding bowls from the table. "Let's let your dad watch the ball game. I'm going to wash these dishes. You want to help, or do you want to get Sam up from his nap? We can talk about all of this later."

"I'll go and get Sam. Unless maybe he's already jumped out of the window. He's getting old enough to work stuff like that out."

She wandered down the hallway of the flat thumping the walls as she went. It made a nice, hollow, echoing sound in the dark hall. Anastasia had noticed that for the first time when she was three or four and had been thumping the walls ever since. There were handprints way down low, from when she was very small; handprints higher up, from when she was bigger (and a dark stain at that height: she had squashed a tomato there when she was nine and very angry about something); and now that she was twelve and beginning to be quite tall, her handprints were appearing at a level that had never had handprints before.

The whole flat had a history, and it was *her* history

and her parents' history and beginning to be Sam's. She had planned to show Sam how to thump the walls with that hollow sound very soon. The thought of moving made her stomach ache.

"And we didn't even have a chance to talk about the *other* stuff!" she called back towards the kitchen, where she could hear her mother washing the dishes. "That we would have to have a *car*, for pete's sake! We would have to do stupid suburban stuff. Probably I would have to be a Girl Guide!"

There wasn't any answer from her mother. In the living room, she could hear her father turn the volume up on the TV to drown her out.

"You could never *ever* wear jeans any more, you know, Mum!" she called. "Ladies in the suburbs only wear pretty cotton dresses from Lord and Taylor's!"

No answer. She stood still for a minute outside Sam's door.

"And they play *bridge* every afternoon! And have affairs with the neighbours' husbands! Do you *realize* that?"

No answer. Her mother was washing the dishes very loudly, which meant that she was getting pretty cross. In a minute she would probably throw a dish.

"Oh, rats," muttered Anastasia to herself, and opened the door to her brother's room. Once, before Sam was born, it had been the dining room. It was true that they were outgrowing the flat. But it didn't matter. Not as much as the other things mattered.

"Hello Sam," said Anastasia. Her brother was

sitting in his cot with a blanket over his head, chuckling. "Stop being so smart," she said. "I have terrible news." Sam took the blanket off his head and looked at her. His face had sleeping wrinkles on it.

"Frank Goldfish is going to die," said Anastasia sorrowfully. "Goldfish can't survive things like moving to the suburbs. Suburban goldfish are different, anyway. They have tanks with all that plastic junk in them: castles and little fake divers. Frank just likes his little ordinary city-goldfish bowl. I am quite certain that Frank will not survive this."

Then she realized that Sam didn't care about that. It was Sam who had flushed Frank the First down the toilet.

"And also," she told him sadly, "I know that your blanky won't survive. Moving men absolutely refuse to move grubby old blankies. I'm sorry to tell you that, Sam." She lifted him out of his cot and took his faded yellow blanket away from him. He grabbed for it, missed, and burst into howls.

"It's really too bad about your blanky, Sam," Anastasia said in a soft, mournful voice. "I suppose we'll have to put it out for the garbage men to pick up."

Sam stamped his small bare feet. "Gimme my blanky!" he roared, grabbing for it. Anastasia held it up higher.

"I'm so terrribly sorry, Sam," she said in a stricken tone that she was imitating from an old movie that had been re-run on TV recently. George Brent telling Bette Davis that she had a brain tumour.

Sam's howls turned into shrieks, and he threw himself on the floor and began to kick.

"Mum? Dad?" called Anastasia. "I've just told Sam the news! Can you hear him? He doesn't want to move to the suburbs either!"

Anastasia went to her room to sulk. She always left the door open when she was sulking. She had perfected the art of sulking, and one of the essential points was that people had to *know* you were doing it. So it was important to leave the door open.

She lay on her bed, which was the best place for sulking, and was visible from her open door. But when no one was walking past her room, sulking was boring. So, to pass the time, she got out the notebook in which she intended to write a mystery novel. She had been intending to write it for almost a year, as soon as she could think of a title. She had decided to write a mystery after she began to think that Nancy Drew mysteries had no relationship to real life. Whose real life, after all, included haunted houses, spiral staircases, or twisted candlesticks? Yet real life – especially Anastasia's real life – was full of mysteries. For almost a year, she had been making notes about the mysteries of her own existence. None of them yet seemed to lend themselves to an entire book. 'The Mystery of Why I Am Not Allowed to Go to X-rated Movies Even Though I have Known All the Facts of Life Since I Was Six', for example, was a legitimate mystery of real life; but she couldn't seem to go on to write a novel about it.

Now, angrily, she wrote, 'The Mystery of Why Some People Make Decisions without Consulting Their Twelve-Year-Old Children'. Then she wrote, 'Chapter One: Decisions about Moving to the (Ugh) Suburbs'.

But she got so angry, just thinking about it, that she didn't write anything else. It was hard to write in a notebook while you were lying on a bed anyway. It was much easier to lie back and sulk.

2

"Daddy?" asked Anastasia, as she stood at the bathroom door that evening, watching her father give Sam a bath. "Have you and Mum ever given serious thought to what a weird baby Sam is?"

It was true, what she said. Right now, for example, Sam was sitting in the bath, and he looked like any ordinary two-and-a-half-year-old baby. He had a fat stomach with a poking-out bellybutton, rosy cheeks, curly brown hair, brown eyes with long eyelashes, and he had soap suds in his ears, which was kind of cute. A minute ago he had squirmed and wiggled and screeched when his father had washed his face, which was an ordinary two-and-a-half-year-old baby thing to do.

But then he had said firmly and with dignity, "Don't get soap in my eyes, please. My eyes are very sensitive."

That was weird. The little boy next door could only say things like ma-ma, da-da, bye-bye, and ordinary baby things.

Sam had *never* said ma-ma or da-da or bye-bye. He had started talking like Walter Cronkite before he was a year old. Anastasia's mother *swore* that one day when he was four months old, he had said, "Thank you", when she fed him some strained apricots; but no one believed her, and she had no witnesses.

"He's not weird," said Anastasia's father, lifting Sam out of the bath. "It's just that people develop at different rates. For example, Anastasia, you are twelve years old, but you are already five feet seven inches tall . . ."

"I *know* that, Daddy. You don't really need to *remind* me of that, Daddy."

"I only bring it up because it is an unusual height for a twelve-year-old girl. You've grown fast, height-wise. But at the same time, your body is still quite straight, up and down. I mean, you haven't yet begun to mature much physically, except for height. You don't yet have *hips*, for example, or . . ."

"*Daddy. Don't be gross.*"

"There's nothing gross about hips. I was just pointing out that different aspects of people develop at different rates. Now in many ways, Sam is still a baby. Cut that out Sam."

Sam was eating toothpaste.

"I like it," said Sam. "I like the flavour."

"Well, it costs a dollar fifty-nine a tube. Cut it out."

He began to dry Sam with a big blue towel.

"See what I mean, Anastasia? He's mischievous, like all toddlers. And he still wears nappies because he hasn't achieved the physical maturity to be toilet-trained. I *wish* you would be toilet-trained, Sam."

"No," said Sam, and smiled sweetly.

"And he still has his security blanket, like many babies . . ."

"Where is my blanky?" asked Sam. "I want it right now."

"Mum washed it while you were having your bath," said Anastasia. "It's in the dryer."

"Well I want it when I go to bed," said Sam firmly.

Dr Krupnik pinned on Sam's nappy and snapped up his pyjamas.

"There you are, old buddy. Go and find your mum."

Sam padded off down the hall.

"It's just that he is verbally precocious," said Anastasia's father, leaning over to scrub out the bath. "He's unusual, that way. But I wouldn't call him – what did you call him? – a weird baby."

"Well, okay then, he's unusual. Don't you and Mum realize what a *disaster* it would be to move an unusual baby like Sam to the suburbs? In the suburbs all babies are alike."

"You're sure of that?"

"Absolutely. All suburban babies ride around in shopping trolleys at supermarkets, and whine, and their mothers slap them."

"Their mothers *slap* them?"

"Absolutely. Their mothers all have pink curlers in their hair. Do you want that to happen to Mum, and to Sam?"

Dr Krupnik sighed. "Anastasia, get me a beer from the refrigerator. As soon as your mum puts Sam to bed, we will talk some more about this move which we are going to make."

"Did I hear the last part of the sentence correctly?"

"Which we *are going to make.*"

"You once told me that this family was a democracy."

"Wrong. I said that this family is a benevolent dictatorship."

"Don't I get any part in the decision making? Is this a fascist state?"

"Not at all. You get a part."

"What part?"

"You're going to help us choose a house."

They sat around the table in the living room, which had once been the dining room table until the dining room had become Sam's bedroom. It was certainly true, Anastasia thought again, that the flat was getting too small. Or maybe they were getting too big. Certainly *she* was getting too big. Five foot seven, for pete's sake. Probably the Celtics would be scouting her for their basketball team before she was fifteen. At this rate she would be almost seven feet tall by then. Already no boys liked her, because she was taller than they were. When she was seven feet tall, it would be even worse.

Not that she *wanted* any boys to like her. Anastasia hated all boys, especially all the boys in class seven of the Bosler Primary School, and most especially Robert Giannini, who carried a briefcase to school every day. She wondered what Robert Giannini did with his briefcase now that school was over for the summer.

Maybe there would be more interesting boys in the secondary school in the autumn. Not that she cared, of course.

And by autumn they might be living in the suburbs. She could feel the thought of it affecting her physically. The stomach-ache was coming back. She could feel her hair beginning to ooze oil, so she would have to wash it again before she went to bed, and she had already washed it that morning. She could feel a pimple beginning to grow on her chin. Her eyes, behind her glasses, began to blur. Terrific. Now she was going blind on top of everything else.

Anastasia pictured herself in the suburbs: seven feet tall, with acne and greasy hair, and blind. She would get a Seeing Eye dog, a ferocious one, and name him Fang. If any boys ever made any remarks to her about her height, she would simply say in a low voice to Fang, "Kill".

That wasn't a bad thought. It made her smile to herself. She pictured her Seeing Eye dog tearing Robert Giannini's briefcase to shreds with his teeth and then starting in on Robert Giannini himself. She grinned. Her vision came back.

"So," said her father, taking out a notebook, "what we need to do is make a list."

Anastasia groaned. Even her mother groaned. Dr Krupnik was always making lists. Once, when Anastasia was younger, *she* had been a list maker too. But then her life became too complicated.

"House," wrote Dr Krupnik at the top of the page. "Okay," he said. "Let's decide what kinds of things we want to look for in a house. Katherine, what's most important to you?"

Her mother thought for a moment, chewing on a strand of her long hair. Her hair was always shiny, like a TV commercial for shampoo. She didn't even wash it every day. She told Anastasia that when she was a teenager she had had oily hair, but Anastasia didn't believe her. Parents always tell you stuff to make you feel better, and when they do it, it makes you feel worse.

"Light," said her mother, finally. "Good light, and a room all to myself, where I can paint."

That made sense. Anastasia had been afraid for a moment that her mother would say, "Coppertone appliances in the kitchen". Anybody who had a kitchen full of coppertone appliances would very soon start wearing pink curlers and worrying about wax build-up.

But light, good light, and a room where she could paint made sense. Anastasia's mother was a very good painter. Long ago, before she was married, she had studied art in New York. Even now some of her paintings hung in galleries in Boston and Cambridge. But her easel and paints were in the tiny room that had once been a pantry. She never complained about that, but it made Anastasia feel a little sad for her.

"Light," wrote Dr Krupnik on the page. "Room for painting," he wrote. "Anastasia?" he asked. "What is most important to you?"

She was thinking. Now that her vision had unblurred, now that she wasn't going blind, she wouldn't need the Seeing Eye dog. Probably there was a law against having a Seeing Eye dog if you could see. Still, she did like the idea of a monstrous dog, straining at the end of a leash, to whom she could whisper, "Kill", if someone like Robert Giannini started making remarks.

"You go next, Dad," said Anastasia. "I'm still thinking."

"Study," he wrote next. "Bookcases," he wrote beside it.

Well, that made sense, too. Dr Krupnik was a professor of English. He also wrote poetry, and each time he had written enough poems to make a book, he sent them off to his publisher, and then a new book was published with his name on it. His picture was on the back of each of his books. Anastasia could never work out why people didn't recognize him on the streets and rush up and ask for his autograph. But they didn't. He said he didn't mind; in fact, he said, he was *glad* that they didn't.

People wrote to him, though. Strangers wrote to him: People who had read his books of poetry. Once, a year ago, Anastasia had got into a *lot* of trouble because of those letters. One night at dinner, when Sam was a much younger baby who kept them all awake at night because he howled and screamed a lot, so they were all feeling tired, Dr Krupnik had said, "There is a stack of mail on my desk that is giving me grey hair."

"Dad," Anastasia had pointed out, "you don't *have* any hair." That was true. The top of his head was quite bald.

"Well, my beard is getting grey, from that mail. When am I ever going to find time to answer it? I have to correct three hundred exams, and the publisher wants revisions on the new book . . ."

"Oh, don't worry," said her mother. "You'll get to it sometime. Those people don't expect answers anyway."

He had just groaned and stroked his beard.

Anastasia had thought about that. She *liked* to write letters, and she never had anyone to write to, because no one ever wrote to her. So the next day, using her father's portable typewriter, she had answered all of the letters. It was fun. To the man in Des Moines, who had sent three poems, asking Dr Krupnik to read them and give his opinion, Anastasia wrote:

Dear Mr Covington,

I read all of your nice poems. They are so very nice. They are not as good as mine, but that is because I have worked a long time at it, and I am quite famous. Maybe if you work at it some more, yours will be better in the future. I certainly do hope so.

A girl had written a very peculiar letter from San Francisco. The letter said that Myron Krupnik's love poems had really spoken to where she was at, and she thought they had kindred souls, and she would like to spend some time with him if he was ever in San Francisco. Anastasia answered her:

Dear Lisa,
I am a married man with two adorable children. And I never go to San Francisco. But thank you anyway.

A librarian in Detroit had written that Dr Krupnik's new book was very popular in her library. It was amazing, she wrote, how often people took it out. Anastasia answered the librarian.

. . . I don't think it is amazing at all. It is, after all, one of the finest collections of poetry published in the twentieth century. I wish you would suggest to them, though, that they *buy* the book. I don't make any money when they take it out of the library. If they buy it, I make 10%.

There had been twelve letters, and Anastasia had answered all of them, and she had mailed her answers. When she had told her father that night what she had done, she had planned to suggest that he might pay her a secretarial salary. It had taken her all day to write the letters. Even at minimum wage, it would be a good chunk of money for her savings account.

Instead, he had gone storming out of the house to the post office to try to get her letters back. The post office people had let him in, even though they were closed, but they wouldn't give him the letters. They told him that tampering with the mail was a federal offence. So he came home and drank two beers, very fast, without offering Anastasia the foam – without even *speaking* to Anastasia, for that matter – and then he stayed up until 2.00 A.M. writing letters to all the same people that Anastasia had just written to.

Anastasia had not worked out why her father was so upset until a few weeks later, when it became very clear. Robert Giannini had slipped her a note in school. The note said, "I like you. Do you like me? Tick one: Yes. No. A whole lot. I hate you. I don't know." She had ticked "I hate you" immediately; then she had decided that was cruel. So she rubbed out her first tick mark and ticked simply, "No". Underneath, she had written, "Sorry".

But she had thought, suddenly, while she was answering it, about how her father might have answered if he had tried to do it for her. Her father didn't believe in what he called "terse negatives". That meant that he didn't like simple nos. He probably would have written some long boring response, beginning "Dear Robert, you are in many ways a fine person, but at this particular time . . ."

Thinking about it, she had begun to realize that people just can't answer other people's mail.

Her parents were looking at her, and she realized that she had been daydreaming again, and not even about the right thing, not about the new house. What a horrible thought, a new house. Even thinking about Robert Giannini was better than thinking about a new house.

"What would happen," she asked slowly, "if we made this list about what we want in a house, and then we couldn't find a house that had those things?"

"Well," said her father, "I suppose we'd have to give up and stay here. But I think we can probably find what we want. Look: we've put down a room for your mum to paint in, with lots of light. And a study for me, with bookcases. While your mind was drifting there, off in space somewhere, we added a garden for Sam. Can't you think of anything that *you* want, Anastasia?"

"Yes," said Anastasia, realizing suddenly that she had solved everything, that they would not have to leave the flat, not have to live in the suburbs after all. "A tower. I want a house where I can have a room in a tower."

To her surprise, her father wrote that down.

*

"The Mystery of the Girl Who Lived in a Tower", Anastasia wrote dreamily.

Then she looked at that title. Good grief. It sounded like a Nancy Drew title. Probably on the library shelf of twelve thousand Nancy Drew books, there was already one called "The Mystery of the Tower Room" or something.

She tore that page out of her notebook and threw it away. It was much harder to write a book than she had ever realized it would be.

3

"Telephone for you, Anastasia!" her mother called from the kitchen.

Anastasia put down her book and walked towards the kitchen, thumping her hand along the wall.

"Who is it?" she asked her mother.

"I don't know. I didn't ask."

"Boy or girl?" What a stupid question. *Boys* never called her.

"Girl." Of course.

She took the receiver and stretched the cord so that she could take the phone into the pantry.

"Hello?"

"Hello, Anastasia. This is Robert."

"*Who?*"

"Robert Giannini."

"Oh. I thought it was a girl."

Good grief. What an incredibly stupid thing to say. It wasn't Robert Giannini's fault that his voice still sounded like a girl's. Anastasia sat down on the pantry floor and wanted to die on the spot.

"No, it's Robert." Maybe he hadn't noticed the incredibly stupid thing she had said.

"Hello, Robert."

"Hello."

If only she had paid more attention to the *Cosmopolitan* article on being a spritely conversationalist. It had a section about Phone Flirtation. Not that she cared.

Robert wasn't very spritely at conversation either, for pete's sake. Now they had each said hello twice, and no one was saying anything.

"I was just wondering the other day," Anastasia said, finally, "what you do with your briefcase in the summer-time." Good grief. What an idiotic thing to say. As if she'd been *thinking* about him, or something.

"I keep stuff in it. I collect stuff."

"Oh."

"Do you want to go and collect stuff with me?"

"What do you mean?"

"Well, do you want to go and ride bikes and maybe go down to the river and see if there's any interesting junk lying around?"

"Oh. Well, okay."

"Today do you want to do it?"

"Yes, okay."

"I'll meet you down at your corner. In about an hour, okay? I could come sooner but I have to have a shower first."

"Okay. Goodbye."

Anastasia groaned after she hung up the phone. If only he hadn't said that about the shower. The absolutely last thing in the entire world that Anastasia wanted to know was that Robert Giannini was going to have a shower, for pete's sake. It was the most embarrassing thing she had ever heard.

She wandered back into her bedroom, looked around at the clothes strewn on the floor, and had a horrible thought. She had nothing to wear. The jeans she was wearing had paint on one knee. Everything on the floor or the bed or the chair – or in the wardrobe, for that matter – was either too small, or incredibly ugly, or else Robert Giannini had already seen her wearing it.

Maybe she should call him back and tell him she couldn't go. But then he would ask why, and she would have to say she had no clothes, and that would be too embarrassing.

She wandered back to the kitchen. Her mother was defrosting the refrigerator. Sam was sitting on the floor, wearing only a nappy and sucking on chunks of ice that had come loose from the freezer.

"I'm eating ice," said Sam matter of factly. Sam had a knack for saying things that were already completely obvious, like, "I've wet my nappy", or "I'm eating my dinner", or "I'm wearing my pyjamas with clowns on them".

"I can *see* that you're eating ice, Sam," Anastasia said sarcastically. "Mum, you haven't by any chance bought me any new clothes recently and forgotten to tell me, have you?"

Her mother brushed back her hair from her eyes with one hand. "No. Why would I do that?"

"I don't know. I just hoped that you had. I don't have anything to wear."

"Are you going somewhere?"

"Yes, I'm just going out to ride my bike with a friend of mine. No big deal."

"What's wrong with what you're wearing?"

"Yucks. Look: paint on my knee. And this shirt has a torn sleeve."

"Well, it's pretty hot out. Why don't you wear your jogging shorts?"

"*Mum.* You can see my *legs* in them."

Her mother looked puzzled. "Of *course* you can see your legs in them. You can see *anybody's* legs in jogging shorts."

"Well, my legs are too skinny, if you must know."

Her mother sighed. "There's a clean pair of jeans in your drawer. If those won't do, I don't have any other suggestions. Unless you want to wear a dress."

Anastasia thumped back down the hall, into her room, and unfolded the clean jeans from her drawer. She put them on. They weren't too bad. She pulled a shirt out of the drawer, started to put it on, suddenly realized what it said, and wadded it back into the drawer. "Boston is for Lovers" was what the shirt said. Good grief. What if she had actually *worn* a shirt that said "Boston is for Lovers" across the front when she went to meet Robert Giannini, the jerk? It made her face feel hot to think about it.

Now she was *quite* sure that a pimple was starting on her chin. Her chin felt huge. She looked in the mirror; nothing on her chin except a couple of ugly freckles. Well, she was sure it was there, lurking, under the freckles. Probably it would *appear* just as she met Robert. She would be standing there and all of a sudden, right when he was looking at her, this *thing* would come bursting out of her chin. Probably he would *say* something about it, that jerk.

Anastasia found a shirt she didn't hate too much, one with a hideous frog on the front, and she pulled it on over her head. Now her hair was a mess. No time to wash her hair. She had washed it last night but already it felt as if she had washed it in oil.

Anastasia groaned, called "See you" to her mother and to Sam, and went off to get her bike out of the garage.

"Hello."

"Hello."

Terrific. It was going to be like the telephone conversation.

"Have you been having a good summer, Anastasia?" Robert sounded just like her great-aunt who called sometimes from Milwaukee.

"Okay, I suppose. I think we're going to move."

"You're going to *move?* Where are you going to move to?"

"Somewhere out in the suburbs, I suppose. We're looking for a house."

Robert wrinkled his nose. Anastasia wasn't sure if he was making a face about moving to the suburbs, or if he had to wrinkle his nose to adjust his glasses. Sometimes she did that to adjust her glasses, especially if it was hot.

"That's lousy," Robert said sympathetically. "You'll have to go to a new school and everything, and you won't know anybody. You won't have any friends."

Boy. Some people really know just what to say to cheer you up.

"I don't think I want to talk about it," said Anastasia glumly.

"Well, come on then," said Robert. "Let's ride down to the river." They got on their bikes. Robert had his briefcase hooked onto the back of his. Typical, thought Anastasia, looking at the briefcase. *Typical.*

The Charles River separated Cambridge from Boston. From their side, they could look across and see the skyscrapers of the city. Anastasia loved Boston, but she loved her side of the river more, where the old brick buildings of Harvard stood. Her father taught at Harvard. He rode a bike to work each day, and he carried a briefcase with him on his bike, but that was okay because he was forty-seven.

Her mother's bike had a little seat for Sam, and that was okay, too. In fact, her parents were perfect Cambridge people. Anastasia thought. Lots of Cambridge men had beards, as her father did, and rode bikes to work. Lots of Cambridge mothers wore jeans and rode bikes with baby seats to the grocery store, as her mother did. Nobody stared, in Cambridge, at her mother's clothes, like the French tee shirt with the picture of the chicken, and under the chicken an oval with the word *oeuf* in it. *Oeuf* meant "egg" in French. Anastasia's mother spoke French. She had spent a year in Paris, painting, before she was married.

Not one single person in the suburbs would know what *oeuf* meant. Anastasia was absolutely certain of that.

The banks of the Charles were filled with people. There were always lots of people there on warm days, all sorts of people. College students lying on blankets, reading. Families with babies and small children. Black people, white people, Chinese people, people who spoke other languages. Anastasia liked looking at the Indians best; the women wore long, flowing dresses that were not really dresses at all, but pieces of bright cloth wrapped around them in a complicated way. Some of them had a single red spot decorating the centre of their forehead. Their husbands wore turbans and had bushy beards and moustaches that came to points at the sides. Two of the turbaned men were throwing a Frisbee back and forth, and between them a dark-skinned baby toddled, wearing Pampers.

Anastasia wondered if there were chemist shops in India, with shelves of Pampers and talcum powder and Crest toothpaste.

She and Robert leaned their bikes against a tree. Near them, two girls speaking French were trying to put a kite together. They were doing it wrong, and Anastasia could have told them how to do it right, but the only French she knew was *oeuf* and *merci*.

Robert had unhooked his briefcase, and she saw him pick something up from under a bush and stash it away quickly in the briefcase.

"What was that?" she asked.

"Nothing. Just junk."

Liar. She had seen that it was a *Playboy* magazine.

"What kind of stuff do you usually find?"

"Last week I found a piece of rope and a plastic wine glass. Once I found a dollar bill."

A dollar bill. That wouldn't be so bad. She walked along beside Robert. There were a lot of things on the grass, but none of them very interesting. Squashed beer cans. Paper napkins. Flattened cigarette packets. A little plastic car with the wheels missing: she picked that up. Sam would like it. She put it in her pocket.

"Robert, you want a sock?"

Robert looked startled, as if she were going to hit him. "What for?"

"No, I don't mean I'm going to sock you. Do you want a *sock*, the kind you wear? There's one lying over there."

"What colour?" He didn't see it.

"Grey. But that's from dirt. I think it's probably white."

"I don't think so. One sock's not very useful."

"You could hang it up at Christmas." Good grief. She wished she hadn't said that. She didn't want Robert to know that she still hung a stocking up at Christmas, like a baby.

But Robert grinned. "I use my mum's tights at Christmas. She wears the stretchable kind."

Anastasia giggled. She happened to know that Robert's mother was quite fat. She wondered if Mrs Giannini wore the kind of tights that Anastasia had seen at the supermarket, the ones called Fat Fanny tights.

Of course she couldn't ask Robert that.

It was weird, the difference between talking to boys and talking to girls. Anastasia couldn't work that out. She could have mentioned Fat Fanny tights to her best friend, Jenny MacCauley. But in a million years she wouldn't have mentioned Fat Fanny tights to Robert.

But her mother didn't seem to have that problem, talking to her father. Or talking to any of their men friends, in fact. Her mother could have said Fat Fanny tights as if it were just an ordinary, funny thing to say.

What made it different, talking to Robert? Anastasia decided to read the *Cosmopolitan* article when she got home, the one about making spritely conversation, to see whether it explained why there are certain people that you have trouble saying stuff to, and why it feels, when you are with those people, as if your tongue is too big.

"Do you want to sit down and watch the boats?" asked Robert. They had walked quite a distance along the river. Robert had collected a few things: the *Playboy* that he thought she hadn't seen; a paperback copy of Shakespeare's sonnets, which he said he would give to his grandmother; a broken belt buckle, which he thought he could fix; and a whole batch of iced lolly sticks, which he said he used for building things like model aeroplanes. Anastasia only had the little plastic car in her pocket and a matchbook from the Hyatt Regency.

They sat down, and Robert began to fool with one of his trainers. Anastasia began to pray. She did not pray very often – only when absolutely necessary – but it was absolutely necessary right now. She prayed that Robert was not going to take his trainers off. Anastasia thought that feet were the grossest things in the whole world. If she had to look at Robert Giannini's feet, she would die, right there on the banks of the Charles River.

But he was only dislodging a pebble. Thank you, God, said Anastasia to herself.

"How is your family?" asked Robert politely.

"They're okay. My father's teaching a couple of summer school courses. And my mother has just finished doing some illustrations for a book about sea shells."

"Don't you have a baby brother? I remember when we were in class five, your mum had a baby."

"Yes. Sam. He's . . ." Anastasia hesitated. It was hard to describe Sam. "He's kind of weird," she said, finally.

Robert looked puzzled.

"He can talk okay," Anastasia said.

"Why is he weird, then?"

Good grief. It would be easy to explain, if she could tell about how Sam wasn't toilet-trained. But she couldn't say *that*, to Robert, any more than she could say Fat Fanny tights. Then she remembered what her father had said about Sam.

"Some parts of him didn't develop as quickly as others," she told Robert. "His brain is in good shape. But some other parts of him aren't so good."

"Oh," said Robert. "I understand."

They sat silently and watched the boats. The river was dotted with small sailing boats, heeled over in the breeze. Anastasia thought that it would be fun to be in a sailing boat. She didn't know how to sail. But she thought that it would be fun just to be a passenger, just to be sitting in the boat, maybe trailing her fingers in the water, while Robert did the sailing . . .

Good grief. Anastasia almost blushed. She had actually been thinking about sailing with stupid Robert Giannini, the jerk. Probably he would bring his briefcase along on a sailing boat, for pete's sake.

"You know," said Robert, "I've never told anybody this . . ."

Oh no, thought Anastasia. I don't want him to tell me something that he's never told anybody, for pete's sake.

" . . . but I have this cousin."

"So?"

"Well, my cousin Pete, he's sixteen years old. He's my aunt Marie's son?"

"Yes."

"And he's retarded."

"That's too bad," said Anastasia politely.

Robert was poking the grass with a twig. "I mean, he's really very severely retarded. He can't even live at home. He lives at a special place. Sometimes Aunt Marie takes him out for the day. Sometimes she brings him to our house. And he's just like practically a baby or something. He can't even feed himself."

"That's too bad," said Anastasia politely again. She felt genuinely sad about Robert's cousin Pete.

"So, well, the reason I told you that is because you shouldn't feel too bad about Sam. Because you said his brain is okay, and that's really the important thing. It doesn't matter that he's deformed. You shouldn't feel embarrassed about that or anything."

Deformed? Good grief. Had she said that Sam was deformed? Why had she said *that?* And now that she had said it, and Robert had made that long speech about his cousin, and he had never told anybody else, for pete's sake, now she certainly couldn't say hey, I made a mistake, I lied, Sam *isn't* deformed.

"Yes, well I'm not embarrassed about it," she said miserably. "It's not that bad."

"And you know they can do a lot of good stuff at the Children's Hospital. Probably your parents have already taken him there."

"Yes, they have." That, at least, wasn't a lie. Sam had had X-rays at the Children's Hospital last year, when he tipped over his high chair and fell on his head. The X-rays were negative. He was fine. It took a long time to wash the oatmeal out of his hair, though.

Robert said goodbye to Anastasia at the corner near her house. He said he was going to go home and make something out of his iced lolly sticks. He also said two other things that made her feel strange.

One was, "If you move to somewhere not too far away, I'll ride out on my bike to see you."

She answered, "Okay."

And the other was, "My family always donates money to the March of Dimes and stuff."

She couldn't work out why he said that. "That's nice," she said, puzzled. "Mine gives money to the Civil Liberties Union."

"The March of Dimes goes to help crippled children, like Sam," Robert explained before he rode away.

Anastasia walked her bike down the street to where she lived. She decided that she would definitely read that article in *Cosmopolitan*. Maybe it would explain how some people got themselves into such stupid situations by simply opening their mouths. Maybe it would explain how to get *out* of those situations.

She wondered how she would go about hiding Sam if Robert did come to visit her in the suburbs.

It was all too complicated, too mysterious. She couldn't begin to make a title out of all the things that were mystifying in her life.

Maybe she should write a letter to "Dear Abby", instead.

"Dear Abby," Anastasia wrote, "There is this boy in my class, I'll call him Richard to protect his identity, and the first thing that went wrong today was that Richard called me, and I said incredibly stupid things on the phone, and then . . ."

She stopped. Dear Abby would laugh. Anastasia had a sudden, horrible vision of Dear Abby, looking glamorous, sitting behind a mahogany desk, reading Anastasia's letter and wiping tears off her cheeks with a lace handkerchief, because she was laughing so hard that she cried. Then she would publish the letter in the newspaper, and everyone in Anastasia's school – everyone in Cambridge, in fact – would read it and would recognize who it was, because of course she would have to write about the briefcase. Everyone in Cambridge would laugh at her.

She turned to a new page in her notebook. "The Mystery", she wrote, thinking in titles again, "of Why Other People Always Think Your Very Serious Problems Are Hysterically Funny".

4

"Run a comb through your hair, sport. The estate agent lady'll be here in half an hour. She's going to take us to look at a house."

"Daddy, I *told* you that I don't want to go and look at houses. *Casablanca* is on TV this afternoon. I'm going to watch it over at Jenny's. You and Mum go and look at the house with the estate agent lady. I'll take Sam with me to Jenny's if you want."

"No. You and Sam are coming with us today. Your mum and I have already looked at seven houses . . ."

Her mother interrupted. "I looked at five others without you, Myron. I've looked at twelve altogether."

"Twelve, then. And this sounds like one that we want you to see. And Sam, too. Where is Sam?"

Anastasia groaned and went to look for her

brother. She found him sitting on his bedroom floor looking at a volume of *War and Peace*.

"Good grief, Sam. Don't tell me you can *read* now!"

"Of course I can't read. I'm only two and a half years old. I'm looking for the pictures. Why doesn't this book have pictures?"

"I don't know. Probably pictures hadn't been invented yet, when it was written. Come on, Sam. Let me change your nappy. We have to go and look at a house."

"Booorrrring," said Sam cheerfully.

"You're right: *boring*. Hey, listen Sam. Do you want to be in a plot?"

"Okay."

"Well, you cry when you see the house, okay? Cry a whole lot, and say you hate it. Say you're *allergic* to it. Say it makes your eyes hurt, or something."

"Okay," said Sam cheerfully. He practised a fake whimper.

"Yes, that's pretty good," said Anastasia as she changed his nappy and buttoned him into a clean sunsuit. "Just keep doing that when you see the house. Maybe you can make real tears."

The estate agent lady had bleached hair and a gross car with push-button windows. Sam fooled with the button on his window and mashed his fingers and began to cry.

"Not yet, Sam," muttered Anastasia. "Save it."

"I think you'll adore this house," said the estate agent lady in a fake voice. "Good neighbourhood, too. Wonderful schools. What class did you say you were in, Anastasia?"

"I'll be class eight."

"Oh, goodness, I thought you were older. Maybe because you're so tall for your age."

Terrific. Didn't anybody ever tell her how rude it is to mention somebody's *flaws*, for pete's sake? Was she going to mention her father's baldness next?

No. She was going to talk about the roof and the furnace. Wonderful old slate roof, needs no maintenance at all, lasts forever; wonderful brand new furnace, just put in last year, hardly uses any oil, blah blah blah. Anastasia could hardly believe that her mother had already been through this twelve times. She tried to think of the most boring thing she had ever done; going to an organ concert at the Catholic church with Jenny MacCauley's family came to her mind. She had almost fallen asleep. She imagined doing it twelve times. No way.

And this was just as boring, maybe even more so. Now the lady was babbling about the plumbing, the wonderful copper pipes, the woodwork, the wonderful woodwork, the interest rates, the wonderful interest rates.

Anastasia's interest rate in this conversation was nought per cent. She leaned back on the gross plastic seat of the gross car and gazed through the window.

The trees and lawns were nice. It was certainly a lot greener than Cambridge.

"Look, Sam," she said, and pointed. Some kids in bathing suits were running through a sprinkler in a garden.

Sam looked. "I would like that," he said thoughtfully.

"Yes, because you like being wet, stupid," Anastasia said pointedly.

Anastasia was beginning to feel very odd. At first she thought maybe she was carsick. Then she realized what it was. It was because she liked what she was seeing through the windows of the car. She liked the trees and the lawns and the flowers. She liked the idea of running through a sprinkler, even with stupid Sam. She liked it that there were dogs and kids and bikes and a kind of nice-smelling quiet out here, wherever they were. But to like those things meant moving, and she loved Cambridge and the flat. So there was a war going on in her stomach.

"Well, kiddos," said the estate agent lady in her Barbie Doll voice, as she turned a corner, "here we are. This is it!"

Sam dutifully burst into fake tears. "I'm allergic to it!" he wailed.

Anastasia didn't even hear him. She was looking at the house, and her stomach felt as if she had been kicked by someone wearing cowboy boots. Her mother had once told her that it was painful to fall in love, and now, suddenly, she knew what that meant. She had expected to feel it for the first time when she fell in love with a *boy*, for pete's sake. But now she was feeling it – the pain in her stomach, her heart beating funny, Mantovani violin music in her ears, and aching behind her eyes as she tried not to cry – because she was falling in love with a *house.*

It was because the house had a tower.

And it happened to all of them as if it were a contagious disease. The main symptoms were speechlessness and silly grins.

The estate agent lady didn't understand that. She thought something was wrong. She became confused when none of them said anything, and she began to apologize for the house.

The study was lined from floor to ceiling, on every wall, with bookcases. And it had a fireplace. Anastasia's father stood in the centre of the study with a silly grin and said nothing.

"I know you wanted a study," said the estate agent lady. "Of course this room seems small, I know. But you could have all these shelves torn out, and that would open up the room quite a bit and make it larger, and . . ."

Her voice drifted away in confusion, because no one was listening to her. Anastasia could read her father's mind. In his mind he was arranging all his books, alphabetically, on the shelves. In his mind, he had a roaring fire in the fireplace; he was sitting in front of it, smoking his pipe, reading.

They moved on to another room, a huge octagonal room stuck onto the side of the house. It was all windows. They stood there, silently, with the same silly grins, and Anastasia read her mother's mind. Her mother was setting up easels in the room. She was doing huge paintings with sweeping brush strokes. She was hiring models to stand there in the brilliant light. She was doing sculpture. Murals.

The estate agent lady began to talk very fast, trying to mend the silence. "Of course, in the Victorian era, when this house was built, they always had these strange rooms that they called solariums. Useless, now. You could close it off to conserve heat. Or, in fact, you could even have this room torn down. It does stick out rather awkwardly from the side of the house, I know. The garden would be bigger if you just had this room taken off, and . . ."

But no one was listening to her. She stopped talking, mid-sentence, confused, and they moved on.

Upstairs, they moved from one bedroom to another. Big bedrooms, with fireplaces and huge cupboards playing hide-and-seek. Their feet echoed in the empty rooms: the heavy, decisive steps of Dr Krupnik's size-twelve shoes; the staccato taps of the estate agent lady's high heels; the duet of Anastasia's trainers and her mother's sandals; and behind them, the pad, pad, pad of Sam's little feet.

Now not even the estate agent lady was saying much. She was embarrassed. She thought they hated the house. Half-heartedly, in a bathroom, she said, "New plumbing. Wonderful copper pipes," but then she fell silent again and looked through her bag for a cigarette.

Finally, she opened a door on the second floor and gestured towards the narrow, curving staircase behind it.

"You could just close this off," she said, and puffed nervously on her cigarette.

Anastasia scuttled up the little staircase alone to the tower room and stood there looking out and down, at the green lawns, the huge elms, the curving streets, and in the distance, the Charles River and the buildings of Cambridge and Boston.

Her parents didn't come up the stairs. They had read her mind and knew that she wanted to be in the tower room alone.

But after a moment she could hear Sam's small feet climbing the stairs. He appeared in the room, looking puzzled, and said, "Do you want me to cry again? Do you want to be part of the plot now?"

But Anastasia said no and took his hand. They went back downstairs just in time to hear her father tell the estate agent lady that they would buy the house.

"The Mystery", wrote Anastasia carefully, "of Why You Sometimes Hate the Idea of Something, but Then You Like the Thing Itself".

Now that had possibilities for a book. She would have to refine the title a little, because it seemed a little complicated. But it had real possibilities.

Below the title, after she reflected on the possibilities, she wrote, "Subtitle: Or Why You Sometimes *Like* the Idea of Something, But Hate the Thing Itself".

Moving, and the new house, seemed to fall into the first category. And Robert Giannini seemed to fall into the second.

5

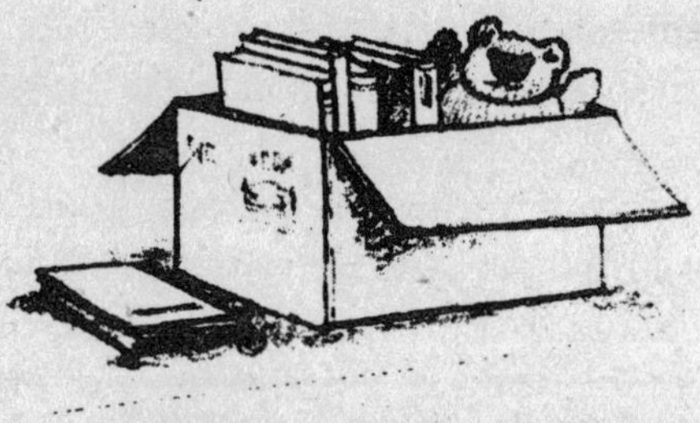

"Boy, Anastasia, I don't know," said Jenny. "I said I'd help you pack. And I *will* help you pack," She put a stack of Anastasia's paperback books into a carton, half-heartedly. "But boy, Anastasia. I really hate it that you're moving. You've been my best friend ever since we started in the infants."

"Yes," said Anastasia glumly. "Except for that one summer, when Lindsay Cavanaugh moved in down the street."

"Yes, Lindsay Cavanaugh, that jerk."

"She was your best friend that whole summer. I wanted to kill myself."

"Yes. You know why it was, though. Her father was a film-maker, remember? He was going to use Lindsay and me in a movie."

"Big deal."

"Yes, big deal. We had to get up at 5.00 A.M., and he took us out to Crane's Beach, and we had to run on the beach with no clothes on while he took movies. When my father found out he did that, he almost broke old Lindsay Cavanaugh's father's neck."

"Yes, I remember." Anastasia giggled. "It wasn't porno or anything, though. You were only seven years old, for pete's sake."

"Actually, it was probably a pretty good movie. The sun was coming up and everything, and we were the only people on the beach. Except birds. Nobody ever got to see it, though, because my father made him destroy the film."

"I hated you that summer. You were so conceited."

"Well, I thought I was a big movie star. Except for that summer, we've always been best friends. Are you taking this, or throwing it away?" She held up a battered arithmetic book.

"Good grief. Where did you find that?"

"It was under your bed."

"I thought I'd lost it. My mother had to pay the school for it. I suppose you'd better throw it out."

The arithmetic book sailed into the big wastepaper basket that was in the middle of Anastasia's room.

"Can I have this picture of you? I don't want to forget what you look like." Jenny had a Polaroid snapshot of Anastasia in her hand.

"Yes, but it's ugly. And you're not going to forget what I look like anyway, Jenny. Aren't you going to come and visit me? Robert Giannini said that he was going . . ." Anastasia stopped talking abruptly, and blushed.

"Who? *Robert Giannini?* What's Robert Giannini going to do?"

"Nothing."

"What do you mean, nothing? Robert Giannini's going to *visit* you, isn't he, Anastasia? He's going to *visit* you! I can't believe it, that jerk!"

"Do you think I should keep this orang-utan poster, or throw it away? I've had it about five years. I'm kind of bored with it."

"Throw it away. And stop changing the subject. Are you going to let that jerk Giannini visit you? Did you *invite* him?"

"No, I didn't invite him. He invited himself. But he isn't so bad, Jenny. He really isn't. He's *kind* of a jerk, but not fully fledged."

Jenny threw herself onto Anastasia's bed, held her stomach, and groaned. "You *like* him, don't you? You actually *like* Robert Giannini! I can't believe it."

"I don't like him. I just don't *hate* him any more."

"Traitor. Traitor traitor traitor. Why didn't you tell me?"

"I forgot."

"You didn't forget. You were embarrassed."

"Yes, I was embarrassed."

Jenny lay on the bed with her eyes closed. "Well, guess what."

"What?"

There was a long silence. Then Jenny took a deep breath. "I don't hate Michael Gottlieb any more, either."

"*That jerk?*"

"He's not really a jerk. Really, he isn't, Anastasia. The other day he came over, and we went down to the store and got iced lollies. He was sort of nice, all of a sudden."

"Why didn't you tell me?"

"I forgot."

"Liar."

Jenny looked at Anastasia and grinned. Anastasia began to laugh. Jenny began to laugh. Anastasia could hardly talk because she was laughing so hard; but finally she spluttered, "Michael Gottlieb! He always wears that stupid baseball cap!" Jenny doubled up, laughing, and gasped, "Robert Giannini! That briefcase! That gross briefcase!"

For the rest of the day, they couldn't look at each other without making the kind of semi-sneezing noise that holds back a brand new laugh.

It was hard, packing. Not hard on the muscles – Anastasia had pretty good muscles – but hard on the head. And hard on the heart.

Anastasia found her mother crying, one afternoon. Not curled-up-on-a-bed, pounding-your-fists-into-the-pillow sort of crying. Just silent, tears-running-down-your-cheeks crying. Her mother was standing in the pantry, packing dishes, and there were tears on her face.

"Did you hurt yourself?"

Her mother sniffed and smiled. "No. I'm just sad."

Anastasia picked up a plate and looked at it. It was an ordinary yellow plate. It made her think of spaghetti and of meat loaf. It didn't make her feel sad.

"If I were you, I would feel good about this plate," she told her mother. "*Most* people in the suburbs eat off plastic dishes."

"Assumptions again."

"No, really. They do. Except when they eat TV dinners. Those they eat right out of the tin tray."

Her mother leaned against the cupboard and began to laugh. "Anastasia, haven't you worked out yet that your assumptions all turn out to be *wrong*? Take the new house, for example. You thought we'd have to move to a split-level house in a development. Instead we found that wonderful house with a tower."

Anastasia shrugged and grinned.

"How did you become such an expert on suburban life, anyway?"

"Told you. Books and TV. Mostly TV commercials. You never see *city* people worrying about ring-around-the-collar."

"Well, we won't worry about it either, not even when we live in the suburbs."

"Why were the dishes making you cry?"

"It wasn't the dishes. I was feeling sad about the stained glass in these cupboard doors. I've always loved this stained glass."

Anastasia looked at the stained-glass windows of the cupboards. She remembered when Sam was a tiny baby, and they had kept his little cot in the pantry. She used to open the cupboard door, stand behind it, and make faces at the baby. The very first time Sam had smiled was when Anastasia had been making a purple-and-amber face at him, wiggling her nose.

Oh, dear. Now Anastasia was starting to feel sad, too.

She wiggled the loose pane of coloured glass. "Maybe we could take it out and take it with us, Mum."

"No. It doesn't belong to us."

"Of *course* it belongs to us! It's always been ours! All my *life* I remember this stained glass!"

"But we don't own this building, or the things that are part of it. So when we leave, we have to leave all these things for the next people who will live here."

Good grief. Anastasia hadn't even thought about someone else living in their flat. All of a sudden, she thought of the wallpaper in her bedroom. She had chosen it herself, when she was eight. It was blue and white, with people riding old-fashioned bicycles on it; some of them were playing flutes and violins while they rode.

She didn't want anyone else to have that wallpaper. But there was nothing she could do.

Well, there was something. She thumped her way down the echoey hall to her room, which seemed hollow and empty now. The rug was rolled up, and the curtains had been taken down. Her desk, usually cluttered with paint boxes and notebooks and comics, was bare, except for the goldfish bowl where Frank swam lazily back and forth, back and forth.

"Frank," she said, "don't tell anyone that I'm doing this." Frank made a kissing face at her.

Anastasia found a pencil stub in the wastepaper basket knelt on the bare floor in a corner of the room and wrote, on the wallpaper, in her best printing: "This is my room forever. Anastasia Krupnik."

That made her feel better.

Then she thumped down the hall to her father's study. He was standing beside his own bare desk by the wall with his back to her, and he jumped, startled, when she came in.

He looked guilty. Anastasia was an expert on guilty looks.

"What are you doing, Dad?" she asked.

"Nothing," he said very quickly.

"Nothing" was what you always said when you were doing something that you felt guilty about and someone came along and asked what you were doing. Anastasia was an expert on that. Either you said "nothing", or you whistled, or hummed.

Her father began to hum. He did a little drumming rhythm on his desk top with his fingers.

"You all packed in here?" she asked, looking around the bare room.

"Yep. All ready for the movers. It looks empty with the books packed, doesn't it?"

"Yes. I suppose someone else will move new

books in. Probably their books won't be as good as yours, though."

"Probably no one else will have first edition of *The Old Man and the Sea*," her father said, and that seemed to make him feel better. "I think I'll have a beer."

He headed for the kitchen. When he was gone, Anastasia saw, suddenly, the place on the wall of the study where, in his best writing, very small, with his fountain pen, he had written his name.

Anastasia found Sam in his bedroom, sitting on the floor, crying silently.

"What's wrong, Old Sam?" she asked.

"I'm feeling sad about my blanky," he said.

"Oh, Sam, I'm sorry. I was just teasing when I said your blanky couldn't come to the new house. Of course it can come."

Tears trickled down Sam's cheeks. "But it wants to live here," he whispered to her. "It told me so."

Anastasia thought and thought. "I have an idea, Sam," she said, finally. She ran to the kitchen and got a pair of scissors. Then, sitting beside Sam on his bedroom floor, she carefully cut his ragged yellow blanket in half.

"There," she said. "Now part of it can live here, and part of it can come to the new house." She folded one half and Sam showed her where to put it: on a dark, narrow shelf in the cupboard. He wrapped the remaining half around his hand, held it against his cheek, and sucked his thumb, testing how it worked with only half. After a moment he smiled. "Okay," he said. "It's okay."

"Good."

"I'm not a baby," he reminded her firmly.

"I know, Sam. I know you're not a baby."

She called Jenny MacCauley on the phone.

"The moving van's coming in about an hour," she said. "So I called to say goodbye."

"Will you have a telephone in the new house?"

"Of course."

"Is it long distance?"

"I don't know. Not long distance like Milwaukee, or anything."

"Well, call me and tell me the number."

"I will."

"And call and tell me everything that happens."

"Yes."

"Like if you meet any boys."

"Okay."

"Or if *Casablanca* ever comes to a cinema out there, call me, and I'll work out a way to get there. Don't ever go to *Casablanca* without me, promise."

"I promise. Don't you, either."

"I won't. And if Old Briefcase ever comes to visit, call and tell me."

Anastasia giggled. "Okay."

"Or if you get any new clothes, or anything."

"Okay. And you, Jenny, if you read any good

books, call and tell me. Or if Michael Gottlieb comes over. Old Baseball Cap."

Jenny giggled.

"I still can't believe you're moving Anastasia."

"Me neither. Come and visit me."

"I will."

"Promise."

"I promise."

Then, suddenly, Anastasia was too sad to talk any more. Very quickly, before she began to cry, she said goodbye and hung up the telephone.

Everything was packed, and the moving van was pulling up to the front door.

But Anastasia hadn't packed Frank Goldfish – she was going to carry him with her, in his bowl, to the new house – and she hadn't packed her notebook.

Now she sat down on the bare floor, beside Frank in his bowl, and looked around. The moving men were coming in, and she could hear their footsteps on the bare floor of the flat. Her entire life was packed into cardboard boxes, except for the life that she was leaving here.

"The Mystery," she wrote quickly, before they got to her room, "of Saying Goodbye."

She re-read it with satisfaction. Now *that*, she thought happily, is a *title*.

6

Anastasia's mother was sitting in the kitchen of the new house in a rocking chair, with her sandals kicked off and her long hair frizzy from the heat.

"Look at me," she said dramatically to Anastasia, who had wandered into the kitchen for a peanut butter sandwich, "and you are looking at someone who is suffering."

"Suffering from what?" asked Anastasia, as she spread peanut butter on a slice of wholemeal bread.

"Angst. And sore feet. And heat stroke."

"And the heartbreak of psoriasis?"

"No. The heartbreak of not being able to find anything. Have you seen a jug? Can you tell me how to make iced tea, which I desperately want, without a jug?"

"No." Anastasia licked the edges of her sandwich to even them off.

"*Damn.*" Her mother stood up and began to look through a half-unpacked carton.

Her father came into the kitchen, wiping his face with a handkerchief. "Did you make the iced tea?" he asked.

"I don't want to talk about it," said her mother tensely.

"I'm not asking you to talk about it. I'm asking you to pour it."

Her mother glowered at him.

"She can't find a jug," Anastasia explained. "Here," she said to her mother, handing her a saucepan. "Use this."

Her father sat down in the rocker, leaned his elbows on his knees, and looked at the floor.

"What's wrong, Dad?" Anastasia happened to know that her father was not at all interested in floors. Whenever he stared at the floor, it meant that something was wrong.

"I was unpacking the records," he said, "and I can't find the Verdi Requiem. I think the movers stole it."

"Dad," said Anastasia patiently. "Those movers have never even *heard* of the Verdi Requiem. Those movers were the sort of people who would only steal Peter Frampton."

Her father wasn't paying any attention to her. He was only paying attention to the floor. "Also," he said, "I hate the car. And the car hates me. It backfires at me. It keeps running after I turn the ignition off, even after I get out, and as soon as I am *behind* it, it backfires at me."

"I don't hate the car," said Anastasia cheerfully. "I thought I would, but I don't. I'm glad you got an old beat-up car instead of a gross Cadillac or something."

"Here," said her mother, and handed them each a glass of iced tea. "If it tastes like aluminium, it's not my fault. I think the movers stole all my jugs."

She sat down in a chair across from Anastasia's father, took a sip of tea, and made a face. Then she put her elbows on her knees and stared at the floor.

"You people are both suffering from Post-moving Depression," announced Anastasia.

"For pete's sake, where did you come up with *that* idea?" asked her mother.

"*Cosmopolitan* magazine."

Her father set his glass on the table with a thud that almost broke it. "Anastasia Krupnik," he said, "we have subscriptions to at least seven magazines in this household, all of them with some intellectual content. Why do you insist upon spending your allowance to buy that garbage?"

"It tells me stuff."

"*What* stuff?"

"Well, one issue had an article about lopsided breasts, how to disguise them, and also an article about wives who get fed up with things and run away. Those might be useful bits of information to me some day."

Her father made a noise like a horse exhaling. He stood up and stomped out of the kitchen.

"Post-moving Depression," said Anastasia to her mother. "It will only last a few days."

Sam padded into the kitchen. "I stood in every cupboard," he said.

"Sam," said his mother. "Where are your trainers? You're going to get splinters if you don't keep your shoes on." She slid her own feet back into her sandals.

Sam thought. "One trainer is in one cupboard," he said, "and one is in a different cupboard. I forget where." He sat on the floor and examined the soles of his feet. "I *like* splinters," he said happily.

"Sam's not depressed," pointed out Anastasia. "Neither am I. I wonder why the neighbours haven't come to visit us, though. Neighbours are supposed to drop in and bring a chocolate cake or something, when you move to a new place."

"I wish someone would drop in and bring a jug," muttered her mother. "This tea tastes terrible."

Sam looked up suddenly. "A witch lives next door," he announced.

"No kidding," said Anastasia. "How do you know?"

"I looked out of a window, and she was looking out of a window."

"How do you know she's a witch? Was she wearing a pointed hat?"

"No," he said, picking some dirt out from between his toes. "She had an ugly witch face."

"Hey," said Anastasia, "I have an idea. We need a jug

until we find ours, right? Why don't I go next door and borrow a jug? That gives me an excuse to meet one neighbour, at least. I'm dying to meet the neighbours."

"You want to meet a *witch?*" asked Sam, his eyes lighting up.

"Why not. You want to come, Sam? Find your trainers and I'll take you with me. I want to comb my hair first."

She was heading out of the kitchen when her mother called her back. "Did it really have that article, the one you said? About wives who just chuck it all and run away? What happens to them? Do they end up happy, living in Malibu or something?"

"Mum," said Anastasia, "just hang in there a couple more days. Post-moving Depression goes away. It really does."

The house next door looked like a Charles Addams house. That didn't bother Anastasia. She even watched the shower scene in *Psycho* without covering her face with her hands, something her mother had never been able to do. She read vampire books and watched late movies about gooey blobs that grew and ate entire city populations, without ever having bad dreams.

But Sam was scared. He wasn't old enough to have developed an immunity to it yet. He held tightly to Anastasia with one hand and tightly to his yellow blanket with another. When they got to the front steps, Sam let go of Anastasia and dropped back to hide behind a bush.

"Dope," she needled him, and left him there. She went up on the porch and pushed hard on the unpolished brass bell. The shrill ring sounded inside the house. After a moment she heard footsteps, slow ones, shuffling.

The door finally opened, and a woman peered out from the dim hall.

Good grief. She really *did* have an ugly witch face. Sam was right. She would have looked perfect on a broom.

"Hello," said Anastasia politely. "I'm your new neighbour. My name is Anastasia Krupnik."

The woman with the witch face stared at her without smiling and didn't say anything. Her grey hair stood out around her face, tangled, like a nest that Anastasia had once seen in a tree in winter.

"What's your name?" Anastasia asked.

The woman stared at her for another long moment. Finally she said, "Mrs Stein."

"My mother was wondering if maybe you have a jug we could borrow, just for this afternoon until we find ours. We're still unpacking, and it's so hot we need something to make iced tea in."

"No," said Mrs Stein abruptly. "I don't have one."

Liar. Everybody has a jug unless they can't find it.

"Oh," said Anastasia. She wanted to say sarcastically, "Well, thanks anyway, you old bat."

But she didn't say that. Instead, she said nicely, "Thank you anyway. I'm sorry I bothered you."

Mrs Stein began to push the door closed. Then she stopped, looked beyond Anastasia, and said, "Who's *that*?"

Anastasia looked. It was Sam, who had come out from behind his bush and was looking at them fearfully, his yellow blanket wrapped around his arm and his thumb in his mouth.

"That's my brother, Sam."

"What is that disgusting thing he's holding?"

"It's his blanky. He holds it when he's sleepy or scared."

"Come here, young man," called Mrs Stein.

Sam climbed the steps to the porch carefully holding the railing. It took him a long time because he still went up stairs the baby way, with both feet on each step at the same time.

"Do you like biscuits?" Mrs Stein asked him.

Sam nodded.

"How can you eat biscuits if you keep your thumb in your mouth?"

Sam removed his thumb and wiped it dry on his blanket.

"Can you talk?"

"Yes," said Sam solemnly.

"My name is Gertrude Stein. Can you say that?"

"Gertrustein," said Sam. He said it the way he said Frankenstein when he was playing monsters.

"Do you prefer chocolate chip biscuits or golden syrup ones?"

"Both," said Sam.

Gertrude Stein began to laugh. "Come in then, and I'll give you one of each."

She looked sternly at Anastasia. "What was it you said you wanted to borrow?"

"A jug."

"You come in, too. I'll give you one." Then, as if she needed to explain something, she said, "I like little children. I do not much care for middle-sized ones."

Anastasia and Sam followed her into the dark house.

"This house smells funny," whispered Sam.

It surprised Anastasia that he whispered it. Why was it that Sam, who was only two and a half, already understood something about manners? Some people Sam's age, or even older, would have said that very loudly, which would have been rude. But Sam whispered it, what he said about Gertrustein's house. Anastasia squeezed his hand.

And yet Gertrustein herself, who was probably eighty years older than Sam, had been rude when she opened the door. Or at least she had *seemed* rude.

Anastasia remebered that her grandmother – who had been ninety-two when she died – had sometimes seemed rude.

Maybe it was just that people who were very old, or very young, were the only ones who said exactly what they thought. If they were young, they hadn't learned yet to worry about what other people might think. And if they were old, they didn't care any more.

And the house did smell funny. Sam was right. It wasn't a bad smell; it was just the smell of being closed up: a no-fresh-air-for-a-long-time sort of smell.

"I walk very slowly," said Gertrustein. Anastasia had already noticed that.

"I do, too," said Sam. "It's because I have small legs."

Gertrustein looked back at him and smiled.

Anastasia was surprised again at Sam. He had said something which made her feel good. What a nice chap Sam was beginning to be.

"I don't have small legs," said Gertrustein. "I have big legs, as a matter of fact. But they don't work very well. The doctor says I should go for long walks."

"Do you?" asked Anastasia. "Do you go for long walks?"

"No," sniffed Gertrustein.

The kitchen was not as dark as the rest of the house because there was sunlight coming in through the windows. But it was very old fashioned. Gertrustein shuffled over to a thick crockery pot with a lid, opened it, and took out some biscuits. She put them on a plate and put the plate on the table.

"There," she said. "Sit down, Sam. You too, girl."

Sam climbed onto a chair and sat with his legs

sticking out straight in front of him. Anastasia sat down next to him, and Gertrustein eased herself slowly into a chair and passed the plate of biscuits.

"Why don't you go for long walks?" asked Sam, with a biscuit in his mouth.

"Because," said Gertrustein, with biscuit in *her* mouth, "I don't have anyone to walk with, and it is boring to walk all alone."

"Couldn't you go for walks with your friends?" asked Anastasia.

Gertrustein glared at her. "All my friends are dead," she said.

Good grief. There wasn't any cheery answer to *that*, not that Anastasia could think of. Except "I'm sorry", which she said softly.

But Sam looked up, grinning, and said, "I could be your friend."

Gertrustein grinned back at him. Her face didn't look quite as much like a witch when she smiled.

"I like to go for walks," said Sam, reaching for a second biscuit. "And also I like to ride in my buggy. I have a buggy that folds up and looks like an umbrella. You could push me in it. It has a pocket where my blanky rides. Biscuits could ride there, too."

"Well," said Gertrustein, "that sounds like a good idea."

When they went home, Anastasia had a chipped jug for her mother. Sam had two biscuits in his pocket and a date to go for a walk the next day.

Anastasia felt funny. She felt the same way she had when Sam was born, when her mother brought him home from the hospital, and friends came to visit them to see the new baby. They brought gifts: little sweaters and stretchsuits and stuffed animals. They stood beside his cot, looking down, and said how sweet he was.

Anastasia had loved him, even then, even when he was just born and only weighed eight pounds and hadn't even ever smiled at her yet. But when all those people had come and talked about how sweet he was, she had gone to her own room and closed the door. She had said to Frank Goldfish, then, "Don't tell anyone this, Frank. But sometimes I hate Sam."

She had a feeling now that she wanted to go and say that to Frank again. She didn't know just why.

On the way home, Sam said happily, "Gertrustein really likes me."

Anastasia smiled sweetly at him and said, "Wait till she finds out you still wear nappies, big shot."

At home, there was loud music playing in the living room. The Verdi Requiem. Her father had found it. He was standing in the centre of the room with his eyes closed, waving his arms, holding a pencil in one hand. Anastasia giggled. She thought her father was the only person in the world who conducted orchestras that he couldn't even see.

She and Sam tiptoed past.

She found her mother in the room that the estate

agent lady had called the solarium. Its name had been changed, now, to the studio. Her mother was there, humming, with a jug – she had found their jug – of iced tea on a paint-spattered table. She was leaning canvases against the wall. An easel was set up.

"Hi!" she said. "How was your visit? Look! Don't you love this room?"

"Yes," sighed Anastasia. "I see you folks have recovered from your depression. But now I've got it."

"What's wrong? Was she really a witch? I see she gave you a jug."

Anastasia curled up in a battered armchair. "No. She looks like a witch, Sam was right about that. But she's just an old woman with very messy hair."

"So why do you look so miserable?"

Anastasia drew patterns with her fingers on the arm of the chair. Finally she said, "She didn't like me. She only liked Sam."

Her mother kissed the top of her head. "Are you sure, sweetie? Tell me about her."

Anastasia told her all that she could.

"She sounds lonely," said her mother, sipping some iced tea thoughtfully.

"Yes. She said all her friends were dead."

"Well forgive me if I sound like Ann Landers for a moment. But I think I can explain something. People who are lonely have usually been disappointed by people. So they become defensive. Do you know what *defensive* means?"

"Yes. Having weapons. Nuclear bombs. Dad's always bellowing about the defence budget."

Her mother chuckled. "Well, it's sort of the same thing. Sounds as if she has a whole arsenal over there. Her big weapon is not liking anyone. That way . . ."

" . . . no one can disappoint her, right?"

"Right."

Anastasia frowned. "But she liked Sam. She *really* liked Sam," she said darkly.

"Sweetie, with all due respect to Sam, he doesn't really qualify as a mature person yet. So she can take the risk of liking him."

"But why not me? I wouldn't disappoint her. I wouldn't let her down."

"Well," said her mother decisively, "maybe you'll have to prove that to her."

Anastasia thought for a long time. "You know what I think I'll do, if Dad will drive me to the shops?"

"What?"

"Well, someone who never ever disappoints me, and who keeps me from being lonely, is Frank. I think I'll buy Gertrustein a goldfish."

Her father still had his eyes closed, so he didn't see her come into the living room. But now he had come to the part in Verdi's Requiem where he always sang along with the record. Anastasia cringed. She lived in mortal fear that some day one of her friends would be there when her father was belting out the tenor solo from the Verdi Requiem, with his eyes closed and sweat on his bald head.

Of course now that they lived in the suburbs where she didn't *have* any friends, that couldn't happen. Her depression came back.

Towards the end, at the very high part, her father stood on his tiptoes while he sang. Anastasia giggled.

He opened his eyes when it ended and bowed to Anastasia, who applauded politely; then he went and switched the stereo to Off. He wiped his damp face with his handkerchief.

"I'm always too exhausted to conduct the next section after I sing that section," he said. "How did I sound?"

"Pretty good. You're getting better, I think."

"'*Inter oves lacum praesta et ab haedis me sequestra*'," he said. She recognized them as some of the words he had sung. "Know what that means?"

"No."

"You will after you study Latin. It means, 'Give me a place among the sheep and separate me from the goats'."

Anastasia laughed. "Okay. You're among the sheep."

"So are you. In fact, I don't know anybody who is among the goats."

"I do. Gertrude Stein."

Her father put his handkerchief away and looked at her in astonishment. "Don't tell me you've become familiar with Gertrude Stein!"

"Yes. Just today. Do you already know her?"

"*Know* her! I teach her in a graduate seminar. Gertrude Stein, Amy Lowell, Ezra Pound, and Henry James."

Anastasia wrinkled her forehead. "She's awfully *old* to be going to school still."

"No, no. She's not a student. She's a *writer*. I teach my students about her writing."

"That's funny. She didn't tell Sam and me she was a writer."

"What are you talking about? How could she tell you and Sam anything? She's dead."

Good grief. Anastasia's stomach felt funny. She's a ghost. I'm living in a ghost story. Gertrustein is dead. No wonder she looks so awful.

"Anastasia," said her father suddenly. "I have a feeling that you and I are talking about two different Gertrude Steins."

"The one I'm talking about lives next door to us. She looks like a witch."

"Oh. Well, the one I'm talking about is dead, and she looked like a car mechanic."

Anastasia started to laugh. "If Gertrustein next door were a car mechanic, maybe she could fix our car so it wouldn't backfire."

Her father chuckled. "Maybe so. Now scoot. I want to conduct this last section of the Requiem."

"After you do that, could you drive me to the shops? I want to buy Gertrustein a goldfish."

One of the things Anastasia loved most about her

father was that when you said something like you wanted to buy a goldfish for the next-door neighbour who looked like a witch, he didn't say "why". He said, "Okay", switched on his stereo, closed his eyes, and began to wave his arms in the air.

Anastasia looked again at the title she had written on the day the movers came. "The Mystery of Saying Goodbye." It still seemed, as it had that day, a wonderful title. She chewed on her pencil rubber for a while.

Then she began the first paragraph of her book.

"Once there was a young girl," Anastasia wrote, "who had had, in her short life of twelve years, to say goodbye many times. Her grandmother had died. And her goldfish had been flushed down the toilet and was irretrievable even though the plumbers had been called.

"She had said goodbye to her grandmother two ways. One, by going to the funeral, which was okay even though it was sad. And two, by keeping her grandmother's wedding ring, which was given to her, and looking at it now and then, which made her remember her grandmother in a nice sort of way.

"And she had said goodbye to her goldfish by holding memorial services over the toilet bowl, and playing taps on a harmonica. Her father had sung 'Many brave hearts are asleep in the deep'.

"But one day, she had to say goodbye to the house she had lived in all her life. Actually it was a flat but flats can *feel* like houses, and this young girl's flat had always felt like a house to her.

"That was the hardest goodbye of all, because there was no funeral, no souvenir to keep, no memorial service, no harmonica music, no final flush.

"Also, it became complicated, because at the same time she had to adjust to a *new* house. This young girl was not a very adjustable person."

Anastasia read that again, and then crossed out the last two sentences. She didn't like the word *adjustable*. It sounded like a training bra.

" . . . she had to *adapt* to a new house. This young girl was not a very adaptable person," she wrote.

She chewed on her rubber again, and watched Frank the Second swirl gently around his bowl. Frank hadn't even seemed to notice that he was living in the suburbs now.

She wondered if whoever published her book would mind if it had footnotes. At the end of the sentence she had just written, she made an asterisk.

Now it said, "This young girl was not a very adaptable person."*

At the bottom of the page, she wrote:

* For reasons that scientists have not yet worked out, goldfish seem to be more adaptable than young girls.

7

Anastasia took the new goldfish up to her tower bedroom. He (she? it was hard to tell, with goldfish) had survived the trip home from the shops comfortably, and she set the little bowl on her desk beside Frank Goldfish's bowl.

"Frank," she said, "this is going to be your next-door neighbour."

Then she opened the little bag of goldfish things on which she had spent most of her savings.

"Frank," she said, "don't be embarrassed about all this stuff. I got it because I thought Gertrustein would probably like it. I know *you* wouldn't like it." And she put into the new goldfish bowl a handful of pink pebbles, a plastic castle, and a little fake man in a diving suit.

Frank made a face as if he had eaten a lemon.

"Yes, I know, Frank. It's really stupid looking. But you haven't met Gertrustein. Her house is full of stuff that you and I wouldn't like. But *she* likes it, and that's what matters. And this is going to be her goldfish."

She sprinkled some fish food into both bowls and watched the two goldfish eat. She wondered if goldfish ever felt lonely. *She* was beginning to feel lonely. On the way to the shops, she had seen some kids her age: a boy mowing a lawn a few houses away and two girls sitting together on a porch. Maybe if she walked past, she could say hello. But what if they didn't say hello back? Or what if they *did?* What would she say next?

She lay on her bed and looked around the room. Through the windows, she could see the tops of trees and a lot of sky. It was nice, being up in a tower. Vaguely she remembered the fairy tale of Rapunzel, who had been locked in a tower, and who had hung her long hair from the window so that her lover could climb up. That was kind of neat.

But then Anastasia ran her fingers through her own hair, which had begun to be pretty long – halfway down her back – but she realized that it needed washing again. Yucks. If a lover tried to climb her greasy hair, he would slide back down.

Not that she wanted a lover, anyway, for pete's sake. But a *friend* would be nice.

Her old furniture was all in this room, but the room didn't feel familiar yet. She began to wish that she hadn't thrown her orang-utan poster away. And she missed her old wallpaper. She had got to know the funny-looking bicycle riders on her old wallpaper quite well. She had even given them names. The lady in the long skirt who rode a unicycle and played a violin was named Sybil. The man on an old-fashioned racing bike who rode no-hands and played a flute was Stanley. Stanley had chased Sybil around the walls of her old bedroom for years. She wanted them back.

This wallpaper was old, with stupid flowers. In some places, in the corners, it was peeling a little.

Anastasia clattered down the stairs and found her mother arranging the kitchen cupboards.

"Mum, I miss Stanley and Sybil."

Her mother frowned at a soufflé dish and finally put it into the cupboard beside the refrigerator.

"Who are Stanley and Sybil? I thought you would miss Jenny MacCauley."

"I *do* miss Jenny. But I'm going to call her on the phone. Stanley and Sybil are the people on my wallpaper.

Her mother smiled. "Oh, of course. I forgot they had names. Stanley had that sexy little moustache. I'm not surprised that you miss them."

"My room doesn't feel like mine. I *like* it. But it's strange, still."

Her mother took a heavy bowl out of the packing carton. "If you were a yellow pottery bowl with squiggle designs on your sides, where would you want to live?" she asked.

Anastasia thought, and then pointed to a cupboard. "There," she said.

Her mother put the yellow bowl into that cupboard. "I have an idea," she said.

"What?" Usually her mother had pretty good ideas.

"I could find out if they still make that Stanley and Sybil wallpaper. And if they do, we could have your room papered with it. We were going to wallpaper that room anyway."

Anastasia thought. "I chose that paper when I was eight. You don't think it would be stupid still to want it when I'm twelve?"

"No. It wouldn't be stupid. It was pretty grown-up paper. I remember thinking when you were eight that it was a sophisticated choice."

"No kidding?"

"No kidding."

Anastasia grinned. "Okay. I'd really like that, to have Stanley and Sybil back."

Her mother nodded and put away a few more dishes. "I forgot to tell you something. I'm sorry. Someone named Robert called, while you were off buying the goldfish."

"*Robert* called?"

"Yes. Who's Robert?"

Anastasia groaned. "Did he have a sort of squeaky voice?"

"Well, maybe it was a little squeaky. He sounded very pleasant, though."

Good grief. It was stupid Robert Giannini. *Typical* of that jerk Robert Giannini to sound *pleasant* to somebody's mother.

"It's a boy who was in my class at school."

"Oh. Well, he wants you to call him back. I wrote his number on that pad of paper by the phone."

Anastasia made a face. "I can't call him. What would I say?"

Her mother looked surprised. Sometimes her mother didn't understand *anything*. "You would say, 'This is Anastasia. My mother said you called while I was out'."

Good grief. What a silly thing to say. Anastasia made another face and wandered off to the telephone. She stared at Robert Giannini's number for a while. She already knew what it was. She had looked it up in the phone book about a hundred times. Just because she was bored. Not for any other reason.

"Robert," she said, when he answered the phone, "this is Anastasia. My mother said you called while I was out."

"Yes. Hello. I got your number from directory enquiries."

"What did you call for? Is anything interesting happening in Cambridge? Have you collected any new stuff?"

"Cambridge is the same as ever. Everything's pretty boring here. It's hot. It's even too hot to ride down to the river."

"Yes, it's hot here, too."

"Have you made any new friends?"

"Robert, I've only lived here for three days. I haven't had time. I've made a couple of new friends." It was only a partial lie. She had met Gertrustein, anyway. And she had *seen* some kids in the street, even though she hadn't met them.

"Girls or boys?"

Good grief. Robert was the kind of person who wanted to know *details*. It was awfully hard to give details when you were telling partial lies.

"One girl and one boy," Anastasia said. "The girl is actually a woman. She lives next door. And the boy lives down the street."

Now she would have to go down the street to where the boy was mowing the lawn and introduce herself. Then it wouldn't be a lie at all.

"Oh," said Robert. "How old is the boy?"

"I don't know. About thirteen or fourteen, I think."

"Oh." Robert didn't say anything else for a minute. Finally he said, "Guess what, Anastasia. I've invented a system to tell the future."

Now *that* was interesting. All her life, Anastasia had wanted to be able to know about the future. The horoscopes in magazines and newspapers weren't good enough. They never gave details. But if Robert Giannini, the Detail Freak, had invented a system – well, that could be interesting. Anastasia sat down on the floor.

"Tell me about it," she said.

"You need a pencil and paper."

"I have some right here."

"Okay. First, write down the alphabet, and then write down numbers by the letters. 1 is A, and 2 is B. Like that, all the way through the alphabet. Z is 26."

That was easy enough. Anastasia did it on a piece of paper. "Okay," she said, when she had finished.

"All right. Now here's what you do. I'll tell you how I did mine and how it came out. First you write down your age. I'm 12, so I wrote down 12."

"Okay. I'm 12, too." She wrote it down.

"Then you write down the day of the month your birthday is on. Mine's September the 20th, so I wrote down 20."

"Mine's 9. October the 9th."

"Now add those together. Next you add today's date."

"What's today?"

"The 16th. Add 16."

"Okay."

"Now add your favourite TV channel. Mine's 5."

"Mine's 56. I like the old movies on Channel 56."

"Okay, add 56."

"Then what?"

"This is the last one. You add the last three numbers of your phone number. Mine are 058."

"I know," Anastasia said. "I just dialled them."

"Now," said Robert triumphantly. "Look at the number you end up with – and then look at the alphabet. There's your future!"

"I don't understand."

"I came out with 111. So look at letter 1 and letter 11. A and K. Your initials, Anastasia!"

Anastasia made a face. "You're weird, Robert."

"What number did you get?"

Anastasia checked her addition. "370." She looked at the alphabet. "C and G. Big deal. I don't know a single person with those initials. Unless Clark Gable is going to come back from the grave."

There was a silence. "Well, maybe if you like some other TV channel. Walt Disney's on Channel 4 on Sunday nights. Don't you like Walt Disney?"

"Yucks. Robert, this is really a silly system you've invented."

"Well it worked for *me*." She could tell from Robert's voice that he was cross.

"I'll do it again tomorrow when the date is different. Maybe tomorrow I'll like a different TV channel, too."

"Okay," Robert muttered.

"I have to go now, Robert."

"I might ride my bike out to see you. I looked on the map, and it's not too far."

"Okay," said Anastasia. "But call first. Because I might be busy with my new friends or something."

She felt like a rotten person after she'd hung up. But honestly. Robert was such a jerk. Your age. The date. Your favourite TV channel. Your phone number. All of those things *change*, for pete's sake. How could anybody know anything about the future *ever*, when everything changes all the time?

Anyway, she thought suddenly, if you *did* know the future, there wouldn't be any *surprises* left.

Back in the kitchen, her parents were measuring the windows so that her mother could make curtains.

Once, several years ago, her parents had had a huge fight about sewing. Anastasia's mother had suddenly said, one day, that she didn't see why she automatically did all the mending and sewing. She was sewing some buttons onto something at the time and had just pricked her finger with the needle, and she had the tip of her finger in her mouth, sucking it, when suddenly she got cross.

"This is the most sexist household in Cambridge," she had announced angrily. "Why is it that the wife gets stuck with the sewing? Myron, you do some of the *cooking*. Will you tell me one good reason why you don't *sew?*"

"Because I don't know how," Dr Krupnik had said, chewing on his pipe.

"I'll teach you, then."

"Thank you, but I don't *want* to know how to sew."

Her mother sat there for a minute, sucking her finger, looking more and more angry. "In that case," she said, finally, "thank you, but I don't want to do any washing any more. Ever."

"In *that* case," said her father, "I don't think I want to be an English professor any more. I have always, if you must know, wanted to be a beachcomber. So I think that from now on I will walk on empty beaches

– all alone, by the way – and recite poetry to myself. Of course that means that there will be no more salary cheques."

Anastasia's mother folded the shirt which was still missing two buttons, very neatly, and laid it on the table. "As a matter of fact, *I* have been wanting for a long time to go to the Cotswolds and live in a small cottage with a thatched roof – all alone, by the way – and paint."

Anastasia had scurried away to her room, terrified. If her father became a beachcomber – all alone – and her mother went to the Cotswolds, whatever the Cotswolds were – all alone – what would happen to Anastasia?

But after a while, she heard her parents laughing. When she went back to where they were, her mother was giggling and had her father's pipe in her mouth, and her father was sewing a button on his shirt.

Since then, her mother had always done all the sewing. Anastasia couldn't work it out. It was something like item number 124 in her list of things she absolutely didn't understand.

Now her mother was about to make curtains for the kitchen. The fabric, bright blue with yellow and orange suns and moons and stars all over it, was unfolded on the kitchen table.

"Those curtains are going to be weird," Anastasia said cheerfully.

Her father turned, with a tape measure dangling around his neck, and said loudly, "That's *it*."

"*What's* it, Dad?"

"That word. Weird. I have heard you use the word *weird* at least four thousand times in the past week."

"But . . ."

"Anastasia, this is a household of verbal, articulate, intelligent people. We have an entire room filled with bookcases. In those bookcases there are dictionaries. Encyclopedias. *Roget's Thesaurus*. Anthologies of obscure Elizabethan poetry. There are a *hundred* words – at *least* a hundred words – that you could substitute for *weird*."

"Name some."

He got a beer from the refrigerator. "*Strange*," he said. "*Dreadful. Formidable. Ghastly. Unearthly. Demoniacal* . . ."

Anastasia could tell, when he got to *demoniacal*, that he was going to go on for quite a while. She grabbed a biscuit and began to back out of the room.

"I'm going to take Gertrustein her goldfish," she muttered.

"*PHANTASMAGORICAL!*" said her father, and took another gulp of beer.

Anastasia closed the door quietly. Sam appeared on the stairs with wet nappies and rosy cheeks, coming down from his room after his nap. "What's the matter with Daddy?" he asked.

Anastasia shrugged and gave Sam half of her biscuit. "He's being weird," she said.

*

"Frank, I'm going to take your buddy next door. I hope you won't miss him too much," said Anastasia. But Frank kissed the side of the bowl and wiggled his behind. He didn't mind.

Her novel in her notebook was open on her desk. Anastasia picked up her pencil and read what she had written so far, concluding with the footnote. It seemed enough for Chapter 1.

"Chapter 2," she wrote on the next page.

"The young girl decided," she wrote, "that one way to adapt to a new house was to make friends. And one way to make friends was to take them a gift.

"A lot of people find that food is a good gift to take to someone. Sometimes people make an apple pie, or a macaroni and cheese casserole, and they take it next door to their neighbours, and after that they are friends.

"But the young girl didn't know how to cook . . ."

Then she crossed that out. It was a novel, after all. It didn't have to be the complete truth.

"But the young girl didn't care much for cooking, although she was very good at it. Also, it was ninety degrees outside, and too hot to turn on the stove. So she decided to take her next-door neighbour a fish. It was not a *cooked* fish."

She read over what she had written, and it didn't sound just right. Anastasia scowled and tore the whole page out. Good grief: it was really *hard* to write a novel, even after you had a good title.

8

It was not easy to push the doorbell without spilling the goldfish bowl, but after a moment Anastasia managed a good shrill ring. Another moment, she could hear Gertrustein's shuffling footsteps and then her voice: "Who's there?"

"It's Anastasia again."

The door opened, and Gertrustein peered out. "Anastasia Again? It looks like Anastasia Krupnik to me! Hah!" The "hah" was a hiccuppy sort of laugh, which was more of a laugh than her silly joke deserved, Anastasia thought.

"I've brought you something. A goldfish."

Gertrustein looked at the goldfish bowl for a moment. Then she nodded and invited Anastasia inside. That was a relief. Anastasia had thought that she would have to *explain* about the goldfish. I suppose when you get old, she thought, you get over being surprised by stuff. So when someone brings you a goldfish, you don't even ask why.

They put the goldfish bowl on a table in the living room next to a plastic vase of artificial flowers. Gertrustein leaned close to the bowl and watched intently as the fish swam in circles, flipping his tail. The little diver stood on the bottom of the bowl, tilted slightly, wearing his huge plastic helmet.

Suddenly Gertrustein began to laugh. Anastasia thought that was rude, to begin to laugh at a gift before you had even said thank you.

"What are you going to name your goldfish?" asked Anastasia politely, pretending not to notice that Gertrustein was laughing.

But she just laughed harder.

"My goldfish is named Frank," said Anastasia. "I don't know if yours is male or female, though."

Gertrustein looked at her, still chuckling. "It's male, of course. It's the funniest thing I've ever seen. I'll name him Mr Stein. He looks exactly like my husband. The same popeyes."

Anastasia glanced around the room for signs of a husband. At her house, there were always pipes lying in ashtrays or size-twelve trainers in a corner. But there was no indication of a Mr Stein.

"Where *is* your husband?" she asked.

"Oh, goodness. I haven't any idea. He's been gone for forty years. He ran off with a lady mandolin player who wore bright blue shoes."

"Well," said Anastasia uneasily, "I'm very sorry he did that."

But Gertrustein was laughing again. "Oh, don't be. He looked like a goldfish, although I never realized it until this afternoon. I was *glad* when he ran off. I never should have married him."

"Why did you, then?"

"I was a spinster. Do you know what a spinster is?"

"Yes. I think I'm going to be one, because I'm so tall, and everything. Boys don't like me, except one boy, and I don't like *him*."

"Nonsense. Give yourself time. How old are you?"

"Twelve."

"Well, I was over *thirty*, and not married. Lived right in this house, the same house where I had been born. Lived here all alone bcause my parents were both dead by then. And along came Mr Stein one day, selling kitchenware door to door . . ."

"Did you buy any?"

"Bought the whole batch. Still have it. It outlasted Mr Stein."

"Excuse me, but why do you call him Mr Stein? My mother calls my father Myron."

Gertrustein began to laugh so hard that the sofa on which they were sitting wiggled.

"His name was Lloyd," she spluttered. "Lloyd Stein. But I'll have to tell you what happened on our wedding night . . ."

Good grief. Anastasia liked reading about people's

wedding nights in *Cosmospolitan* magazine or in Gothic novels. But she certainly didn't want to hear about a *real person's* wedding night.

Gertrustein took a deep breath so that she would stop laughing. Then she said, "The night that we were married, Mr Stein said to me, 'Gertrude, are you familiar with the word which is spelled L-L-A-M-A?' I thought for a moment, and then I said, 'Of course. Llama. It's an animal with a sad, smiling sort of face.'"

Anastasia nodded. It was the same way she would have described a llama.

"Then he said, 'Gertrude, your description is correct, but your pronunciation is wrong. When a word begins with a double L, the double L is pronounced as Y. Therefore the correct way to say *llama* is in fact *yama*, don't you see? Very few people know that,' he said. 'Well,' I told him, 'I certainly never knew that'."

"I didn't either," said Anastasia.

"Then he told me, 'So you can see, of course, that the correct pronunciation of *Lloyd* is, actually, *Yoyd*. I would prefer that you pronounce my name correctly, now that we are man and wife. Please call me Yoyd from now on'."

"Good grief," said Anastasia, beginning to giggle.

"Good grief indeed. How on earth can you call someone *Yoyd*? I wanted to hit him over his silly, pompous, popeyed head with one of the aluminium saucepans that he had sold me. I didn't, of course. But you can see that it was somewhat fortunate that the mandolin player came along. In three years I had never called him by name. He hated laughter. And I could never have said Yoyd without laughing. When I had to speak to him at all, I called him Mr Stein."

"A magazine that I read a lot would call that a Brief and Unfortunate Marriage."

"Yes. It was certainly a Brief and Unfortunate Marriage."

"Did you ever look up *llama* in the dictionary? To see if maybe he was right?"

"Of course not. Of course he wasn't right. He was an idiot with goldfish eyes."

"Well, I'm sorry that you married him."

"Me too. But it was understandable, I suppose. I was over thirty, after all, and all alone. I liked his aluminium kitchenware. And the man I loved had married someone else."

Now *that* was romantic and interesting.

"What was *his* name?"

Gertrustein looked a little bit sad. "Edward Evans. We had grown up together. As a matter of fact, Anastasia, Edward lived in your house, when he was a boy."

It was always hard to imagine old people being *young*. Anastasia looked for a long time at Gertrustein and just couldn't see even the smallest fragments of a young face. Sam had been right: she really did look like a witch.

"I don't mean to be rude or anything," Anastasia

said, "but you know, Gertrustein, you really would look much nicer if you would fix up your hair differently."

Gertrustein held up her hands. They were twisted and misshapen. "It's all I can do to hold a hairbrush," she explained. "My arthritis is so bad."

"Well," said Anastasia, "tomorrow, when you take Sam for a walk, why don't you walk down past the shops? And buy some curlers, and when you come back, *I'll* fix your hair for you!"

Gertrustein thought about that, frowning. "All right," she said, finally. "We'll give it a try, now that there is a new Mr Stein in the house."

In his bowl, the new Mr Stein gazed out with bulging eyes, swished his tail, and swooped around the plastic diver. Anastasia, who was an expert on goldfish emotions, could tell that he was quite happy.

"Mum, I have something important to talk to you about."

"How do you like the new curtains so far?"

One of the new curtains was hanging at one window. The others were still spread out on the kitchen table beside the sewing machine.

"Fine. They look pretty good. Can you stop sewing for a minute?"

"Of course. What's on your mind?"

Anastasia sat down on one of the kitchen chairs, opposite her mother, and wrapped her feet around the rungs. "This is sort of embarrassing," she said. "Promise you won't tell anyone."

"Okay. I promise."

"Well, I feel sort of weird about this. I'm sorry, but there isn't any word except weird for it. But I think I'm going to have to marry Robert Giannini."

Anastasia had always thought that it was only in books that people's mouths fell open in surprise. But her mother's mouth fell open in surprise.

"Anastasia! That's *impossible!* How could that be? You're only twelve years old! You can't possibly . . ."

"Mum," Anastasia said impatiently. "I didn't mean *now*. I mean *years* from now, after I've been to college. But I might as well start getting used to the idea now. And that's what makes me feel weird. Because I can't *stand* Robert Giannini. I had sort of decided that maybe I could learn to like him, because I do like him a little bit sometimes. But I was just talking to Gertrustein, and she was telling me how she married someone she couldn't stand, although she liked his aluminium kitchenware, but she'd never learnt to like him because he wanted her to call him Yoyd, and then he ran off with a mandolin player, and . . ."

"Hold on. Hold everything. I very rarely want a beer in the middle of the afternoon. But suddenly I want a beer. Can I get you something?"

"Are there any iced lollies?"

Her mother came back from the refrigerator with a can of beer and a green iced lolly. Anastasia peeled off the paper and began to lick the iced lolly carefully.

"Now, for starters. Why do you think you're going to have to marry Robert Giannini in ten or fifteen years?"

"Because he loves me. And he's the only boy who ever has or ever will. Now don't feel bad about this, Mum, because it isn't your fault, but I *am* a sort of freak. In class six I was the tallest girl, but the boys were taller, most of them. But in class seven I was the tallest *person*. There weren't any boys as tall as me, and I was even taller than the teacher. By the time I finish high school, I will probably be one of the world's tallest human beings. I also have the world's most hideous hair, in case you haven't noticed.

"Now for some reason Robert Giannini doesn't seem to mind what I look like. He's the only male in the world who will ever feel that way, so probably I'm lucky to have found him. The trouble is, I think *he's* revolting. I hate his squeaky voice. And I hate it that he carries a stupid briefcase everywhere. I can't *stand* it that he wears a Sea World tee shirt. But I have to work out how to adjust to those things if I'm going to marry him, because I certainly don't want to have a Brief and Unfortunate Marriage, for pete's sake . . ."

"Whoa. You're going much too fast for me, Anastasia. Wait a minute." Her mother sipped at the beer and looked puzzled. "First of all, what makes you so sure you want to get married at all? Lots of women never do and are perfectly happy."

"Would you be?"

"No, I like being married. But that doesn't mean that *you* have to."

Anastasia sucked on her iced lolly and thought for a long time. She thought about the time that her mother had had the flu and her father had taken cups of tea to her and sat beside her bed, not minding that he might catch the flu, too.

Then she thought about what it would be like to be in bed with the flu if there were no one to bring cups of tea and sit beside your bed. It made her feel lonely, just thinking about it.

Then she thought about the day that Sam was born, and her father took her mother to the hospital and stayed there with her while Sam was being born, and he came home, he was so excited that he couldn't remember if the baby weighed eight pounds and four ounces or four pounds and eight ounces; and she and her father smoked cigars to celebrate, only hers was a chocolate cigar.

She thought about what it would be like to have a baby if you weren't married, and nobody stayed with you while the baby was being born and smoked a cigar afterwards to celebrate. It made her feel lonely.

She thought about not ever having a baby at all. That made her feel even lonelier.

"I really do want to get married some day," she said, finally.

"Okay," said her mother. "First of all, then, about Robert. I've never met him, but I'll take your word for it that some things about him right now are revolting. But he's how old? Twelve?"

"Yes."

"Well, I didn't know your dad when he was twelve. But I'll bet you anything he had a squeaky voice. Robert's voice will change. He'll grow taller. And I can guarantee that within the next year, his mother will be using the SeaWorld tee shirt as a cleaning rag. Do you know what I was using as a cleaning rag just this very morning?"

"What?"

"A pink tee shirt with ruffles on the neck and daisies embroidered on the sleeves."

"Oh, *gross*. I'd forgotten that shirt."

"Well, you loved it when you were eight or nine. People's tastes change. Robert's will, too."

"Yes, probably he won't even like *me* after a while." Anastasia caught the last piece of green iced lolly just before it slid off the stick. She fired the empty stick into the paper basket with a long, arching basketball shot.

Her mother laughed. "Well, maybe not. But other boys will."

"Hah," said Anastasia gloomily.

"Hah. Trust me. I promise you that will be true. Did you just hear something? I thought I heard a buzzer."

"The doorbell. It's the first time anyone has rung the doorbell since we moved in! I'll get it."

The boy at the front door was the same boy that

Anastasia had seen mowing a lawn down the street. She had walked past him twice, trying to get up the nerve to say hello. Now he was standing right here on the front porch, looking at her. He was looking *down* at her, because he was a little taller than she, and he was wearing cut-off jeans and a rugby shirt. He looked a little like Luke Sky-walker. When he said hello, she noticed his voice was a little squeaky, like Robert's.

His voice will change, she thought happily.

"Hello," she said.

"My name's Steve Harvey. I live down the street, and I saw that you people moved in, and I wondered if you wanted your lawn mowed. I've got my lawn mower right outside."

"Well, I'll ask my mother, but I'm absolutely certain she'll say yes. She was just saying this morning that the grass needed to be cut." What she had said, actually, at breakfast, was, "Myron, we have to buy a lawn mower and cut this grass."

"My name is Anastasia Krupnik," she added, before she went to get her mother.

"What form are you in?"

"I'll be in the eighth."

"Me too. You'll probably be in my classroom because they do it alphabetically."

"Oh. Well, it'll be nice to know someone in my classroom before I start school."

"Yes. It's lousy to be the new kid. I know, because I just moved here last year. But it doesn't take long to make friends. Do you play tennis?"

"Not very well."

"Me neither. But there are courts down behind the school. You want to play later?"

"Yes. Wait here a minute, and I'll go and ask my mum about the lawn."

Her mother was standing in the kitchen, grinning.

"Mum, there's a boy at the door who . . ."

"I know. I was eavesdropping."

"We *do* need the grass cut. You were just saying to Dad this morning that . . ."

"Anastasia, up in my bathroom there's a brand new bottle of shampoo. You'll have time to wash your hair and dry it while he's doing the lawn."

"Do you think maybe I should shave my legs?" whispered Anastasia.

"The last time you tried to shave your legs," her mother whispered back, "you practically needed blood transfusions. I'd forget it if I were you."

"*Cosmopolitan* magazine says that it's fashionable not to, especially if you have blonde hair, like me."

"Fine. Wonderful. Now scoot. I'll get him started on the lawn."

Hmmm, thought Anastasia, as her hair dried, and she practised her backhand, standing in the centre of her tower bedroom. Maybe it's true, what Mum said. Maybe other boys besides Robert Giannini will like me.

Maybe *this* boy will.

Maybe my hair will look okay when I go to play tennis.

Maybe my legs aren't quite as skinny as they were last month.

Maybe I will think of something intelligent to say to him. And maybe I won't hit the ball into the net every time, the way I usually do.

I think I will have a hyphenated name, she thought, when I get married. Anastasia Krupnik-Harvey, she thought. That doesn't sound too bad.

Anastasia peeled a strip of the old, loosened, flowered wallpaper from the wall of her room, exposing an even older layer of paper underneath. She rolled the strip into a ball and shot it into the wastepaper basket.

Outside, she could hear the clatter of Steve Harvey's lawn mower.

Maybe I will start feeling at home in this room before too long, she thought.

Maybe the suburbs aren't as bad as I used to think.

Maybe I was making premature assumptions.

Anastasia picked up her notebook and began a new version of Chapter 2.

"After she moved to her new home," Anastasia wrote, "the young girl began to be more adaptable than she had been in the past. She began to take up tennis, as a hobby."

9

The phone rang, and it was Jenny MacCauley.

"Jenny! I've called you twice, and you weren't home either time."

"Oh. I suppose I was out."

"Yes, your mother said you were out. How are things in Cambridge?"

"Booorrring," said Jenny mournfully.

"Yes, here too. Booorrring," said Anastasia.

"Do you hate it there?"

"Well, sort of," Anastasia lied. "When are you going to come and see me?"

"I thought Robert and I might ride our bikes over next Saturday. He said he'd looked at a map and worked out how to get there."

"Robert *Giannini*? When did you talk to *him*?"

Jenny hesitated. "Well, yesterday he came over and we rode our bikes down to the river."

"That jerk."

"Yes, that jerk Giannini. Anyway, we sat by the river for a while because Robert was doing one of his surveys. We were counting joggers. How many old joggers and how many young. How many male and how many female. How many wearing special jogging shoes. How many female joggers wearing bras and how many not. Robert's going to send the results of his survey to *Psychology Today*."

"That idiot."

"Yes. Anyway, after that we went over to the Brattle Theatre and saw *Casablanca*."

"JENNY MACCAULEY! YOU TOLD ME THAT WE WOULD GO AND SEE THAT TOGETHER. YOU KNOW I'VE ONLY EVER SEEN IT ON TV!"

"Well, you weren't *here*, Anastasia."

Anastasia glowered. "Funny that you said things were boring in Cambridge, Jenny. It certainly doesn't *sound* boring."

There was a long silence. Finally Jenny changed the subject. "Have you met anyone out there?"

"Yes. The woman next door. She takes Sam out for a walk every afternoon."

"Any boys?"

"Yes, as a matter of fact. A boy named Steve Harvey. He's going to be in class eight, and he's tall and good-looking. I've played tennis with him three afternoons now."

Jenny interrupted her. "You're a terrible tennis player. You always hit the ball into the net."

"That's because I never had a good partner before, Jenny MacCauley, you rat," said Anastasia angrily. "It just so happens that when I play tennis with Steve Harvey, I hit the ball over the net at least fifty per cent of the time. We're playing again today. Probably by the end of the week I'll hit the ball over the net *eighty* per cent of the time, and probably—"

Jenny interrupted her again. "Anastasia," she said pointedly, "you promised me you'd *call* me if you met any boys."

"I *did* call you. You were always *out*. You were always out seeing *Casablanca* with Robert Giannini, probably."

"So? You're always out, playing tennis, it sounds like. Funny that you said things were boring *there*."

There was another long and uncomfortable silence.

"Are people like you expected in the suburbs?" asked Jenny finally. "Do they wear pink curlers and eat TV dinners and have bowls of artificial fruit?"

Anastasia thought about the past three afternoons, when she had gone to Gertrustein's house after tennis and rolled Gertrustein's ragged grey hair up in pink curlers so that she would look nicer. On one of those days, Gertrustein had put a TV dinner into the oven while Anastasia was there. She had explained how she very seldom did much cooking any more, because it was so lonely to cook for just one person.

"Yes," said Anastasia to Jenny. "The lady next

door is just like that. Pink curlers. TV dinners. Artificial fruit. The whole bit."

"Sick-o," said Jenny.

"Yes," said Anastasia vaguely. "I suppose so."

"Listen, I've got to go. But Robert and I'll ride over next Saturday, okay?"

"Okay. Hey, did Robert ask you anything about Sam? Did he say anything about Sam, well, not having any legs, or anything like that?"

"Good grief. Why would he ask me that? Sam has *legs*. He kicked me once, because I hid his blanket as a joke."

"Oh," sighed Anastasia, "it's too complicated to explain. I'll see you on Saturday."

"Don't forget to watch TV tonight. *The Maltese Falcon* is on."

After Anastasia had hung up, she thought, I should have asked her if she was going to watch it on TV. Or if she was going to go and see it at the Brattle Theatre. With Robert Giannini, that jerk.

She decided that maybe this afternoon she would get the tennis ball over the net more easily, and *harder*, by pretending that it was Robert Giannini's head. Whammo.

One of the things Anastasia liked about her tower room was that her parents didn't very often come up to it. So it was very private.

Not that she ever did anything subversive in her room. A lot of kids she knew sometimes smoked cigarettes in their rooms and then sprayed air freshener around so their parents wouldn't know; but Anastasia thought smoking cigarettes was gross.

And some kids she knew occasionally drank beer in their rooms. But there was always beer in the Krupniks' refrigerator, and whenever her father drank a beer, he gave it to her first, so that she could sip off the foam, because he didn't like the foam. So she was actually pretty bored with beer, and it never seemed like a big deal, the way it did to some kids.

And of course lots of kids read dirty books in their rooms and hid them under the mattresses. But Anastasia's house had always been filled with books, and some of them had sex in them, and she had always been allowed to read whatever she wanted. Anastasia thought that dirty books were generally not as gross as cigarettes, but rather like beer: interesting now and then, in small doses, but no big deal.

So there was not, really, anything private in her room except her private notebook, and she didn't even need to hide that. Her parents had told her once they would never read her private notebook. So she had tested them a few times, by leaving it around the house conspicuously, with an almost invisible hair on it, which would be dislodged if anyone opened the notebook. She had learned that trick from spy novels. But the hair always remained in place. Her parents really *hadn't* opened it. Sam had, once, and scribbled with crayons on a few pages. But Sam couldn't read yet.

Still, even though she didn't need a private place for subversive stuff, she did like having a room that was very private. It was quiet. It was a good place to read, or to think, or to daydream, or to be sad.

Right now she was lying on her bed, wondering what to do next Saturday when Robert Giannini showed up in the suburbs.

First of all, it was a problem because she didn't want Steve Harvey to know that the Other Man in her life carried an idiotic briefcase everywhere and wore a SeaWorld tee shirt.

It was okay for Steve Harvey to know that there *was* an Other Man. In fact, it was probably a good thing. It made her seem *desirable*, at least, and according to *Cosmopolitan*, that was a good thing. "Keeping Him on His Toes" was the title of the article that had pointed that out.

But keeping Steve Harvey on his toes was one thing; keeping him doubled over, laughing, when he *saw* Robert Giannini was something else again.

She reached out and peeled another strip of old wallpaper from the wall, while she thought. Her wastepaper basket was almost full of crumpled bits of old wallpaper.

Second – Anastasia almost groaned aloud – was the problem of what to do about Sam, when Robert Giannini came. Probably that jerk was going to show up with a get-well card and a March of Dimes contribution for Anastasia's poor crippled, deformed brother.

Downstairs, she could hear the familiar padding sound which was Sam wandering around the big house in his little red trainers. On his two very sturdy, healthy legs.

Maybe she could just shut him in his room while Robert was visiting. But that wouldn't work, she knew. Sam never stayed in any place where you put him. He was always popping out of doors, doing his Ed MacMahon imitation. "Heeeeeere's Johnny!" Sam would announce loudly and wait for applause.

Maybe if she fed him a lot of beer, he would just go to sleep for a long time. But Sam didn't *like* beer. He didn't even like foam. It made him sneeze.

Maybe she could convince him to just sit in his buggy with a blanket over his legs. But it was ninety degrees outside. Nobody in his right mind would sit in a buggy with a blanket over his legs when it was ninety degrees.

Anastasia sighed and pulled off another strip of wallpaper. There were three layers of wallpaper. After she pulled off a piece of the top layer, she could see green flowered paper underneath. If she picked at that and peeled it off, there was a blue striped paper under that. Finally, behind the blue striped paper, there was bare plaster. It made kind of interesting designs, as she poked and peeled at the three layers.

"Anastasia? You up there? May I come up?" It was her mother calling.

"Yes. Come on up."

Her mother appeared in her room, puffing from

two flights of stairs, but grinning. "Guess what! They still make Stanley and Sybil! I've just been to the wallpaper shop."

"No kidding!"

"No kidding. It costs more than it used to, but that's okay. I ordered three rolls, and it'll be in next week. We'll have to strip off the old stuff. Oh, I see you've already started!"

"Yes, I was just lying here thinking, and I was kind of peeling while I was thinking."

"I like to have something to do with my hands, too, while I'm thinking. Usually I knit. But I can see where peeling wallpaper would be okay, too." Her mother picked at a corner and pulled back a strip of the top layer. "What are you thinking about?"

One of the good things about Anastasia's mother was that she never laughed at you. Especially not at your problems. Anastasia always imagined Dear Abby bent double most of the day, laughing at people's problems and having to bite her tongue in order to keep a straight face while she wrote what sounded like a very serious answer.

But her mother was definitely not like that.

"I have a real problem," she said to her mother gloomily. "It's about Sam."

"About Sam? Has he been colouring in your notebook again? Or poking at Frank Goldfish? It's been at least six months since he's flushed anything down the toilet – I think the last time was my silver earrings, and that was just after Christmas . . ."

"No, no. It isn't anything that Sam has done. It's that . . . well, you know how weird Sam is."

"Not *weird*, Anastasia. Unusual, maybe. Precocious."

Anastasia groaned, "Well, anyway, when we were still living in Cambridge before we moved, I was talking to Robert Giannini – who really *is* weird, by the way, I'm sorry, but there isn't any other word for Robert Giannini – and he asked me how my brother was. He's never seen Sam. And I was trying to describe Sam to Robert Giannini. And somehow, I haven't worked out how, I *never* will work out *how*, Robert got the idea that Sam was deformed . . ."

"Deformed? *Sam?*"

"Yes. It was because I was trying to explain how Sam grew at different rates, because that's what Dad told me, that his brain developed faster than some other parts of him. That's *true*, Mum. You know he talks like Einstein, but he still sucks his thumb and wears nappies . . ."

"Yes, but that's not *deformed*, Anastasia."

"I know that, and you know that. But for some reason Robert Giannini got the idea that poor old Sam is crippled . . ."

"Handicapped," corrected her mother.

"Okay, handicapped. And he started being very sad about it and telling me about his retarded cousin and asking if we had taken Sam to the Children's Hospital and telling me about the March of Dimes . . ."

"Good grief."

"Mum, you know what? Robert Giannini was making premature assumptions."

"And you were letting him, Anastasia."

Anastasia sighed. "I know. But I don't know how it happened. And now, guess what."

"I'm not sure I want to guess what. You mean there's *more?*"

"Mum, Robert Giannini is going to ride his bike over here next Saturday."

Her mother groaned.

It was at this point, Anastasia was quite sure, that Dear Abby would take a deep breath in order to stop laughing and would write: "Dear Confused, It is very simple to solve this ridiculous problem. You must simply explain to your friend that it was a matter of poor communication, of misunderstanding, of premature assumptions. Tell him the truth about your brother. A real friend will understand."

But Anastasia's mother didn't say any of that. She didn't laugh. She just groaned.

"Do you want to hear a story about a terrible thing I did once?" she asked, looking embarrassed.

"Yes." For some stupid reason, when you had done something stupid, it always made you feel better to hear about stupid things that other people had done.

"Well, do you remember what my name was before I got married?"

"Yes. Katherine Klein."

"Well. When I was in art school, when I was oh,

maybe nineteen, I had a terrific crush on a man in one of my classes. One evening he asked me to go out and have a cup of coffee with him.

"Now, do you know that little framed print that's hanging in the hall, near the telephone? The one that's black and white, very abstract?"

"Yes. It looks like an ink blot. Like a psychiatrist would ask you what you see in it."

"Well, that's a copy of a painting by Franz Kline."

"Is he related to you?"

"No. That's the point. The name isn't even spelled the same. But Franz Kline was a very, very well-known expressionist painter. Now, we were all young art students, and we used to sit around talking for hours about painters. That's what this boy and I did that night. And somehow, in the course of the evening, he got the idea that I was Franz Kline's daughter."

"*Mum!* You didn't tell him that, did you?"

"Of course not. I just let him make the assumption. But I also didn't tell him that my father was Joseph Klein, insurance man, from Hartford, Connecticut. By the end of the evening, this boy thought that my home was in a loft in New York City, with my famous painter father."

"Good grief."

"Good grief is right. Because – as you know – there's a point at which you can say, 'Hey, no, you've got it wrong.' But if you don't say it *then*, it gets harder and harder to say it, and you get in deeper and deeper."

"Did he ever find out the truth? *Did he ever come and visit you at your house?*"

"No. He kept wanting to. He kept hinting that he wanted to, because of course he wanted to meet my father, or who he thought was my father. I kept making excuses."

"What happened?"

Anastasia's mother groaned, remembering. "Well, one thing that happened was that I flunked an important exam. Franz Kline *died* that year. It was in the *New York Times*, of course. So for two days I had to hide. I couldn't go to any classes – and missed an exam, so I got a fail mark – because of course I wanted this boy to think that I had gone home to the funeral and everything."

"That's *terrible.*"

"Of course it's terrible. And it's something like your situation right now. What are you going to do when Robert comes next Saturday?"

"I don't know."

"Maybe we could talk Sam into lying in bed all day with a blanket over him."

"It's too hot. I've already thought of that."

"*I* know."

"What?"

"Simple. Mrs Stein and Sam really get along very well. I'll ask her if she can babysit on Saturday. Sam can go to her house for the day. But listen, Anastasia . . ."

"What?"

"Robert Giannini's not going to come and visit *often*, is he?"

"No. Absolutely not. This is the last time. I can't stand him."

"Unfortunately," continued Anastasia in Chapter 2 of her novel, "just as the young girl began to live a new and well-adapted life, her past crimes began to catch up with her."

Then she crossed out the word *crimes*.

" . . . her past sins began to catch up with her," she wrote.

Then she crossed out the word *sins* and chewed on her pencil rubber.

Finally she wrote, " . . . her Past began to catch up with her, and to get tangled up with her Future."

10

"It's Anastasia again," Anastasia called, after she had rung Gertrustein's doorbell. "I've brought you something!"

"Hello there, Anastasia Again," said Gertrustein, when she opened the door. It was amazing how Gertrustein's disposition had changed in a short time. Anastasia remembered how grouchy she had been, the first time they had met. Now she answered the door cheerfully, always smiling.

It had to do with her hair, thought Anastasia. Now that her hair looked pretty, Gertrustein felt cheerful. Anastasia had noticed that she *herself* felt more cheerful now that she was washing her own hair twice a day with special shampoo for oily hair. She had been doing it ever since she had met Steve Harvey. The better her hair looked, the better she felt.

Now *that* was something worth sending into *Psychology Today*, instead of a stupid Giannini survey on joggers.

She would have to work out, though, how people like her father fitted into her theory. Her father was almost always cheerful even though he was bald.

"Hey, Mr Stein is getting fat!" Anastasia peered into the goldfish bowl at the plump goldfish who stared back at her silently.

Gertrustein laughed. "I know. I think I'm feeding him too much. It's so nice to have someone to *feed* that I get carried away sometimes."

"Gertrustein," said Anastasia very seriously. "You absolutely have to make an effort to make some friends. You could invite friends over for dinner, or you could go to their house for dinner. It's not healthy to stay all shut up in your house, feeding too much to a goldfish."

But Gertrustein got a very stubborn look on her face. "I do not like people," she said, with dignity.

"Ridiculous. You're only pretending that because you're *scared* of them."

"What are you, some kind of *social worker?*"

"No. But I know what I'm talking about. Because look at me: when I moved here, I pretended that I wasn't going to like anyone in the suburbs. You know why? Because I was scared they wouldn't like *me!* And then I met you, and you like me . . . you do like me, don't you?"

"Yes," said Gertrustein reluctantly.

"And then I met Steve, and Steve likes me, at least I think he does. And now I can't wait to meet more people. Steve's going to have a barbecue at his house, and invite a lot of kids my age, and I'm really looking forward to it. It was all my imagination that I didn't like people in the suburbs. And it's all *your* imagination, Gertrustein, and what you should do is . . ."

"You said you brought me something. What is it? Gertrustein changed the subject.

"Oh, I almost forgot. Look!" Anastasia held up a piece of paper. "A gift certificate!"

Gertrustein took the paper and frowned at it.

"A lady came to the house," Anastasia explained, "to welcome my mother to town. She brought lots of free stuff that the town gives to new people. Two free passes to the movies – Steve and I are going to use those – and, let's see, my father gets a free oil change for the car at some petrol station, and my mum gets a discount on a leg of lamb at the supermarket. We get dinner for four at some restaurant, if we go on a Tuesday night. And then there was this one, which Mum said I could give to you, because she and I don't need it: a free permanent wave, your hair will look nice all the time, without my helping you to put it in rollers."

Gertrustein looked dubious. "Well . . ." she said.

"Hah. I *knew* you'd say that. So I've already called and made an appointment for you at the Clip 'n Curl. It's right next to the chemist's, close enough for you to walk, and your appointment is for ten o'clock on Saturday morning."

"You're taking over my whole life, Anastasia Krupnik."

"No, I'm not. I'm just helping you to get your life started. I'm sorry if it's rude to say this, Gertrustein, but I think your life ended when Mr Stein – the man, not the goldfish – ran off with his mandolin player. And that was forty years ago!"

Gertrustein smiled suddenly. "You're right, Anastasia, but you're also wrong. My life ended when Edward Evans married the local nursery school teacher forty-seven years ago. Too late to start it up again now. But all right. I'll go and have a permanent wave at ten o'clock on Saturday morning."

"Then you'll make new friends, and . . ."

"Hold on there. I will have a permanent wave. Then I will come home and feed my fish and watch TV. One thing at a time. I'm too old for any more changes."

"Good grief," said Anastasia suddenly. "I forgot something. Mum wanted you to babysit for Sam on Saturday. And it's really important. Maybe I should call and change that appointment . . ."

"No. Sam can come with me. I'll need the moral support."

The thought of someone who wears Pampers being moral support was a little startling to Anastasia, but it did seem to solve the problem.

And she was beginning to have another idea.

Maybe it would be meddling in Gertrustein's life. On the other hand, she had *already* meddled in Gertrustein's life quite a bit, and it had seemed to work out okay. If *this* idea worked . . .

"I have to go somewhere," she announced. "I'll see you later, Gertrustein."

She ran to the garage and wheeled out her bike.

Anastasia had already been to the small library. It was one of the first things she had done after they moved, finding the library and getting a library card.

In Cambridge, there had been a branch library not far from the Krupniks' flat. Anastasia had been going to it since she was Sam's age: not by herself at that age, of course, but holding her mother's hand. Once, just before she moved, she had worked out that – if she had taken out eight books every week from the time she was two – she had taken more than four thousand books out of that library. That was a little puzzling, because the branch library was so small that she didn't think it *had* four thousand books. But her mother had pointed out that sometimes she took the same books over and over again.

In Cambridge, they knew her so well at the branch library that they called her Anastasia Again, the way Gertrustein was beginning to.

At this new library, they didn't know her at all, at least not *yet*, which was a little depressing. But they would. She had looked through their card catalogue and discovered they were missing some of her favourite books, so she was planning to write them a letter. One book that had been her favourite for years, in Cambridge, described all the symptoms of leprosy in great detail. She had taken it out regularly once every few months, just to be sure once again that she didn't have leprosy. Sometimes it was hard to tell, because one of the symptoms was itchy ear lobes. Every now and then Anastasia had itchy ear lobes. When she did, she always took out the leprosy book so that she could read the other symptoms and be certain she didn't have them, too. Now that she lived in a town whose library didn't contain the leprosy book, she didn't know what she would do when her ear lobes itched. So she was going to mention that in her letter to the local library – politely, of course.

But right now she was headed, on her bike, for the building that she had noticed next door to the library. It was called the Senior Citizens Drop-in Centre.

The door was open, and people looked up when she entered. It was probably pretty obvious, she realized, that she wasn't a Senior Citizen. Anastasia was not, in fact, a Senior Anything. She had dropped out of Girl Guides as soon as she realized how awful she looked in a Girl Guide uniform, so she would never be a Senior Girl Guide. And she had given up swimming lessons just after she passed Advanced Beginners, because it was such an effort not to sink. So she would never get her Senior Lifesaving badge.

Inside the door was a notice board, and Anastasia read announcements of painting classes, a trip to a flower show, a Great Books discussion group, lectures by a financial expert, and a course in gourmet cooking. There was also a notice of a lost cat named Boots, who was wearing a red flea collar and there was a wedding announcement. The people who had got married were named Ida and Harry, so Anastasia knew that they were Senior Citizens. No one young was named Ida or Harry.

Most of the people in the Senior Citizens Drop-in Centre had grey hair, except for one woman whose hair was bright orange and one man who had no hair at all. Some of them were playing cards, although they stopped when Anastasia came in and looked over at her, still holding their cards. "I said 'Four spades'," one woman said, but the others didn't answer her. Two men were playing Ping-Pong, and they stopped, too, and looked at Anastasia. They were all pretty friendly looking, but they seemed surprised to see her there.

A young woman came out of the back room, saw Anastasia, and smiled.

"Hello there. I'm Fran McCormick, the director. Can I help you? Are you looking for someone?"

Anastasia introduced herself, and Fran McCormick shook her hand.

"I have a friend," said Anastasia, "who is a Senior Citizen."

"Oh? What's her name? I know everybody pretty well," said Fran McCormick.

"Well, her name is Gertru . . . Gertrude Stein. But

you wouldn't know her. She never goes out of her house except sometimes to take my little brother for a walk."

Everyone was listening. Even the card players had put their cards down, although the lady who had said "four spades" looked a little impatient. One of the Ping-Pong players suddenly hit the ball across the net, and it went past the other player, who wasn't paying attention. "Hah! Gotcha!" said the man who had hit the ball, smugly. Then he turned, too, to listen to Anastasia, and the little plastic ball rolled into a corner of the room.

Well. With so many people watching her now, Anastasia began to feel as if she was making a speech. She had never liked making speeches. When they had to give oral reports in school, she had never once got a mark better than a B-minus, because she became nervous and said "ah" too often.

"Well, ah, let me start over," she said, when she realized so many people were listening. "My friend Gertrude Stein lives next door to me, and she's a Senior Citizen. But she's lonely. She eats all by herself, so she only eats TV dinners, and except for me and my little brother, she doesn't have anyone to talk to, although she's *interesting* to talk to, and, ah, her goldfish is getting fat because she feeds him too much, and she does it just because it makes her feel good to feed somebody, even if it's only a goldfish . . ."

For a moment, Anastasia felt as if that had been a stupid thing to say. But then she noticed that the

Senior Citizens were nodding, as if they understood. Probably some of them had goldfish, too.

"Well, why don't you send her down here to us?" asked the man who had hit the Ping-Pong ball.

"She wouldn't come. She'd be scared. Maybe it sounds stupid to be scared when you're all grown up, and even *old*, but . . ."

But they interrupted her, murmuring to each other and nodding again. They all seemed to understand about being scared, even if you were old.

" . . . and she pretends she's not scared, by being grouchy," Anastasia went on. They all nodded again.

"Let's send her an invitation to the square dance!" called out one of the card players.

"She'd throw it away. She'd say 'junk mail', and throw it away," Anastasia explained.

"What do you suggest that we could do for her?" asked Fran McCormick.

"Well, since you're called a Drop-in Centre," began Anastasia, "I thought maybe some of you could drop in on her. I could give you the address. It's not very far away."

But they all began shaking their heads.

"Not uninvited," said a tiny white-haired lady wearing a pink pants suit. "Really, that just isn't done. I wouldn't want anyone to drop in on *me* unexpectedly!"

The others agreed. Anastasia was surprised. She *liked* having unexpected guests. But apparently the Senior Citizens disagreed.

She thought for a minute. "Well then, *here's* an idea. Why don't you drop in on *me*? I live right next door. And you wouldn't be unexpected, because I'm inviting you. I'll make lemonade and everything. And then . . ."

Some of them were beginning to nod their heads. "And then you invite *her* over!" said the man with no hair.

"Right! And you can all make friends with her!"

"I'd come," said the orange-haired woman.

"Me too," called out some others.

"When?" asked someone.

"Well," said Anastasia, "she's having a permanent wave on Saturday morning. The first time she's been to a hairdresser's in maybe thirty years."

"Saturday afternoon, then!" announced the bald man. "How many people could make it on Saturday afternoon?"

Hands shot up, and Fran McCormick counted. Fourteen.

Anastasia wrote down her address. A thought nudged itself into the back of her head.

"By any chance," she asked the Senior Citizens, "are any of you named Edward Evans?"

But no one was. No one had ever heard of Edward Evans. Well, that would have been asking too much.

Pedalling home, Anastasia felt pretty good. She was sure her parents wouldn't mind. Her mother would help her make lemonade. Her father would dream up some kind of entertainment, although she'd have to tell him tactfully not to conduct Verdi's Requiem for the Senior Citizens. But maybe he could read some of his poetry to them.

Then she thought of something and almost rode her bike into someone's shrubbery. Good grief. Saturday.

What on earth was she going to tell Robert and Jenny?

Chapter 2 was not very long, Anastasia realized, reading it over. Only one sentence. But she liked the way it ended, with a mysterious reference to the young girl's Past and her Future. It was important to be very subtle in a mystery novel, so that readers wouldn't know exactly what was happening too early in the book. It was one of the troubles with Nancy Drew books, that they weren't subtle enough. Agatha Christie, now: *those* were subtle. In Agatha Christie books, you never knew who was bad and who was good. That was important.

"Chapter 3," she wrote. "In her new life, the young girl began to meet new people. A tall tennis player with blue eyes. An old woman who looked like a witch. A mysterious band of people who held regular meetings, and who were stricken with astonishment when the young girl showed up unexpectedly at their hide-out one day.

"At the same time, people from her past were still on her trail. The young man with the puzzling briefcase had found out where she lived, and she received a message that he was on his way. He was bringing with him an Irish woman with a chipped tooth."

There. Now she had a whole cast of characters, and the reader would not know yet who were villains and who were heroes.

Anastasia didn't know yet, either; but she would worry about that later.

11

"No. Absolutely not. I won't, under any circumstances." Anastasia's mother stood in her studio, with a paintbrush behind one ear and her hands planted firmly on her hips.

Anastasia glowered. "Why *not?*"

"Because it's a lie, and I won't tell anyone a lie on your behalf. And on top of that, it's the *stupidest* lie I've ever heard."

Anastasia was astonished. She had thought it was a terrific idea. "What's so stupid? Look, all you have to do is call Jenny, and sound very sad, and tell her that she and Robert shouldn't come on Saturday because you've just found out that I have leprosy and I've had to go to a leper colony very suddenly."

"That's ridiculous."

"Maybe it's not so ridiculous. Maybe I really do

have leprosy, as a matter of fact. My ear lobes itch. They've been itching all afternoon. It's an early symptom."

"It's a symptom that you haven't washed your ears. With all that hair washing you've been doing lately, you'd think you'd remember to wash your ears."

"Mum. That's gross."

"Not as gross as lying to your friends. Why don't you want them to come, anyway?"

Anastasia groaned and flopped down in an old stuffed chair covered with painty rags. "Oh, it's complicated. I invited some other people over on Saturday. Some new people I've just met."

Her mother looked at her, smiled, took the paintbrush from behind her ear, and set it on the table. She sat down on the arm of the chair and stroked Anastasia's head.

"Oh, sweetie, I'm so glad. Dad and I haven't wanted to say anything, but we've been worried about your making friends. Except for Steve, you haven't really met any other kids yet. That's wonderful, that now you have, and I'm delighted that you've invited them over."

Good grief. Anastasia felt, suddenly, the way she had when Robert Giannini told her about his retarded cousin: as if suddenly, before you knew it, it was too late to explain.

"No kidding, Anastasia, I'm really thrilled. And Robert and Jenny will fit right in, I'm sure. Listen, we can have a barbecue or something. How many people are coming over?"

"Fourteen."

"Goodness, that's a lot for a barbecue! But I think we could manage hot dogs. And I could make a big potato salad . . ."

"Mum, really, just lemonade will be fine. I told them it would just be lemonade."

"Well, whatever you think. But you know, we've been talking about getting a badminton set. We could get it before Saturday, and then . . ."

Anastasia pictured the Senior Citizens playing badminton. She pictured the ambulance pulling up, to cart away the ones with broken hips and heart attacks. She groaned.

"Mum, you know what I'd really like best? I'd really like it best if you and Dad would go off to a movie or something. Saturday afternoon."

Her mother stopped stroking her hair. Anastasia could tell that her feelings were hurt.

"You mean that you don't want Dad and me to be here and meet your new friends? All of a sudden you're embarrassed to have us old people around?"

"Oh, Mum," she groaned, "it's not that. It's . . . Oh, for pete's sake, I need to think."

Anastasia pulled herself up out of the chair and started up to her room. In the hall, Sam was flicking a flashlight on and off. He'd been playing with it all day.

"Flash!" said Sam, shining the light at her and laughing.

"Knock it off, Sam," Anastasia muttered.

Sam's lower lip began to quiver as he decided

whether or not to cry. Anastasia walked past him and headed up the stairs to her room. Her ear lobes really did itch. She began to wish that she really *did* have leprosy. Goodbye, cruel world. Life was just too confusing.

"Flash! Flash!" called Sam after her, blinking his light.

Anastasia slammed her door and decided to stay in her tower for a long time. Like the rest of her life.

But the phone rang. Whenever you decide to lock yourself in a tower for the rest of your life, for pete's sake, the phone always rings.

Anastasia's mother called from the first floor. "Anastasia?"

"What? Is it for me?"

"Come down here a minute, would you? I want to talk to you."

Anastasia clumped down the stairs. On the second floor, Sam swooped out of his bedroom, yelled "Flash!" and blinked his light at her.

"KNOCK IT OFF, SAM!"

Sam grinned and scooted off into a cupboard. She could see his flashlight blinking beneath the closed cupboard door.

"What do you want? Was the phone for me?" she asked her mother.

"Not really. But it was puzzling. It was someone named Fran McCormick . . ."

"Then it *was* for me!"

"Well, she said she didn't need to speak to you. She wanted to check with me to make sure that it was all right with me that all these people were coming over on Saturday. I must say, that was considerate of her. I can't remember that any of your *other* friends ever thought to ask my permission for anything."

"What did you tell her?"

"I told her yes. I told her we were planning to make a lot of lemonade. But, Anastasia . . ."

"What?"

"Then she said that if it wasn't too much trouble, could we please use artificially sweetened lemonade. Because Edna and Morris and Ernest have diabetes. That seems strange, Anastasia. I remember there was a child in your fourth class who was a diabetic, but for three kids out of a batch of fourteen to have diabetes? Well, that seems very peculiar to me. Where did you meet these kids?"

Anastasia was tempted to burst out laughing and to tell her mother that the "kids" were all Senior Citizens and that Edna and Morris and Ernest were all in their seventies or eighties. But she was cross with her mother. She was cross with her for worrying about her ability to make friends, for pete's sake.

"They have a kind of club," said Anastasia airily. "I was walking past where their clubhouse is, and I just decided to go in. They were all in there playing cards. So we started talking, and I invited them over. I have a knack for making friends, you know," she added meaningfully.

"What do you mean, a kind of club? What do you mean, they were in there playing cards? Were they playing poker or something? Have you got yourself involved with some sort of *gang*, Anastasia Krupnik?"

Anastasia looked angrily at her mother. "I suppose you could call it that. You could call it a 'gang' if you want to. I myself don't like to make that kind of stereotyped statement."

"Anastasia Krupnik, if those fourteen people arrive here on Saturday on *motorcycles* . . ."

Now Anastasia almost *did* laugh. But she was still cross with her mother. She looked down her nose, which was not hard to do because of her height.

"I don't believe any of them will arrive by motorcycle," she said haughtily, and turned to go back upstairs.

Sam ambushed her on the landing.

"FLASH!"

"MUM!" Anastasia yelled. "*Why* is Sam blinding everybody with that blasted flashlight?"

"Sam, put your light away for now," said her mother. "He and Mrs Stein have a plan," she explained to Anastasia. "They're going to flash lights at each other from their bedrooms after dark. Don't ask me why."

"Ask *me* why," grinned Sam.

"Why, stupid?"

"Because we're playing Flasher. Gertrustein used to play Flasher when she was a little girl, and she had a friend who lived right in this house."

"Yes, I know about her friend. Edward Evans. Some friend. He grew up and married someone else, and now all she has is a goldfish."

Sam wasn't listening. He had unscrewed the end of his flashlight and was examining the batteries.

"Anyway, stupid, you know what a *real* flasher is?"

"What?"

"Some jerk of a man who goes out wearing nothing at all but a raincoat, and then he jumps out unexpectedly and opens up his raincoat at people."

"Oh," said Sam, with interest. "Does he say 'Flash'?"

"How should I know? I've never seen one."

"Well, *I* say 'Flash'," said Sam, losing interest. "I'm a flasher with a flashlight. FLASH!" He shone the light in Anastasia's eyes again and ran off when she made a half-hearted attempt to grab him.

Anastasia let him go and plodded back up to her bedroom to peel more wallpaper.

But the telephone rang again. This time it was for Anastasia. Her mother called her from downstairs. She could tell from her mother's voice that she was still cross. Well, that was okay. Anastasia was still cross too.

"Is it the motorcycle gang? Did they ask for the gun moll?" Anastasia asked her mother sarcastically.

"It's Steve Harvey," said her mother coldly. "I should have told him you were out stealing hubcaps."

"Ha ha. Very funny." Anastasia took the phone and disappeared into a cupboard with it.

"Hello, Steve."

"Hello. Listen my mum had an idea. She's been wanting to welcome your family to the neighbourhood. So she thought maybe your family and mine could go together for a picnic on Saturday. Maybe to Sturbridge or somewhere."

Oh, rats. Oh, *rats*. Anastasia had been dying to meet Steve's family. His father was a sports commentator who actually knew a lot of famous athletes personally. His mother was a lawyer in the district attorney's office, and she had prosecuted an axe murderer once. And his older sister, who was home for a visit, was almost six feet tall, Steve said. She was a ballet dancer in New York. Her real name was Anne, but she went by the name Anya professionally. Anastasia thought that was the most terrific, wonderful thing she had ever heard.

Anastasia had once wanted to be a ballet dancer herself. She had taken lessons when she was nine and ten, but her feet never seemed to work right. One day she had tried to show her mother the dance she was practising for a recital. She had twirled around on one toe, and her other leg knocked over a floor lamp, which hit the TV and bent the antenna; the antenna knocked a picture off the wall, and the picture hit a cup of coffee, which overturned on a book called *Treasures of the Louvre*. Anastasia grabbed for the book, but she tripped on a wrinkle in the rug and fell against the coffee table, breaking one of the table's legs and spraining her own ankle. She had to have X-rays and to wear a bandage for three weeks, and she had missed the dance recital and stopped taking ballet lessons.

Her father had said, at the time, that she should be in the *Guinness Book of World Records* because she had done three hundred dollars worth of damage in twenty-seven seconds. But she had checked in the *Guinness Book of World Records* and found that a tornado in Hastings, Nebraska, had beaten that record in 1947.

Still, she was dying to meet Anne Harvey. She was dying to meet a female who was almost six feet tall and hadn't become a professional basketball player.

But instead, on Saturday, instead of going to Sturbridge with the remarkable Harvey family, Anastasia was going to be serving lemonade to fourteen senior citizens, and to creepo Robert Giannini, and to traitor Jenny MacCauley, who had gone to see *Casablanca* without her.

She felt like having a tantrum, the way Sam did sometimes, kicking the floor and shrieking.

But twleve was too old for that; and anyway, she didn't want Steve Harvey to hear her kicking the floor and shrieking. Steve had already said, once, that she seemed very sophisticated for twelve.

She had explained, when he said that, that probably it was because she grew up in Cambridge, which was a more sophisticated place than the suburbs.

Steve had agreed. But then he had said something surprising. He had said that before he met Anastasia, he had thought everyone who lived in Cambridge was weird. He had thought that they were all intellectuals who sat around in the evenings drinking rose hip tea and playing recorders.

Anastasia had confessed that before she met *him*, she thought that everyone who lived in the suburbs was boring and preppy, that they all wore shirts with alligators and went to Bermuda for the spring holidays.

Steve said that he'd never been to Bermuda in his life, and that he always ripped the alligators off his shirts.

Anastasia said that she hated rose hip tea more than anything in the world except liver.

It had been kind of nice to find out that they were wrong about each other, that they had – it now occurred to her – made premature assumptions.

So she certainly wasn't going to screech and kick the floor now, even though she certainly felt like it.

Instead she said, "I'm really sorry, Steve, but we won't be able to come on Saturday. I have a couple of friends from Cambridge coming over to visit me that day, and there are some other people coming, too."

"Well, maybe some other time," Steve said cheerfully.

Yes, thought Anastasia glumly. She happened to know that his sister was going back to New York on

Sunday, to start rehearsals for a new ballet. Probably with Nureyev, for pete's sake.

"My life is ruined, and it's all your fault," she muttered to her mother, who was in her studio again, painting different shades of blue onto a large canvas. She had a blue daub on her chin.

"Why *my* fault?" called her mother after her, as she headed back up the stairs.

Anastasia didn't really have an answer for that. Since Steve Harvey couldn't hear her, she gave a very unsophisticated answer.

"Because I didn't *ask* to be born!" she bellowed.

And her mother had a very unsophisticated answer to *that*. "Nyah nyah," she called, and stuck out her tongue.

"Who was the young man with the mysteriously blinking light?" wrote Anastasia, at the beginning of Chapter 4.

"And what role was the cruel, subversive woman with blue paint on her chin going to play in all of this?" she went on.

It didn't seem fair to leave out her father. So she continued Chapter 4 by writing, "The tall, bearded stranger sipped thoughtfully at a beer, with his eyes closed, listening to Mozart."

In an Agatha Christie book, Anastasia realized there had always been at least one murder by Chapter 4.

So she wrote ominously, "Mozart was dead."

12

Anastasia woke up early on Saturday morning, and before she opened her eyes, she heard a sound that sounded like Frank Goldfish.

"Frank?" she said sleepily. "What are you doing? Cut it out. It's too early to be playing. Go back to sleep."

But the sound continued, and Anastasia woke up a little more, opened her eyes a tiny bit, and realized it was raining. High up here, in her tower room, wet tree leaves were blowing against her windows.

Anastasia grinned. Terrific. Robert and Jenny wouldn't be able to ride their bikes over here in the rain. Probably her dad would be willing to drive Gertrustein down to the hairdresser's. Maybe the Harveys wouldn't go to Sturbridge, and maybe Anastasia could walk over and meet Anne, at least, before she went back to New York. And in the afternoon, all the Senior Citizens could come; Fran McCormick would bring them in the van that was painted with a gross name: Oldster Roadster.

She turned over, hugged her pillow, and went back to sleep.

But when she woke again, later, the rain had stopped.

Downstairs, her mother was brushing Sam's hair.

"Sam's going with Mrs Stein to the hairdresser's," she said, "so I thought he'd better look glamorous."

"Don't let them cut your hair, Sam," said Anastasia, buttering a piece of toast.

"Do my curls look pretty?" asked Sam anxiously.

Good grief. There was so much that Sam didn't know yet.

"Not pretty, Sam," Anastasia told him. "Handsome. Boys aren't supposed to look pretty, only handsome."

"Oh."

"You're not taking your flashlight, are you?"

"No, it's in its hiding place. Tonight we play Flasher."

Anastasia's mother looked out of the window. "It looks as if it might rain again. The sky's pretty grey." She went to the wardrobe, got Sam's little raincoat, and buttoned him into it. "There you are, old buddy. Your buggy's over at Mrs Stein's. Have a nice time. And behave yourself."

They watched through the window as Sam trotted across the garden and climbed the steps to Gertrustein's porch.

"Now. What's next? Lemonade. Anastasia's mother got the lemons out of the cupboard. "Might as well make it now, so Robert and Jenny can have some when they get here. Be sure to tell them to leave plenty for the Mafia."

"*Mum!*"

Her mother chuckled. "Okay, I'm sorry. I'm sure your new friends are actually very nice, Anastasia. I was just in a rotten mood yesterday. I've been working on a painting for a week now, and it just isn't going very well. You know how grouchy your father gets when he's writing a poem that doesn't seem to work? And he blames us, even though we've never seen the poem?"

Anastasia laughed. "Yes. I've been writing a novel for about three months now, myself. It took me 2½ months just to think of a title. And now the novel doesn't seem to have much connection with the title."

"Goodness. That would be a problem."

"Also, I'm having a hard time getting all the ingredients in."

"Ingredients?"

"Mmmmm. It's a mystery novel. I finally put in lots of mysterious characters. Then I remembered I needed a dead person. So I got that in, at the end of Chapter 4. But there's no sex yet."

"Sex? Are you sure you need sex in a mystery novel?"

Anastasia thought. Nancy Drew books had no sex. Nancy's boyfriend was a little retarded that way. Anastasia thought. He was old enough to *drive*, for pete's sake, but he went on for book after book after book, without ever developing any interest in sex. But that was one reason why Nancy Drew books were boring.

Agatha Christie books had hints of love affairs, but nothing explicit. Anastasia wanted her mystery novel to be even more interesting than Agatha Christie's.

"Yes," she said. "I need some explicit sex. Maybe in Chapter 5."

"Stir."

"Stir my novel?"

"No, stupid. Stir the lemonade."

They filled several old cider jugs. "There," said her mother. "We can add ice cubes when we serve it."

"Probably my gangland friends will sneak some vodka in, too."

"*Anastasia*. You're not serious, are you?"

Anastasia groaned. "No, Mum. I was only kidding."

Watching from the front window, Anastasia saw them as they came around the corner. She grinned. Actually, it would be fun to see Jenny again. She had missed Jenny. Probably, if the situation had been reversed, she would have gone to see *Casablanca* herself, she had to admit.

But she groaned when she saw Robert. Good old jerko Giannini. Right here, right here at her very corner, for pete's sake, he had stopped his bike and was consulting a map. Anastasia could see that Jenny was pointing to the house and yelling at him. But Robert was busily consulting his map, which he then folded very carefully and put back in his pocket. Typical of Robert to be able to fold a map. He was the only person Anastasia had ever met who could fold a map.

And he had his briefcase, of course. She could make out its rectangular outline, even though it was wrapped in something. Of course. Dark green plastic. Typical, that Robert had wrapped his briefcase in a rubbish bag so that it wouldn't get wet. Gross.

And his feet. What was wrong with his feet? Anastasia squinted, so that she could see them more clearly. Oh, no. She couldn't believe it. Sick SICK.

Robert Giannini was wearing galoshes.

"Hello, Jenny!" Anastasia said, and made a special face at her which meant: look at Robert, wearing galoshes.

"Hello," said Jenny, and made a face back which meant: I know, it's the grossest thing I've ever seen.

"Well," said Robert Giannini, "we made it, Anastasia."

"I can see that, Robert. Come on in."

Robert and Jenny loved Anastasia's new house. It made her feel good, showing it to them and seeing it in a new way herself, as she did. She felt a little like an estate agent, opening doors and saying "This is the study" and "This is the studio where my mother paints" (although she closed that door again quickly, when she realized that her mother had been working on a nude).

Especially she liked taking them up to her tower room. Even with the wallpaper partly peeled off, the room was exciting, set up high in the tops of the trees, with a view that stretched so far that they could see the tall Hancock Building in Boston in the distance.

Robert said, "You know, Anastasia, when you pull off these layers of wallpaper, you peel away a whole history of your room. Who lived in the house last?"

Anastasia shrugged. "Some doctor and his wife. They had five kids."

"Well, probably one of the kids lived up here, don't you think? So this top layer of paper belongs to that kid."

He pulled off a section of that paper near the window. "Now, look," he said. "Green, with flowers, under that. Wonder who lived here then."

"Maybe a young couple," said Jenny. "Maybe the husband beat the wife, so she used to come up here to hide from him."

"That's really old-fashioned paper," said Anastasia, looking at the pattern more closely. "Probably it was way back in the 1930s or something, when everything was different. Maybe the wife wanted to go out and get a job instead of staying home and cooking. That's why he beat her."

"The rat," muttered Jenny.

"What's underneath?"

Robert picked with his fingernail at the green flowered paper until a piece of it came loose. "Blue. With a sort of striped pattern. This one's *really* old." He pulled more of the green away. "Wonder who lived here then."

"A family that had a crazy uncle. They kept him chained up here in the tower," suggested Jenny.

"Yes," said Robert. "He used to keep track of the days and weeks by making marks on the wall. Look! Right here is a mark he made!"

Robert was right. At the edge, still partly covered by the green paper, was a mark made with pen and ink.

"It probably says 'Help I'm being held captive in this tower!'"

"Be careful, Robert. Don't tear it!"

Anastasia laughed after she said that. Telling someone who wears galoshes, carrries a briefcase, and folds maps correctly to be careful. Really stupid.

He finally lifted up a strip of green paper and exposed all of the faded writing. They leaned over and tried to work out what it said. It was certainly not the marks of a madman counting the days of captivity.

Anastasia made it out and opened her mouth in

astonishment. "I know what that is! Good grief! Wait till . . ."

But she was interrupted. Her mother called from the bottom of the tower stairs.

"Anastasia! You get down here *right away!* Two vans have just pulled into the drive. Your guests are here!"

An hour later, some of the confusion had subsided. Everyone was on their second cup of lemonade, and Anastasia's mother had opened the box of imported biscuits that she'd been saving since last Christmas for a special occasion (although Edna, Morris, and Ernest, being diabetic, couldn't eat them).

Anastasia's father was in the study, showing off his first editions to Harry, who had once taught European literature at Tufts University, and to Jeanette, who years ago had managed a Boston bookshop.

Robert had opened his briefcase and was showing some rocket plans to Morris and Fred, who were retired engineers, and they were arguing over whether the rocket Robert had designed could possibly make it to the moon.

Edna and four other ladies were showing Jenny photographs of their grandchildren.

Someone was playing "Alexander's Ragtime Band" on the piano, and a tiny lady with snow-white hair was dancing around and around the dining room all by herself.

In the studio, the man with no hair at all was looking wistfully at the half finished painting of a nude.

Someone kept asking if the Krupniks had a croquet set. Or a badminton set. Or a volley ball.

In the kitchen, Fran McCormick was helping Anastasia's mother make some more lemonade, and they were both laughing so hard they were almost crying.

" . . . and I thought she meant a motorcycle gang," Anastasia's mother sputtered. Anastasia wandered into the kitchen.

"Anastasia," laughed Fran, "I think your mother is going to clobber you after we leave."

Anastasia perched on a kitchen stool, chewed on a biscuit, and grinned. "This is a good party," she said. Even Robert Giannini is a hit. I think Robert is really an eighty-year-old man in a twelve-year-old body."

"Is everybody okay in there? The new lot of lemonade's almost ready," said her mother, stirring.

"Everyone's fine. Someone wants to play croquet. Some other people are having a contest over who has the best looking grandchildren, so there are photographs all over the place. The chap with the bald head wishes you had painted the breasts bigger on the nude."

"Tell him to go and buy a *Playboy*."

"I did. And Mum, I've just seen Gertrustein and Sam go into her house. The point of this party was to introduce Gertrustein to everyone. How shall we get her to come over?"

Her mother went to the telephone and dialled.

"Mrs Stein? This is Katherine Krupnik. How did it go at the hairdresser's?"

"Don't tell her there are *people* here," hissed Anastasia, "or she won't come." Her mother gestured to her to be quiet.

"Oh, Gertrude, I'm sure it looks *lovely*. You just aren't used to it."

Anastasia remembered something. "Tell her," she whispered. "that I have something I absolutely *have* to show her."

Her mother gestured: Shut up.

"Of course you're not going to wear a hat for the rest of your life," her mother was saying into the phone. "He *what?* That little beast!"

She put her hand over the receiver and whispered to Fran and Anastasia, "Sam told her she looks like Art Garfunkel."

"Sam *loves* Art Garfunkel," said Anastasia.

"Gertrude, Anastasia tells me that Sam loves Art Garfunkel," her mother said into the telephone. "So he means it as a compliment. Listen, Gertrude, why don't you bring Sam over here now? I want to see your permanent wave, and Anastasia has something that she says she absolutely has to show you."

After she hung up, she said apprehensively to Fran and Anastasia, "This may be a terrible mistake. She says she intends to put on a large hat and go to bed in a dark room for the rest of her life."

"*Mum*," Anastasia pointed out, "she's saying that for the same reason she says she doesn't like people. She's *scared*. Is she coming over?"

"Yes. In fact, there she is now, coming out of her house with Sam. You go and greet her at the door, Anastasia."

They watched through the window as Gertrustein and Sam came across the garden, and Anastasia ran to open the door.

Gertrustein was, as she had said, wearing a large green hat which covered her hair.

"Good afternoon, Anastasia," she said. "I've brought your brother back. And your mother says you have something to show me."

The piano began again, with "You Are My Sunshine". People began to sing. There was a thump in the dining room, and Anastasia cringed; the white-haired lady had bumped into the table as she danced.

Sam looked startled at the noise. He dropped Gertrustein's hand, said, "I'm going to hide," and scooted up the stairs.

"I wasn't aware that you had guests," Gertrustein sniffed. "I'll come back another time."

"No, no, it's okay," said Anastasia casually. "It's just some friends who are visiting us. Come on in." She took Gertrustein by the hand and practically dragged her into the living room.

"Everybody," announced Anastasia in a loud

voice, "I would like you to meet my friend Gertrude Stein."

The Senior Citizens clustered around Gertrustein, introducing themselves. Someone put a paper cup of lemonade into her hand. The woman with orange hair sat back down at the piano and began to play "As Time Goes By", the song from *Casablanca.* "A kiss is just a kiss . . ." Edna and Fred began to sing.

"Here's lookin' at you, kid," said the bald-headed man in a not-too-bad Humphrey Bogart voice to Gertrustein, and held up his cup of lemonade in a toast.

Anastasia saw that Gertrustein's mouth was beginning to twitch at the edges into a smile.

The doorbell rang.

At the door was Steve Harvey, with the tallest, most beautiful girl Anastasia had ever seen.

"I didn't realize you were having so many people," Steve said loudly, to make himself heard over the noise. "This is Anne. We didn't go to Sturbridge because of the rain this morning, and Anne wanted to meet you before she goes back to New York."

Anastasia grinned, shook Anne's hand, and brought them inside. She thought for a minute that she would try to explain about the guests. Then she looked in the living room, saw seven Senior Citizens, plus Gertrustein still wearing her big green hat, arranging themselves into a circle to do some sort of dance, and decided that it would be impossible to explain.

"My parents are outside in the car," explained Steve. "Do you think . . ."

"Yes," said Anastasia. "Bring them in."

Finally, the noise had lessened. Everyone was worn out, and the lemonade was almost gone. Anne Harvey had demonstrated a dance from a Broadway musical, and when she had asked politely if she could wear Gertrustein's green hat for the dance, Gertrustein had finally taken the hat off. Everyone had admired her new mass of silver curls. There had been a long discussion about Art Garfunkel, and they had played an Art Garfunkel record on the stereo.

Mr Harvey had done an imitation of Groucho Marx. Anastasia's father had read a poem about baseball. Then Mr Harvey had read the same poem in his Groucho Marx voice.

The man with the bald head was now wearing the big green hat.

Everyone was exhausted from laughing and singing. For the first time in two hours, the house was quiet, as they all gathered their breath in order to say goodbye.

There was the soft padding sound of bare feet coming down the stairs.

"It's my brother," said Anastasia softly. "I wondered what had happened to him."

Sam appeared in the doorway, and everyone said, "Oooooh," the way people do when they see a curly-headed baby.

But Anastasia's heart sank. No, Sam, she said silently. Don't do it, Sam. She cringed. The instant she saw that Sam was wearing his raincoat and that below it his legs and feet were bare, she knew what was coming. I'll kill you, Sam, she thought.

Sam grinned and stood in the doorway looking at the room full of senior citizens, and Gertrustein, and his parents, and the Harveys, and Jenny, and Robert.

"FLASH!" he said loudly and opened his raincoat. Then he scampered away, naked.

Everyone sat politely silent for a moment. Then the Senior Citizens began to giggle. Anne Harvey started to laugh. Gertrustein laughed so hard that her Art Garfunkel curls shook. Mr Harvey announced, "Ladies and gentlemen, an astonishing thing has happened", in his Groucho Marx voice.

It was time for everyone to go home.

"Gertrustein, I really do like your hair," said Anastasia, "and I'm glad you had fun at the party."

"Hmmmph," said Gertrustein.

Sam had been tucked away for his nap, and they were cleaning up the kitchen.

"Mum, do you know what Robert Giannini said, when he and Jenny were leaving?"

"What?"

Anastasia giggled. "He came over to me privately and said in this serious voice, 'Anastasia, I thought that your brother had a birth defect. I didn't realize that you meant he was emotionally disturbed. I'm really sorry'."

"That jerk," said Anastasia's mother. "Of course, Sam really was obnoxious, I'll admit."

"It was probably my fault," pointed out Gertrustein, "since it was I who suggested to him that we play Flasher."

"Gertrustein!" said Anastasia. "I've just remembered! I really *do* have something to show you. Do you think you could climb up all the stairs to my room?"

Gertrustein groaned. "Can't you bring it down?"

"No. Come on. We can go slowly."

The two of them climbed the staircase to the second floor; then, puffing, Gertrustein made it up to the tower.

"Actually," she said, "I think the dancing helped my arthritis. I think maybe I'll enroll in their folk-dancing class."

"Look!" said Anastasia. "Kneel down here, Gertrustein, so you can see."

They knelt side by side, and Anastasia pointed to the faded writing on the oldest layer of wallpaper.

"'Edward loves Gertrude. Always'," Gertrustein read aloud. "My goodness. I wonder when he wrote that."

"There's no date."

"Well, it really doesn't matter when he wrote it, I suppose. It's nice to know that he *did*." Gertrustein blushed a little.

"I wonder where he is now."

"Probably being a Senior Citizen somewhere."

"Maybe you could find him."

But Gertrustein hooted. "I wouldn't even want to, now. He's probably fat. Better just to remember him. Of course, it would be nice if . . ."

"If what?"

Gertrustein patted her curls. "If he could see my new hairdo," she laughed.

"Chapter 5," wrote Anastasia at the top of a new page. She had begun to be a little bored with novel writing, so she decided that Chapter 5 would be the final chapter. That meant, she knew from Agatha Christie, that she had to bring all the characters together, preferably in a locked room, and solve the mystery.

And she also had to put the sex in.

She realized that it was not entirely clear just what the mystery *was*. But it was in the title. "The Mystery of Saying Goodbye." Okay. She just had to connect the title with the plot.

Anastasia spit out some rubber bits that she had nibbled off accidentally and began to write.

"All of the characters," she wrote, "were in the same room. Suddenly, creeping down from the tower came a naked man."

Then she frowned, crossed out "man" and wrote "little boy".

But that was no good. There was nothing at all sexy about a little boy, naked or not. Well, she thought, it *is* a novel. It doesn't have to be exactly true.

So she wrote again, "Suddenly, creeping silently down from the tower, came a naked man. All he was wearing was a trench coat, and he carried a flashlight.

"He threw open the door to the room, opened his trench coat, laughed an evil laugh, and disappeared."

There. So much for the sex. Now to connect the title. "The tall bearded man said to everyone, 'Goodbye. I am going to take a nap now.'

"The blue-eyed tennis player said to the young girl, 'Goodbye. Do you want to play tennis later if it doesn't rain?'

"The young girl said, 'Goodbye. Yes, I do.'

"The tall ballerina said, 'Goodbye. I think I will go to New York now, to be in a ballet.'

"The cruel and subversive housewife, who actually turned out to be pretty nice, said, 'Goodbye. I am going to wash the lemonade jugs.'

"The woman who looked like a witch, except she didn't any more, said, 'Goodbye. I will help you wash the lemonade jugs. Where is my green hat?'

"The bald man who was wearing her green hat took it off and gave it to her. 'Goodbye,' he said. 'Maybe we could have dinner together some night soon.'

"A whole batch of old people said, 'Goodbye', and they went home. Some of them had to babysit for their grandchildren.

"The strange young man wearing a SeaWorld tee shirt said, 'Goodbye, everyone. I am sorry about the naked, emotionally disturbed man. Where is my briefcase?'

"The Irish woman with the chipped tooth said, 'Here it is. Don't forget your stupid galoshes. Goodbye, all.'

"The famous sports commentator said, 'This is Groucho Marx wishing you goodbye after what has proved to be an eventful afternoon.'

"The lady lawyer who had once prosecuted an axe murderer said, 'Will you stop that ridiculous Groucho Marx imitation! Goodbye, everyone. Thank you so much for including us.'

"The young girl realized, after they had all left, that there were many different ways to say goodbye. That solved the mystery."

Anastasia read Chapter 5 again. It was the longest chapter of her novel. But she realized it was lacking something still.

Two things, she decided. The sex was not *quite* explicit enough. And there should have been another mention of the corpse.

But those things were easy to add. She wrote two more sentences.

"The naked man had a poking-out bellybutton. And Mozart was still dead."

Then she wrote, "The End" and went to get her tennis racket.

Anastasia At Your Service

For Ben and Grey

1

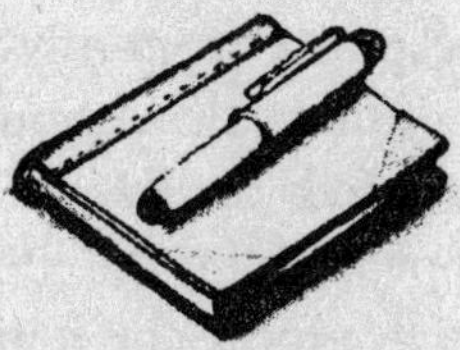

"Groan," said Anastasia Krupnik feebly, and kicked the living room couch with one trainer. She was lying on the living room floor. She was terribly depressed. She was so depressed that she had been acting out all the deathbed scenes she could think of. Beth, in *Little Women*. (A few small coughs, and then, weakly, "Farewell, my dear sisters.")

Juliet. (A gulp of poison, a horrible face because poison probably tasted terrible, and then, sadly, "Sorry things didn't work out, Romeo.")

Charlotte, in *Charlotte's Web*. (No final words, because spiders couldn't talk. But a few writhes. Probably spiders would writhe, dying. Then all eight legs – or six? Anastasia couldn't remember – straight up in the air. Tough to act that one out, when you had only two legs.)

She wondered what would happen if her parents found her dead on the living room floor. Probably her mother would say, "For Pete's sake, I just cleaned this room yesterday, and *now* look at it."

She groaned again. "Groan." Feebly, still, but a little louder.

There was no response from anywhere. Deathbed scenes weren't any fun at all without an audience.

"GROAN," she roared, finally.

Her mother appeared in the doorway with an orange potholder mitten on one hand.

"Did you call me?" she asked cheerfully. "I thought I heard someone call 'Mum'."

"I was groaning, for Pete's sake," said Anastasia. "Can't you even recognize a groan when you hear one?"

"Do it again."

"GROAN," roared Anastasia. Then she went on, dramatically, "I am dying. I have clasped an asp to my bosom."

"Must have been a heck of a disappointment for the asp. You hardly even *have* a bosom."

"*Mum*!" Anastasia sat up and threw a cushion at her mother.

"Sorry. That *was* a rotten thing to say. You've got the groaning wrong, though, incidentally. You don't *say* "groan" when you're groaning. A good groan sounds like this: 'Arrgghh'."

"Hey, that's pretty good."

"You try it."

"Arrggghhhh."

"Not bad. I would have come right away if I'd heard that. Do it again, louder."

"AAARRRRGGGGHHHHH."

"Terrific. Wait a minute while I get my cup of coffee and then I'll ask you what's wrong."

Anastasia followed her mother to the kitchen and poured herself a glass of lemonade.

"Now then," said her mother as she stirred her coffee, "what seems to be the problem?"

"Severe depression." Anastasia sighed.

"Well, I can *see* that. What's causing the depression?"

Anastasia thought, while she sipped her lemonade. "Boredom," she said. "And also poverty. Extreme poverty."

"I can relate to that," said her mother. "At least to the poverty part. Your dad and I have never been rich. We never *will* be rich. English professors don't make very much money, and he's always going to be an English professor, because he loves it. And I'm always going to be an artist, because that's what *I* love, and artists never make much money."

"Mum," said Anastasia patiently, "I'm not talking about that kind of poverty. I'm talking about twelve-year-old, extreme, desperate, two-dollar-a-week-allowance kind of poverty. If I really *did* want to kill myself with an asp, I wouldn't be able to, because I wouldn't be able to *afford* an asp."

"True," said her mother. "Asps don't come cheap in Massachusetts."

"And as for the boredom . . ."

"Yes. Tell me about the boredom. I can't remember ever being bored. Also, Anastasia, I can't remember *you* ever complaining of boredom before. Just last week you were in and out of the house all the time, with a million things to do. You were playing tennis every day, and you were off riding your bike, and when I wanted you to help with the dishes I could never *find* you. Now I can *always* find you, because you're always lying on the floor saying, 'Farewell, cruel world.' What's happened?"

"Steve Harvey." Anastasia sighed. "The only person I *know* in this town. At least the only person my age. My tennis partner. My bike-riding companion. My only *friend*, for Pete's sake."

"I'm your friend," said a very small voice. Anastasia's brother, Sam, padded into the kitchen, with his shoes untied, and climbed into a chair. "I want some lemonade. I want my friend Anastasia to pour me some lemonade, please," he said.

"Oh, for Pete's sake," said Anastasia. She poured some lemonade into Sam's plastic clown cup. "Here. Don't spill it."

"You're right, Sam," said her mother, smoothing his curly hair. "You are Anastasia's very dear friend. But right now she's not talking about two-year-old friends. What's happened to you and Steve, Anastasia? Did you have a fight?"

"No, of course not. But he's the only person my age that I've met since we've moved here. And he was going to introduce me to other kids before school started. He was going to have a big barbecue at his house. He was going to have it next *week*, in fact . . ."

"And now he isn't?"

"Now, for Pete's sake, he's *gone* all of a sudden. Somebody phoned his father, some big-deal sports figure, and asked if Steve would like to go to a basketball camp in New Hampshire. They gave him a full scholarship, for Pete's sake. Nobody's ever offered me a full scholarship anywhere, except that time Dad offered to buy me a one-way ticket to reform school."

"He was only kidding, Anastasia."

"No, he wasn't. He was really cross."

"Well, yes, that's true, he *was* really cross . . ."

"Because I left his stupid Billie Holiday records on the radiator and melted them."

"But he didn't mean it about reform school."

"I know." Anastasia sighed. "Watch it, Sam. You're going to spill that if you're not really careful." Sam had picked up the jug of lemonade and was pouring himself another cup.

"No I won't," said Sam sweetly. Then the jug slipped out of his hand. Lemonade poured over the kitchen table and into Anatasia's lap. Her best jeans. Her favourite shirt. Sticky. And *cold*.

"AARRRGGGGHHHH," said Anastasia.

Sam climbed out of his chair quickly. "I'm going out to play," he said. "I'm going to play in the garden." He scooted through the back door.

Her mother grabbed two towels and a sponge and began to mop the table.

"AARRRGGGGHHHH," said Anastasia again, holding her cold, sticky shirt away from her body.

"Sam," called her mother through the kitchen window to the back garden, "while you're out there, look around in the bushes, would you? See if you can find an asp for your sister!"

"Ha, ha," said Anastasia, dripping sarcasm along with lemonade.

Anastasia loved supper-time. Especially when they had lasagna, as they did tonight. Her mother was the best lasagna-maker in the whole world. If ever there were a National Lasagna Bake-Off Contest, her mother would win, she was quite certain.

She had told her mother that once. But her mother had made a terrible face, with her eyes crossed and her tongue sticking out. Apparently her mother didn't want to win a National Lasagna Bake-Off Contest. Anastasia could understand that. Probably the prize would be an apron or something.

Even when they didn't have lasagna, Anastasia loved supper-time, because the whole family, all four of them, were there, and they talked a lot. Often they talked about their problems, and it was absolutely amazing, Anastasia thought, how problems seemed less monumental if you talked about them while you ate lasagna. Or even pot roast, or tuna-fish casserole.

When she was older, and her spelling had improved

a bit, Anastasia planned to write an article for the *Journal of the American Psychiatric Association.* In it, she was going to tell all the psychiatrists in America that if they served dinner to their patients, preferably lasagna (though pot roast or tuna-fish casserole would be okay), their patients would be cured of all their problems much faster.

("Oh, Doctor," Anastasia imagined a psychiatric patient saying, "I see purple leopards lurking behind the furniture. I will commit suicide if they don't go away."

"Hmmmm," the doctor would say. "Would you like some grated cheese on your lasagna? Tell me more about the purple leopards."

"Leopards? Were we talking about leopards? Funny, I don't remember anything about purple leopards. I would like more salad, though. And would you pass the rolls, please?")

"Dad," asked Anastasia as they ate, "do you have your notebook with you?"

He looked surprised. "Of course I have my notebook. I *always* have my notebook with me. Every writer does. You never know, if you're a writer, when you might have to take notes on the human scene." He took his small leather-bound notebook out of his pocket.

"No kidding. What does that mean: notes on the human scene?" asked Anastasia.

He thought for a minute. "Well, I eavesdrop and observe people. Then I make notes about what I see and what I overhear. After a while, I use some of that stuff in poems."

That was fascinating to Anastasia. She had tried and tried to be a writer, but somehow she had never succeeded very well. Yet her father, when he was not busy being an English professor, was a pretty successful writer of poetry. She had never worked out just how he did it. And now it turned out to be so simple. Notes on the human scene.

"Read me some," she suggested.

He put down his fork and flipped through the pages of his little notebook. "Well," he said, "here's what I wrote just this morning. 'Sam looks like his mother when he sleeps'."

Anastasia's mother smiled. Sam smiled.

"'They both sleep with their mouths open, and their bottoms sticking up in the air'," he went on.

Anastasia's mother stopped smiling. "Myron!" she said. "If you *ever* use that in a poem, I will sue for divorce!"

Dr Krupnik grinned. "Just observations," he explained. "Notes on the human scene. Why did you ask if I had my notebook, Anastasia?"

"Because I have a problem. You always seem to need your notebook when you help me solve my problems."

"True," said her father. "I'm a list-maker. Most problems can be solved by making lists." He uncapped his fountain pen.

"I have a problem too!" said Sam suddenly, in a stricken voice. "Make me a list, *quick*!"

Anastasia groaned. Sam was always interrupting her serious discussions.

"What's your problem, Sam?" she asked in a bored voice. If they didn't deal with this first, he would keep interrupting.

"A pea in my nose," he said, sounding frightened

"You put a *pea* in your nose? Sam! Why on earth did you do *that*?"

"Sometimes it's not important to ask why, Anastasia," said her mother. She picked Sam up and carried him away to the bathroom. After a moment they were back.

"Operation Pea Removal successful," announced Mrs Krupnik. "Sam, do not *ever* do that again. It is very dangerous to put anything into your nose."

"Also your ears," said Anastasia. "Don't ever put anything into your ears."

Sam sat there looking guilty. He didn't say anything. It was unusual for Sam not to say anything.

"Sam?" said Anastasia's father.

Sam didn't answer. He was looking down into his lap. A very guilty look.

"Sam? Do you have peas in your ears?"

Sam shook his head.

"What's wrong, then?"

"My bellybutton," Sam whispered.

His father leaned over and lifted Sam's little shirt. There was a pea, slightly squashed, stuck on Sam's bellybutton.

Sometimes it was very, very difficult to have a serious meal with Sam around.

"Now," said her father finally, with his pen poised over his notebook, "back to your problem, Anastasia. Sam, you eat your dinner. No more fooling around."

Anastasia listed her problems once again, for her father, the way she had for her mother that afternoon. Boredom. Poverty. Depression.

Dr Krupnik wrote Boredom, Poverty, Depression in his notebook. He drew a box around them. He drew arrows pointing to the box. He drew a small flower. He drew three squiggly lines in a row. Finally he wrote one word with a flourish, underlined it, and put an exclamation point at the end of the word.

"There you are," he said. "Easy solution."

Anastasia pushed her glass of milk to one side so that she could see what he had written.

"*Job*!" it said at the bottom of the page.

Anastasia groaned.

"That sounds easy to you, Dad," she pointed out patiently, "because you're forty-seven years old and you *have* a job. You have a job teaching English at Harvard. And Mum, *you* have a job doing illustrations for that textbook on photography . . ."

"It is *not* easy," said her mother. "I spent all morning trying to draw the inside of a diffusion enlarger. If you think that's *easy*, Anastasia . . ."

"I didn't mean that. Of course the work isn't easy. But it's easy for you to get a job because you went to art school and everything. You have qualifications. Twelve-year-old people don't have qualifications for anything. Nobody gives a job to a twelve-year-old person."

Her father turned to a fresh page in his notebook.

"Now the list-making really starts," he said happily.

"What do you mean?"

"Start thinking of the kinds of things you'd like to do. Things you'd be good at. Things someone might need someone to do. Then you'll start your own business, providing those services."

"Not babysitting. I hate babysitting."

Sam gave her a dirty look.

"Well, maybe I wouldn't mind babysitting if it were with a really well-behaved baby. But don't put babysitting down. Not until the very end, in case I'm desperate."

"Okay. Babysitting goes last. What shall I put first?"

Anastasia thought for a minute. "Well," she said at last, "promise not to laugh?"

"Anastasia!" said her mother. "We *never* laugh at you."

That was true. It was one of the things she liked about her parents.

"Okay. Here goes. What I'd really like to do – and I'd be good at, too – is to be a companion to an old lady. A really rich old lady. Like in mystery books by Mary Roberts Rinehart. Those really rich old ladies hire young girls – maybe not twelve, but I could do it just as well as someone older – to hang around and help them out with stuff. Read their mail to them. Make tea for them. Maybe polish their diamond bracelets and stuff like that. Of course, in the books they have to help solve mysteries, and I don't suppose anyone in this town needs mysteries solved. But there are all sorts of things that I could do for a rich old lady."

"Does she have to be rich?" asked her mother. "There are certainly a lot of *poor* – or even just average – old ladies who could use someone to help them out."

"Yeah," Anastasia acknowledged. "I know. But Dad asked me what I really wanted to do. And I think I'd really like to work for a *rich* old lady. We can put poor ones and average ones down as a separate category."

Her father nodded. He was busily taking notes.

"Goodness," said her mother. "What if some wealthy old woman really hired you, Anastasia? Wouldn't you be nervous? What would you say when you knocked on the front door? What if a *butler* answered?"

"Well, I guess I'd just say, "Here I am: Anastasia Krupnik, at your service!"

Sam giggled. His mouth was full of peas. "Anastasia atcherservice!" he said.

Dr Krupnik was still writing things down.

"Tell you what," he said after a minute as he tore the page with the notes out of his notebook. "Instead of making a whole list, let's concentrate on this one at first, since it's what you want to do most. You write up a sort of résumé . . ."

"What's a résumé?" asked Anastasia.

"All the reasons that you'd be good at the job. Your past experience that makes you qualified."

"But I don't have any past experience."

"Well, if you think about things you've done in the past, you'll think of things that have some relevance. You've made tea plenty of times, for example. Would you call Anastasia an expert at making tea, Katherine?"

"Sure," said Mrs Krupnik. "When I had the flu last winter, she made me endless cups of tea. And there was only that one disastrous cup . . ."

"That was *Sam's* fault!" objected Anastasia. "I'm not going to take the blame for that! Sam put the goldfish in without my even knowing! He thought it would be funny. And it *wasn't*. Poor Frank Goldfish practically went into *shock*, for Pete's sake! It was lucky he didn't *die*!"

"It was lucky *I* didn't die from shock," said her mother. "I thought I was having some horrible kind of hallucination when I picked up the cup and Frank Goldfish was floating beside the lemon slice."

Sam scrambled down from his highchair and left the dining room with dignity. "Excuse me," he said, at the door. "I'm full."

"Anyway," muttered Anastasia, "that doesn't reflect on my tea-making. I'm not going to put that in my résumé. It still makes me cross to think about it. Some day I'm really going to clobber Sam."

"I know the feeling," said her mother. "Sometimes

I want to myself. A pea in his nose, for heaven's sake. How in the world did I give birth to a child who puts a pea in his nose?"

"Or a goldfish in a cup of tea." Anastasia glowered. *My* goldfish."

"And remember that awful time he . . ." began her mother.

"Come on, ladies," said Dr Krupnik. "That's all beside the point. You put your qualifications down, Anastasia, after you think of them. Then write a job description."

"What's that?"

"All the things you want to do in this job. You've already listed some of them. Then put down your fees. And your phone number. Then I'll xerox it for you at the office, and we'll work out how to distribute the copies in places where rich old ladies might see them."

"That's easy," said Mrs Krupnik. "There's a notice board at the library, and I've seen that one old lady, the one who lives in that huge mansion over on the river, at the library. Also, the Bon Appétit . . ."

"What's that?"

"The gourmet grocery shop. I went in there the other day to buy saffron. There were chauffeurs there, picking up grocery orders. And there was an old woman at the meat counter, wearing three big strands of pearls and a silk dress, carrying a cane and complaining that her lamb chops weren't thick enough. Lamb chops, incidentally, cost $5.79 a pound at the Bon Appétit."

"That's just the kind of old lady I need," said Anastasia. "I'm going to go up to my room right now and write my résumé."

"What about the dishes?"

Anastasia groaned. "Mum, what's more important? The dishes? Or my entire future?"

"If I wash them, will you come down later and dry them?"

Anastasia bowed dramatically. "Anastasia Krupnik, at your service," she said.

"Anastasia atcherservice," said her father, laughing, imitating Sam with his mouth full of peas.

"Anastasia Atcher Service," said Anastasia. It sounded kind of good. Distinctive. Maybe some day it would be a worldwide corporation.

ANASTASIA ATCHER SERVICE

Available: Companion to elderly, wealthy woman, like in mystery novels by Mary Roberts Rinehart (you can find these at the public library if you have never read one). This Companion is a young woman of good breeding, but her family has fallen on hard times so she needs to earn her living. Her duties are that she is always patient and kind to her employer even if the employer is sometimes grouchy. She pours tea a lot. She reads aloud to her employer, like Gothic novels and stuff, and after each chapter they can discuss romance and give each other advice about love if either one of them has an admirer. The Companion advises her employer about what jewellery to wear, like if three diamond necklaces at one time is tacky, the Companion would tell her so, in a kind and tactful way of course. The Companion pulls down the blinds when the employer wants to take a nap in the afternoon, and then she wakes her up if necessary, like if the Vicar comes to call or something. And if the employer is in a wheelchair, the Companion pushes it.

Résumé: This part is supposed to be about experience and qualifications. I don't have a lot of experience with wealthy women, but I do with elderly women because once I had a grandmother who lived to be ninety-two. I was always very patient and kind with her, and sometimes we talked about romance, even though at that time I was only ten and hadn't experienced any romance yet. Now I am twelve and have been through some things, so I know more about it. I am good at making and pouring tea if nobody messes around and louses it up. I have never pushed a wheelchair, but I know I would be good at it because I pushed my brother's pram for about one million hours and never once dumped him out. And I come from a family of good breeding, although they have hard times because my father is an English professor and my mother is an artist, so they don't make much money and can't raise my allowance, which is why I desperately need a job.

I could ride to the employer's mansion on my bike, so the chauffeur wouldn't need to pick me up, unless maybe if it was raining really hard.

Anastasia Krupnik Salary negotiable
797 – 8119

2

"I'm scared stiff," said Anastasia. "I'm so nervous, I might faint. What is that pill that people take to calm their nerves? Valium? Do you have any Valium?"

"Good heavens," said her mother. "Of course I don't. I've never taken Valium in my life. I never even take aspirin. Why are you so nervous? Just the other day you said you wouldn't be, if you got a job."

"Well, I misjudged. I've never in my entire life had a job before, and now I do, and I'm scared stiff. What if she doesn't like me? Old ladies have to *like* their Companions, because they entrust them with their jewels and their personal mail and stuff."

"Anastasia. Of course she'll like you. *Everybody* likes you."

"Do I look all right? I haven't had a dress on in about two years. The last time I wore a dress was to

Grandmother's funeral, I think. It's a good thing you bought me some dresses and skirts last spring."

"You didn't think so at the time. I practically had to bribe you to get you to try them on at the shop. I *did* have to bribe you, come to think of it. I had to buy you that terrible tee shirt, the one with the fluorescent vampire on it."

"That was a good shirt. Too bad it shrank in the wash. Anyway, thank you for making me get the dresses. Seriously, do I look okay?"

"You look terrific, Anastasia. You really do. You're going to be a very beautiful woman some day."

Anastasia made a face. "I wish I could see without my glasses. Can I get contact lenses when I'm older?"

Her mother groaned. "Anastasia, we need a new refrigerator. The roof needs repairs. Don't talk to me about contact lenses."

"Well, now that I have a job, I can start saving money. Maybe I'll buy you a refrigerator. I'll buy myself some contacts. I'll get Sam an electric train. And I'll buy Dad that stereo he likes at the Radio Shack. And I'll buy . . ."

"Anastasia. Don't go overboard. What is she paying you, anyway?"

"I don't know. She said we would discuss it today. But I'm sure it'll be a lot. She's *very* rich. You should see her house. Did I tell you I rode my bike past her house?"

"Anastasia, you described her house in detail at

dinner last night. Nobody else got a chance to say anything at dinner last night. I spent most of yesterday afternoon trying a new recipe. Cannelloni alla romana. It took *hours*. And nobody even got a chance to say they liked it, because you were going on and on about Mrs Bellingham's house."

"I'm sorry. I liked it. I must have liked it, because I ate it. Did it really take hours to make it?"

"Hours. There are two separate sauces. You didn't even notice. One of them had chicken livers in it, and . . ."

"Mum! Did that have *liver* in it? You know I hate liver! Did you sneak liver into that? And I *ate* it? Why didn't you tell me it was liver? You rat!"

"You never gave me a chance. You talked non-stop the entire meal. Mrs Bellingham's house. Mrs Bellingham's cars. Mrs Bellingham's gardens. Mrs Bellingham's this, Mrs Bellingham's that . . ."

"I can't believe you did that to me. Liver. That's treachery. It really is: treachery. Do you think I still have some in my stomach? I might have to throw up."

"You don't have time to throw up. You're going to be late for your first day at work if you don't leave right away."

Anastasia stomped off, muttering. "What are we going to have for dinner tonight?" she called from the front door. "*Brains*?"

"Meat loaf," said her mother. "You're safe."

"If I make enough money, I might start eating in

restaurants," called Anastasia, as she headed to the garage for her bike.

Mrs Ferris Bellingham had called on Saturday, two days before. Anastasia had spent Friday pinning her advertisement up on notice boards around town. At the Bon Appétit gourmet grocery shop. In the vestibule of the Unitarian Church. In the library. The country club. The hospital. Every place she could think of where rich old ladies might hang out.

Someone who had lost a Siamese cat had had the same idea. Every place Anastasia pinned her notice, there was one that offered a reward for a Siamese cat, wearing a red collar, who answered to the name of Sari.

Anastasia thought the cat person really had the wrong idea. A Siamese cat wouldn't be hanging around the library or the country club. A Siamese cat would be in the back alleys, by the rubbish and garbage, or at the dump. The owner should have hung the notices in those places. Some people don't think things through very carefully.

Anastasia had, though. And on Saturday the telephone had rung.

"Hello?" said Anastasia.

"Willa Bellingham here," said a very loud voice. "Mrs Ferris Bellingham."

It took a second for Anastasia to work out how to respond to that. "Anastasia Krupnik here," she said, after a hesitation. "Anastasia Atcher Service."

"You're twelve," said Mrs Bellingham's loud voice. "That is not very old."

Anastasia shrugged and said the first thing that came into her mind. "It's older than eleven," she pointed out.

"You're seeking employment," said the voice. "You have a rather whimsical way of going about it."

Anastasia didn't know what *whimsical* meant. "Yes, I guess I do," she said. "But it works. At least you called me up."

Mrs Ferris Bellingham chuckled. "Indeed. Be here on Monday at two."

"Be where?" Anastasia asked.

There was a silence. "Are you perhaps new in town?"

"Yes. We moved here last month from Cambridge."

"Bellmeadow Farm. Ask anyone how to find it. I will see you promptly at two. I will discuss the terms of employment with you at that time. Be properly dressed."

"Yes, ma'am," said Anastasia.

Mrs Ferris Bellingham hung up without saying goodbye. She didn't even say she would send her chauffeur if it rained on Monday. Or what she meant by properly dressed.

Anastasia had gone out on her bike to Bellmeadow Farm on Sunday, just for a reconnaissance trip. To look it over. She leaned her bike against the stone wall and stood on tiptoe to peer over it. "Farm" was a fake name, she had decided. There were no cows, no hayfields, no tractors. There were acres of green lawn like a golf course, with sprinklers whirring everywhere; and at the end of a long, curving driveway lined with trees she could see the immense stone house, so large it looked like a school or hospital. Two large black cars like presidential limousines were parked in the driveway.

Anastasia remembered a book she had hated when she was younger. *Rebecca of Sunnybrook Farm.* She made up a new book title. *Anastasia of Bellmeadow Farm.* She liked the sound of it.

Now, riding to her first day on the job, she decided that if Mrs Ferris Bellingham wanted to adopt her, she would probably say yes. She was still very, very cross with her mother about the liver.

Anastasia went directly to the back door. It seemed about three miles around the huge house, and it certainly would have been easier to ring the front doorbell. But she had decided, on her way, that it would be appropriate to go to the back on her first day. Later, after she was fully installed as Companion, of course she would enter by the front. Probably she would have her own key.

Later, too, she would call Mrs Bellingham by her first name, Willa. But in the beginning she would call her Mrs Bellingham, she decided. Probably at first Mrs Bellingham would call her Miss Krupnik. Until they became close friends.

She leaned her bike against a tree and knocked on the back door. After a moment it was opened by a very fat woman. Anastasia was startled. She hadn't expected Mrs Bellingham to be fat. She hadn't sounded fat on the phone. Also, Willa sounded like a tall, thin name. But names could be deceiving, Anastasia knew. Sam Krupnik for example sounded like a tall, bearded man. In reality, Sam Krupnik was a two-and-a-half-year-old brat who still wore Pampers at night. Eventually he would grow into his tall, bearded name; in the meantime, he was a pain in the neck.

"Hello, Mrs Bellingham," she said politely. "I'm Anas—"

The woman interrupted her. "I'm Edna Fox," she said. "I'm the housekeeper. And you're the girl Mrs B's taken on. Good thing. We're up to our ears. Come on in."

Mrs Fox led her into a kitchen that seemed as large as the entire downstairs of the Krupniks' house.

Two women wearing aprons were standing near a large double sink, peeling carrots and potatoes. They looked over and smiled at Anastasia. Anastasia smiled back. It was important for the Companion to stay on good terms with the kitchen help, she knew from the novels she had read.

"Rachel and Gloria," said Mrs Fox, indicating the two aproned women.

"How do you do," said Anastasia politely.

"Hi, there," said Rachel and Gloria.

"Here's an apron for you," said the housekeeper,

handing a flowered apron to Anastasia. "Let's get you started. We are out straight. Two of the helps left last week, without any notice at all. And there's a party tomorrow. You can start on the silverware. The polish is over there."

Anastasia unfolded the apron, puzzled. A Companion wasn't supposed to wear an apron. Especially an apron like this. It was the kind that went on over your head, the kind old ladies wore. Also, it was much too big.

She put it on, tied it behind her back, and stood there, embarrassed. Heaped on a wooden kitchen table that looked roughly the size of a football field was a mass of silverware larger than any pile of silverware Anastasia had ever seen.

"I wonder if there's some mistake," she said timidly to Mrs Fox. "I thought I was supposed to . . ."

"Mistake isn't the word for it," said Mrs Fox. "Disaster is what it is. To invite ten people for lunch, with two of the helps gone. Madness. Catastrophe. Here are some rags."

Mrs Fox thrust a handful of cloths into Anastasia's hand and disappeared through a door.

Of course. Anastasia sorted it out in her mind, and she understood. It was an emergency situation. Even the Companion had to pitch in and help in an emergency.

Well, okay. She was a good sport. Companions always were. Anastasia picked up the first of twelve million spoons and began to polish.

She polished.

And polished.

And polished.

"I don't mind doing this kind of thing in an emergency," she said cheerfully to Rachel and Gloria, who continued their peeling silently.

One rag after another turned black as Anastasia polished. After what seemed hours (but it wasn't; she looked at her watch, and only half an hour had passed), there was a large pile of polished spoons and forks beside her on the table. There was a still larger pile of unpolished ones still in the centre. But she made a bundle of the finished ones in her apron and took them over to the sink to wash off the polish.

"Excuse me," she said to Rachel and Gloria, "I'm just going to rinse these off." And she dumped them into the sink.

There was a sudden, deafening crunch.

"Omigod," said Rachel. Or maybe it was Gloria. One of them pushed Anastasia aside and flipped a switch. The crunching noise stopped. The kitchen was very, very silent.

"The waste disposal was running," said Rachel.

"For the peelings," said Gloria.

"Oh," said Anastasia.

One of them reached into the drain and pulled out a silver spoon. Or what had once been a silver spoon. Now it looked like a piece of abstract sculpture that Anastasia had once seen at the Institute of Contemporary Art.

"I didn't know the disposal was on," she said miserably.

"Obviously," said Mrs Fox, who suddenly appeared behind her and took the mashed spoon out of her hand.

"It has a kind of interesting shape now," said Anastasia.

Rachel and Gloria turned away and began peeling again. Mrs Fox didn't say anything.

"Good thing there are a billion more spoons," said Anastasia.

Mrs Fox left the kitchen again.

Anastasia slowly rinsed and dried the rest of the polished silverware. She arranged it on the table, picked up a clean rag, and began polishing again.

"This is a good way to get in practice," she said after a while, "because I suppose I'll be polishing Mrs Bellingham's jewellery when I start my regular job."

Rachel and Gloria looked at her curiously and went on peeling carrots and potatoes.

"Of course I won't drop her diamonds down the disposal," said Anastasia. She meant it as a joke. But neither Rachel nor Gloria laughed.

It sure was *boring*, working in a kitchen with people who had no sense of humour. Much as Anastasia hated doing dishes at home, still she and her mother always laughed a lot. If Sam came in the kitchen while they were washing dishes, they put soap suds on his chin and made him a beard. Sam liked that.

Anastasia began to feel homesick for Sam.

She remembered a silly thing her mother sometimes

did. Sometimes her mother picked up a plate, looked into it, and said, "I can *see* myself in this china!" – imitating a TV commercial.

Anastasia picked up a small silver tray she had just polished, looked into it, and said dramatically, "I can *see* myself in this china!"

Rachel and Gloria glanced over at her as if she were crazy. Neither of them laughed.

Anastasia put the tray down and sighed. She *had* seen herself in the tray. She had silver polish on her nose. Her hair was a mess. She looked like a household drudge.

She felt very, very homesick.

She picked up the millionth fork and polished.

And polished.

At four o'clock Mrs Fox came back into the kitchen. Rachel and Gloria had finished their peeling. They were working silently at something in another corner of the kitchen. The pile of silverware was almost finished.

Mrs Fox nodded to Anastasia. "Mrs B wants to see you now," she said.

At last. Anastasia didn't mind being a good sport in an emergency, but two solid hours of silver-polishing was enough. She was ready to get on with her real job.

She took off her apron, wiped the silver polish from her nose with a damp cloth, and smoothed her hair.

She followed Mrs Fox out of the kitchen. Down a

hall. Through a door. Down another hall lined with paintings. Through an oak-pannelled room with wall-to-wall bookcases. Across another hall. Into a sunny room filled with plants, where a grey-haired woman sat in a wicker chair, working on a piece of needlepoint.

Mrs Bellingham. At last. And she was exactly as Anastasia had pictured her. Everything was going to be okay. Starting now, she could forget the drudgery of the emergency silver-polishing, and she and Mrs Bellingham could get on with the business of Companionship. If she were older, Mrs Bellingham would offer her a glass of sherry now. Probably she wouldn't offer sherry to someone who was twelve. But that was okay. Anastasia didn't like sherry anyway. She'd settle for some iced tea. Mrs Fox had disappeared. Probably Mrs Fox was getting the tea.

Mrs Bellingham lit a cigarette. Anastasia hoped she wouldn't offer her one. To be polite she would have to take it, but she really hated cigarettes.

But Mrs Bellingham snapped the silver cigarette case closed and inhaled her cigarette without offering one to Anastasia.

"Well," said Mrs Bellingham, "we didn't give you much time to break in, did we? Put you right to work!"

Anastasia smiled. "I understand about emergencies, Mrs Bellingham. Everybody has to pitch in. And I enjoyed getting to know the kitchen staff. That's important, I think." It was sort of a lie – she hadn't enjoyed Rachel and Gloria at all – but it seemed the right thing to say.

"Indeed. Did Mrs Fox tell you about the luncheon tomorrow?"

"She told me that there was a party tomorrow."

"A family lunch. My granddaughter's birthday."

Anastasia smiled. That was wonderful, she thought. She could just write off the silver-polishing afternoon as a bad beginning. Tomorrow she would get to know the family. She would begin her Companion duties for real. Tonight she would have to think seriously about Conversation Topics. Not politics or religion, she knew. Literature, probably. Tonight she would review in her mind all the books she had ever read. *Gone With the Wind* was one of her favourites. She could talk to people at the luncheon about *Gone With the Wind*. Why Scarlett didn't marry Ashley Wilkes. Stuff like that.

What a terrific job I have, thought Anastasia happily.

"I would like you here promptly at eleven A.M.," said Mrs Bellingham.

Suddenly Anastasia thought of a problem. She had nothing to wear to a luncheon. She was already wearing her only decent dress, and it had smears of silver polish on it. What she needed was a Basic Black dress. Never in a million years would her mother take her out tonight to buy a Basic Black dress.

She couldn't borrow a dress from Mrs Bellingham. They weren't the same size. And their taste seemed to be a little different.

"Do you have a dark skirt?" Mrs Bellingham asked. She had read Anastasia's mind. What a terrific relationship they were going to have, Anastasia thought.

"Yes," she said. "A dark blue denim wraparound."

"Well, that will do, I suppose. Wear it with a tailored white blouse. Those sandals you're wearing will be all right."

A denim skirt and a white blouse didn't seem too terrific for an elegant luncheon. Maybe Mrs Bellingham planned to lend her some jewellery, thought Anastasia.

"Mrs Fox will give you a white apron," said Mrs Bellingham.

A *white apron*? Anastasia had been thinking along the lines of a diamond necklace. Suddenly she had a strange feeling that things weren't exactly what she thought they were.

Mrs Bellingham inhaled her cigarette again. "The luncheon will be buffet," she said, "so you won't have to serve at the table. But be sure to empty ashtrays, keep water glasses filled, that sort of thing."

Anastasia's vision of herself discussing Scarlett O'Hara with the guests at lunch faded and blurred.

I'm the *maid*, she thought in despair, realizing the truth in a horrible sudden flash.

Mrs Bellingham was making some notes on a pad of paper. Anastasia stood there watching, stricken with disappointment. In her mind she began to compose a letter. She would write it tonight and deliver it in the morning. "Dear Mrs Bellingham," it would say, "I have decided to go into another profession."

"Now," said Mrs Bellingham, looking up, "do you have any questions?"

Yes, thought Anastasia angrily. What right did you have to answer an ad for a Companion, for Pete's sake, and then turn someone into a scullery maid, without even *asking* her? Who the heck do you think you *are*?

She almost said those things aloud. "Yes," she began, in a firm voice. "What—"

"Oh, of course," Mrs Bellingham interrupted her. "Your wages. You will be paid two-fifty an hour and since you arrived at two this afternoon . . ."

Wait a *minute*, thought Anastasia, getting crosser by the second. Two-fifty an hour? That's babysitting pay, for Pete's sake! I was thinking in terms of ten dollars an hour. I might be willing to settle for seven-fifty, but . . .

Mrs Bellingham was going on and on. " . . . so today you have earned five dollars. However . . ."

And after the "however", she reached under her needlepoint and held up the mashed silver spoon. Anastasia's heart sank. Five hundred billion silver spoons in that kitchen, and Mrs Bellingham was – she could hear it coming – going to charge her for that one spoon? Probably it cost as least five dollars, too. Her whole crummy afternoon's pay!

"The price of this at Shreve's is thirty-five dollars," Mrs Bellingham was going on.

THIRTY-FIVE DOLLARS? Anastasia couldn't believe it. It was too horrible to be happening to her. It was a nightmare.

"So that debacle will cost you twelve more hours of work," Mrs Bellingham said firmly. It was what she had been calculating on her notepad.

A what? thought Anastasia. A *bockle*? She didn't even know what a bockle was. It looked like an ordinary silver spoon to her. Just her luck to put a bockle down the waste disposal.

She stood there numbly and said nothing. Surely Mrs Bellingham was finished with her now. She couldn't possibly think of any more humiliations.

Wrong. She could, and did. One more.

"You're going into class 8, I suppose?" Mrs Bellingham asked.

Anastasia nodded.

"So is my granddaughter, Daphne," said Mrs Bellingham pleasantly. "Tomorrow is her thirteenth birthday. So you'll have an opportunity to meet one of your classmates."

It was worse than the thirty-five-dollar silver bockle. Much worse. It was the ultimate humiliation. She was going to meet one of her classmates – someone who might have been her *friend*, for Pete's sake, in a town where she knew practically no one – and she would be wearing an apron and refilling the water glasses.

Anastasia cried as she rode her bike home. It was starting to rain, and the light drizzle mixed with the tears rolling down her cheeks.

Once, she thought bitterly – only a few hours ago – I thought that if it rained, the chauffeur would drive me home in a car.

Her mother was in the kitchen when Anastasia came through the back door.

"Meat loaf in an hour!" called her mother cheerfully. "How did your first day at work go?"

Anastasia headed up the back stairs towards her room on the third floor.

"Just fine!" she called down the stairs in a fake happy voice.

In a million years – in a million *billion* years – she would never let anyone know.

3

Exactly one hour and twenty-seven minutes after she had vowed never to let anyone in the entire world know, ever, what a disaster her day her been, Anastasia burst into tears at the dinner table.

Anastasia had not burst into tears at the dinner table for six and a half years. She could remember the last time, even though it was so long ago. She had had a big fight with her very best friend, Jenny MacCauley, that afternoon. Just before dinner, Jenny had called her on the phone and said, "You are no longer invited to my birthday party Saturday, nyah nyah."

Anastasia had said, "Nyah nyah to you, too", and hung up. But she had burst into tears at the dinner table. She was in class 2 then.

But now she was almost thirteen. It was incredibly

embarrassing to start to cry in public when you were almost thirteen. Even if the public was just your family.

"Excuse me," said Sam very quickly, with a wide-eyed look, when Anastasia began to cry. "I have to go to the bathroom, I think." And he climbed out of his highchair and left the dining room, still wearing his bib.

Even through her sobs, Anastasia knew Sam was lying. Normally it took bribes and threats to get Sam to go to the bathroom. As bright as he was, Sam still liked to wear nappies. It was the one thing he was still babyish and stupid about. That, and his ragged security blanket.

Her parents both stopped eating and stared at her in dismay.

"Sweetheart, what's *wrong*?" asked her mother.

Anastasia couldn't talk. She just kept crying.

Her father left his chair, came around to Anastasia's side of the table, and put his arms around her. He rocked her back and forth.

Through her tears, Anastasia could see Sam peeking at her from the dining-room door. He had wrapped his security blanket around his hand and had his thumb in his mouth.

"Make Sam stop staring at me," she said, weeping.

"Sam Krupnik," said her mother sternly, "either come in here and sit down, or go away. Don't peek around the door like that."

Sam scampered away.

Finally Anastasia's sobs turned to gulps and deep breaths.

"She made me wear an apron," she wailed, "not a cute apron like Dad wears when he grills steaks, but a flowered apron like a cleaning lady wears, and I was just like a maid, I had to stay in the kitchen with the maids, and I wasn't a Companion at all, I had to clean five billion pieces of silverware, and I didn't mean to but I dropped a bockle down the disposal, I thought it was just a spoon, but it wasn't, and she said it cost thirty-five dollars at Shreve's, and now I owe her thirty-five dollars, so I have to be a maid *forever*, and tomorrow I have to be a maid when her granddaughter is there, and her granddaughter is thirteen, she might have been my *friend*, for Pete's sake, and she didn't offer me a glass of sherry or anything—"

"Whoa," said her father. "I'm confused. The granddaughter is thirteen and was supposed to offer you a glass of sherry?"

"No! You're not listening!"

"Well, can you talk a little more slowly?"

Anastasia took a very deep breath. Her crying spell seemed to have ended. Thank goodness. Anastasia hated to cry. It made her look as if she had Troubled Skin, for Pete's sake, and she *didn't*. She had stringy hair and skinny legs, but she did not have, and never *had* had, Troubled Skin.

She wiped her eyes and told the whole story, very slowly.

"Holy Moley," said her father.

"*Dad*," said Anastasia angrily. She hated it when her father said Holy Moley. It was left over from his childhood, or some weird thing.

"Sorry," said her father apologetically. "It was what Billy Batson, the young reporter, used to say in comic books. When things were absolutely awful, he would say, 'Holy Moley!' Then he yelled, 'CAPTAIN MARVEL!' and he turned into Captain Marvel and could solve everything with his super powers."

"Myron," said Mrs Krupnik meaningfully. She had noticed Anastasia becoming more and more impatient.

"No," Myron Krupnik went on, "maybe it wasn't Billy Batson who said Holy Moley. Maybe, come to think of it, it was Freddy Freeman, the crippled newsboy. He was in the same comic books."

"*Dad*! Stop it!" Anastasia was almost beginning to cry again.

"Well, it's just that I wish I could turn into Captain Marvel. It would be easier to solve your problem if I were Captain Marvel."

"Daddy," said Sam, who had crept quietly back into the dining room. "*I* think you're Captain Marvel."

His father lifted Sam onto his lap. "You know, Anastasia," he said, "that woman – what's her name again?"

"Mrs Bellingham."

"Mrs Bellingham. Right. You know, she really

took advantage of you. You had described clearly on your advertisement exactly what kind of job you were looking for."

"Right. Companion."

"And she put you to work at something different, without asking your permission."

"She put me right to work as a *maid*."

"Yes, I think it's fair to say that. And under other circumstances you certainly would be justified in leaving."

"What other circumstances?" asked Anastasia. "The circumstances are that she made me be a *maid*."

"That's true. Unfortunately, you mashed something in the waste disposal. I didn't exactly understand what you said it was."

"A bockle."

"Well, I don't know what that is. But let's assume that she was correct, that it was worth thirty-five dollars."

"Why do we have to assume that? Maybe she was lying. Mum, would you call Shreve's? Ask Shreve's if a bockle really costs thirty-five dollars?"

Her mother looked at her watch. "It's six-thirty. Shreve's is closed. Anyway, Anastasia, you said it was silver, didn't you?"

"Yes. It was definitely silver. I know because I polished it. It looked like a spoon."

"Well, if it was silver and came from Shreve's, it was thirty-five dollars. Frankly, Anastasia, you're lucky it wasn't a hundred and thirty-five dollars."

Anastasia groaned.

"So," said her father, "you do owe Mrs Bellingham thirty-five dollars."

"Only thirty," Anastasia pointed out angrily. "I worked five dollars' worth today."

"Thirty, then. I don't suppose you have thirty dollars to pay her back, do you?"

"Dad," said Anastasia wearily, "the reason I was looking for a job was because I am broke."

Her father lifted Sam down from his lap. "Sam," he said, "climb up in your highchair and finish your dinner, will you?"

Sam trotted around to his highchair, climbed in, and ate a bite of meat loaf. "I have four pennies," he said. "You can have my four pennies, Anastasia."

"That's okay, Sam," said Anastasia. "Thanks, anyway."

"Anastasia," said her father, "I feel sorry enough for you that if I had thirty extra dollars I would pay for the blasted bockle myself. But frankly, moving out here cost so much, what with having to buy a car and a lawn mower and everything, that I'm flat broke, too. Katherine, I don't suppose you . . ."

"No," said Mrs Krupnik sadly. "I won't get paid for these photography illustrations until I finish them. And I'm barely halfway through. I'm really sorry, Anastasia."

"Oh, Mum. Dad. That's okay. I was the one who mashed the bockle. I guess I'm just going to have to keep working for old Bellingham."

"Bellybutton," Sam giggled. "Old stupid Mrs Bellybutton."

Anastasia laughed. It was the first time she had laughed all day.

"I'll just have to work out a way to survive it. Being a *maid*, for Pete's sake. And tomorrow her granddaughter's going to be there. How humiliating. Has anything that humiliating ever happened to you guys?"

Her parents thought.

"Yes," her mother said finally. "A couple of years ago a publisher in New York phoned and asked if I was interested in illustrating a book about Houston rockets. They were paying a lot of money. I said yes, I thought I could do that very well. So they asked me to work up some sample drawings and bring them down to show to the author.

"I was lying when I said I could do that very well. I didn't know anything at all about rockets. But I got a lot of books about rockets and missiles and the space industry. And I spent about a week making rough sketches of jets and guided missiles and engines and launching pads and satellites and various kinds of rockets. Then I put them all in my portfolio and went off to New York. I really thought they were pretty good."

"What happened? Weren't they any good? Did the people laugh when they saw them?"

"Well, we all met in a fancy room at the publishing company. A couple of editors and the art director and the author. They were all sitting around a mahogany table. I was wearing my tweed suit, I remember. I don't think I've worn that since," her mother said.

"What *happened*?"

"I opened my portfolio and took out all those sketches and spread them out on the table. I was really pretty proud of them. But there was a terrible silence."

"Why? Why was there a terrible silence?"

"And then one person started to laugh. Then another. In a minute they were all laughing. They couldn't stop laughing. The fat one – the art director, I think it was – had tears rolling down his cheeks. Someone had to bring him a glass of water, because they were afraid he was going to have a heart attack from laughing."

"Why were they laughing? You're a good artist, Mum!" Anastasia felt terribly sorry for her mother, being humiliated that way.

Her mother began to laugh. "Because they were doing a book about a basketball team! The Houston Rockets is a basketball team!"

"I knew that," said Sam. "I see them on TV."

"Oh, Mum!" said Anastasia. "The rats! That wasn't fair! They should have told you! They shouldn't have laughed!"

"Well," said her mother, "it was humiliating. But I survived it. They found someone else to do the basketball book. And they gave me a job doing a book about the astronauts."

"How about you, Dad? Have you ever been humiliated?" Somehow it was making Anastasia feel better, knowing that other people had been humiliated.

Her father blushed. You could always tell when he was blushing, because he was bald. When he blushed, the top of his head turned red.

"Of course I have," he said with dignity. "No one lives to be forty-seven years old without being humiliated a few times."

"What happened?"

He was still blushing. "I don't want to talk about it," he said.

"That's not fair. Mum told about hers. And I told you about what happened to me today."

He groaned. "Promise you won't ever tell anyone."

"I promise."

Her father looked around the dining room to make sure there were no spies listening. He looked down at his plate for a minute, embarrassed. Then he looked up.

"Last term I gave an hour-long lecture on Social Comedy in Eighteenth-Century England. The students – there were eighty-seven students in the lecture hall – kept laughing."

"But that was okay. You were lecturing about comedy," said Anastasia.

"That wasn't why they were laughing." Her father began playing with his fork.

"Why were they?"

He leaned his elbows on the table and put his face into his hands. The top of his head was bright pink.

"My fly was unzipped," he said after a while. "The whole hour. I didn't realize it until afterwards."

"Dad! That's terrible! Someone should have *told* you! That wasn't fair, for them to laugh!"

But next thing she knew, Anastasia was laughing herself. So was her father. And her mother. Sam wasn't; he was busy trying to make an aeroplane out of a piece of lettuce.

"Well," said her father, still chuckling. "I survived, just as your mother did."

"I guess I will too, then," said Anastasia. "I'll survive being a maid."

"What are you going to say to Mrs Bellingham when you go to work tomorrow?"

Anastasia thought. "I'll smile," she said, "and I'll say, 'Anastasia Atcher Service'."

But much later, as she was going to bed, she thought of something else. Not that she would say. But that she would *do*.

4

The worst part of the problem, Anastasia had realized, thinking about it the night before, was not the humiliation of being a maid. She could survive that, the way her mother and her father had survived their humiliations and had even been able to laugh about them afterwards. Some day Anastasia would be able to tell her own children about the summer she was a maid, and she would be able to laugh about it.

What she might not survive was being a maid in front of Daphne Bellingham, who would be her classmate in class 8 this autumn. *That* was the problem she would have to solve.

And she had decided to solve it by going to work in disguise. She would disguise herself as a middle-aged woman.

*

By ten in the morning, no one was at home except Anastasia. Her father was off teaching his summer school class, and her mother had taken Sam to visit the nursery school he would be going to in the autumn.

Stupid old Sam didn't understand about nursery schools. He thought that he was going to learn to read. He had insisted on going off with volume one of the *Encyclopaedia Britannica* in his pushchair with him. He wanted to learn to read the part about aeroplanes.

Well, thought Anastasia with some satisfaction, maybe today Sam will be humiliated. Maybe the nursery school people would laugh.

Anastasia went into her parents' bedroom and opened one of her mother's chest of drawers. She felt a little guilty, because she wasn't ordinarily a sneaky sort of person.

But this was a very necessary part of her disguise.

She took out one of her mother's bras. Then she went into the bathroom and put it on. Carefully she stuffed each side of it with Kleenex. Then she put on the white blouse that Mrs Bellingham had told her to wear.

But when she looked at herself in the mirror from different angles, she realized the Kleenex didn't work. It looked lumpy and gross.

So she took the Kleenex out and threw it away.

She thought for a minute and went back to her mother's chest of drawers. This time she snitched two pairs of pantyhose.

Back in the bathroom, she put a pair of pantyhose into each side of the bra. They were rounder, softer, more natural-looking than the Kleenex.

But when she looked at herself sideways in the mirror, she groaned.

It looked like Dolly Parton.

Also, it made her feel funny. She couldn't even see her feet, because she had to look over the mountain of pantyhose. So she took them out and thought some more.

After a few minutes, feeling even more guilty, because now she was going to owe her mother at least $1.49, she found a pair of scissors and cut one pair of pantyhouse in half. She stuffed one rolled-up half into each side of the bra.

Now she looked into the mirror and smiled. It was perfect. She walked around the bathroom a bit to make sure the pantyhouse didn't come loose or shift around, but they seemed quite secure. Maybe because her blouse buttoned so tightly over them.

Next, she opened the bathroom drawer where her mother kept make-up.

She took out the mascara and took off her glasses in order to colour her eyelashes.

But she couldn't see without her glasses. Her face in the mirror was blurred.

She put her glasses back on. Now she could see her eyelashes, but she couldn't reach them with the mascara.

"Rats," said Anastasia to herself, and she sat down on the rim of the bathtub to think. How on earth did Helen Keller put on mascara?

Braille.

Anastasia took off her glasses, and put mascara on her eyelashes without looking. Then she put her glasses back on. It didn't look too bad.

She darkened her eyebrows with an eyebrow pencil, reaching around the rims of her glasses. When she leaned forward towards the mirror, her pantyhose bosom bumped into the bathroom sink and squashed; but Anastasia noticed that it puffed right out again when she stood back. Much better than Kleenex.

Finally, very carefully, she sprinkled Johnson's Baby Powder on her hair and smoothed it in with her hands. Then, with a rubber band and a handful of bobby pins, she twisted her hair into a bun and pinned it at the back of her head. Her light hair looked grey from the powder.

She dabbed a little pink lipstick on her lips, straightened her blouse and skirt, and went to stand in front of the full-length mirror that was on the back of her parents' bedroom door.

With greyish hair, dark eyebrows, pink lipstick and the pantyhose bosom, she thought she looked about forty years old. From her mother's wardrobe, she borrowed a large black leather handbag and hung it over her shoulder. Now she definitely looked forty years old. She could be elected President of the League of Women Voters without any trouble at all.

It was twenty to eleven. Anastasia Krupnik, aged forty, with the black handbag thumping against her hip, got on her bike and rode to Bellmeadow Farm.

*

"Good," said Edna Fox at the back door, "you're right on time. There's lots to do. You can hang your bag in that cupboard there. You don't have a lot of money in it, do you? I'm not going to take the responsibility if . . ."

"No," said Anastasia, and rolled her eyes. Good grief. In debt for thirty dollars, working as a maid in order to pay back thirty whole dollars, and someone asks if you have a lot of money in your purse. If she had a lot of money, for Pete's sake, she'd pay it to Mrs Bellingham for her crummy bockle, get on her bike, and be gone so fast they'd never know what had happened.

Too bad she had to put her handbag in the cupboard. It was part of her middle-age disguise. Still, maids didn't usually carry their handbags around while they served lunch, Anastasia realized.

Edna Fox handed her an apron.

Good grief, thought Anastasia. Yesterday's apron had covered her whole body. She didn't want to hide her pantyhose bosom. It would ruin the whole effect.

But the apron was a tiny white one, one that tied around the waist and had no top to it. Good. She tied it carefully, with her back to Mrs Fox, and to Rachel and Gloria, who were at the sink. She had to hold the bosom up with one hand while she arranged the waistband of the apron. The bra was a little loose. The bosom was a little lower than she would have liked. Still, maybe that would make her look even older. Anastasia had noticed that old ladies' bosoms began to be pretty low sometimes. Maybe she looked fifty instead of forty. Fifty was even better.

"You look different," said Mrs Fox. "Are you okay?"

"I'm just wearing my hair differently today," said Anastasia. "I'm fine." But she realized that Mrs Fox was looking at the bosom, not the hair.

Well, tough. It was not, Anastasia thought, unheard of for a girl to grow quite quickly in that respect. Once, years ago, she had had a babysitter named Marcia, who practically *overnight*, for Pete's sake, had changed from flat-chested to—

But Mrs Fox interrupted her thoughts.

"The guests are all here," she said. "They're on the terrace, having cocktails. You can start taking trays of food to the dining-room table."

Anastasia carried a large silver platter of sliced turkey and ham into the dining room. Wide glass doors were opened onto the flagstone terrace, and she could see the people sitting there. She could see Mrs Bellingham, her arch enemy, sitting in a wrought-iron chair that resembled a throne. Typical, thought Anastasia.

She moved quietly to the side of the glass doors and stood where she was hidden by the folds of an opened curtain. Peeking out, she found Daphne Bellingham, who was sitting on the stone steps, sipping a Coke and looking very bored.

Anastasia had been secretly hoping that Daphne Bellingham would be very ugly, with crooked teeth and Troubled Skin. But she wasn't. She had short, curly blonde hair, and tiny gold earrings in pierced ears. She wasn't beautiful. But she was kind of cute.

Rats. Anastasia's parents wouldn't let her have her ears pierced. Not till she was thirteen, they said. She had tried to do it herself once, anyway, with a needle, but her hands kept getting sweaty and the needle slid around too much.

Daphne Bellingham was wearing a yellow-and-white-striped jersey dress, and there was a funny little mark on it. Anastasia squinted at the mark. Of course. The dress had had an alligator on it once, and Daphne Bellingham had pulled the alligator off.

Oh, *rats*. Daphne Bellingham was someone Anastasia would *like*.

Anastasia kicked the carpeting angrily and went back to the kitchen for another tray of food.

"Here," said Edna Fox, and put a large platter into Anastasia's hands. "*Hors d'oeuvres*. Pass these around, will you? Don't forget to serve the women first."

"I know about stuff like that, Mrs Fox," said Anastasia with an icy smile.

The platter was filled with some of Anastasia's very favourite things. Devilled eggs. Artichoke leaves with little shrimps on them. Chicken wings. And Anastasia was starving. Her stomach rumbled. She hadn't eaten any breakfast at all because she'd been too busy planning her disguise.

Going through the dining room to the terrace

doors, she decided that she might faint if she didn't eat something. Not a chicken wing, because she would be left with the bone. Not an artichoke-and-shrimp, because she'd be left with the artichoke part that you didn't eat.

She set the platter on the table for a minute, stuffed a devilled egg into her mouth, rearranged the other things to cover the empty space, and headed for the terrace.

She held her mouth very carefully so that no one would notice there was half an egg inside it.

"There you are, dear!" said Mrs Bellingham in a loud voice. "I want to introduce you to everyone! This is Anastasia . . . What was your last name again?"

Anastasia swallowed the egg whole, and said, "Krupnik", in a strangling voice. Then she hiccuped.

"Excuse me," she said, miserably.

She could hear Daphne Bellingham giggle. Quickly she began passing the platter to the guests. She could hear Mrs Bellingham rattling off everyone's names. My sister, Mrs Aldrich Forbes. My daughter-in-law, Caroline Bellingham. My son, John Bellingham. Blah blah blah. Anastasia wasn't even listening. She was trying desperately to keep from hiccuping again. The devilled egg was lodged in her throat somewhere.

"I especially want you to meet the birthday girl. This is my granddaughter, Daphne. Daphne, Anastasia is—"

Anastasia knew exactly what she was going to say.

Anastasia is going into class 8. Couldn't Mrs Bellingham *see* that it was all a mistake, that she was actually middle-aged?

She hurriedly interrupted Daphne's grandmother and said, in her forty-year-old voice, around the remains of the devilled egg and a whole batch of potential hiccups, "I'm glad to meet you, Miss Bellingham. Would you like some *hors d'oeuvres*?"

She leaned over to offer the platter to Daphne Bellingham. She could hear Daphne stifle a giggle. In a hideous, horrible instant of perception she knew what was happening, and it was too late to do anything about it.

Her whole pantyhose bosom – both sides – was leaning into the platter. It was resting right on the *hors d'oeuvres*. There were devilled eggs stuck to the bottom side of it.

The other people were talking. They hadn't noticed. But Daphne had. Daphne was almost choking on her Coke. Her shoulders were shaking.

"Whoops!" said Daphne suddenly. "I've spilled some Coke on my dress. Anastasia, would you come and help me wash it off?"

Mrs Bellingham tsked-tsked. "Daphne, when will you outgrow that clumsiness? Give her a hand, Anastasia. There's cleaning fluid in the bathroom if you need it."

Anastasia put the platter of *hors d'oeuvres* down in the dining room. The tops of the eggs were a little mashed, but not too badly. You couldn't tell they'd been mashed by a bosom. She followed Daphne through the house to a bathroom off the huge front hall. If she walked stiffly, you couldn't see the egg yolk on her front; it was all kind of on the underneath side.

How on earth did Dolly Parton pass a plate of devilled eggs, she wondered grouchily.

"Now then, Miss Bellingham," said Anastasia briskly, in her middle-aged maid's voice, when the two girls were inside the pretty blue-and-green bathroom, "let me take care of that stain for you."

Daphne Bellingham hooted with laughter. "Knock it off, Anastasia, whoever you are!" she said. "I didn't spill any Coke. I was just trying to rescue you. What on *earth* do you have stuffed inside your blouse: Kleenex? I did it once with Kleenex when I was trying to get some boy on the high school football team to notice me. But it didn't work. It looked really gross. All my friends laughed, and I ended up pulling it all out in the school library, behind the reference shelves. I wadded it all up and left it hidden behind a volume of *World's Great Scientists*. What *is* that you have in there?"

"Pantyhose," Anastasia confessed. "I was trying to look forty years old because I didn't want you to know I was going to be in class 8. Because your grandmother forced me to be a maid, and it was so embarrassing. Actually, it's even more embarrassing to end up with egg yolk all over my blouse."

Daphne giggled. "Here, I can get the egg off. It's

not as bad as you think. Take your blouse off a minute and I'll wash that part. Why on earth did my grandmother make you be a maid? She's such a creep."

Anastasia gave her the blouse, stood there in her mother's bra, and told Daphne the whole story. The night before, it had made her cry. Now, it made her laugh.

"I still owe her thirty dollars," she explained, at the end of the story. "I'll have to be her maid forever." For some reason, the thought of being a maid forever seemed very funny now. Daphne was laughing as she washed the egg smears off the blouse. Anastasia couldn't stop laughing. She was still hiccuping from the devilled egg she had swallowed whole; now she was choking with laughter as well, and tears were running down her face.

"I could take the bosom off" – she giggled – "but what would I do with it? I'd have to carry it back in there. What if your grandmother saw me walking through the dining room with a bra full of pantyhose in my hand?"

"Maybe she'd think it was a new *hors d'oeuvre* Mrs Fox had dreamed up," Daphne suggested. "She's so stupid. Hey – you could just stuff it in one of the drawers here, and leave it. Like my Kleenex I left in the library. You and I could be the only two people in town who hide fake bosoms everywhere!"

"No," Anastasia decided, even though she liked the idea of being Bosom Phantoms, "I can't, because it's my mother's bra. I have to sneak it back into her drawer. I guess I'll just leave it on for now." She took the damp blouse from Daphne and put it on.

"Anastasia, your face!"

"What's wrong with my face?" Anastasia looked in the mirror and groaned. The tears from laughing had made the mascara run down her cheeks, and she was smudged with black.

"Here," said Daphne. "Take off your glasses and I'll wash your face. For heaven's sake, Anastasia, you need a nursemaid. Good thing I was here."

"If you hadn't been here," Anastasia pointed out, "none of this would have happened, because I wouldn't have worn a disguise."

She dried her face and put her glasses back on. "There. Now back to being a maid again."

"You want a cigarette before we go back?" asked Daphne. "I know where my grandmother keeps them."

"No," said Anastasia, startled. "I hate cigarettes."

"Me too." Now Daphne giggled. "But I smoke them because it drives my parents up a wall. I'm practically a juvenile delinquent."

"That's weird," said Anastasia. "I drive my parents up a wall all the time, but I do it accidentally. Why would you do it on purpose?"

"Because of who my parents are, I guess."

Anastasia had forgotten for a moment who Daphne was. Of course. She was Daphne Bellingham. "It must be really weird to be rich," she said. "My parents can't even afford a new refrigerator."

"We're not *rich*," said Daphne.

"Liar. How many rooms in this house – twenty-five? How many servants? How many Cadillacs?"

"This is my grandmother's house," Daphne pointed out patiently. "My grandmother's rich. Super-rich. But don't you know who my father is?"

"John Bellingham," said Anastasia. "Your grandmother introduced me. I was choking on an egg at the time, in case you didn't notice."

"The *Reverend* John Bellingham," said Daphne, in an ostentatiously solemn voice. "Rector of the Congregational Church. Ministers are never rich. They're poor. They're also *good*. They never do anything bad. It is so incredibly boring, being a minister's kid."

Anastasia thought about that for a minute. "My father doesn't do bad stuff either," she said. "But he's not boring."

"Doesn't he ever swear?"

"Well, he's not foul-mouthed or anything. But *occasionally* he swears. Like when I melted his Billie Holiday records."

"See what I mean? If I melted my father's Billie Holiday records, he wouldn't swear. He'd forgive me or something."

"Oh," said Anastasia. "My father has never forgiven me for that."

"Does your father smoke?"

"A pipe," said Anastasia.

"See? My father doesn't smoke anything, ever. He's too good. Does your father ever get cross?"

"Sure. So does my mum. They yell and stuff."

"My parents don't. Not ever. They're nice, absolutely all the time. Can you imagine how *boring* that is?"

Anastasia wasn't certain. Actually, it sounded sort of pleasant. But she nodded her head.

"So," said Daphne, as if it were all quite logical, "I specialize in being practically a juvenile delinquent."

"Oh," said Anastasia. "Is it fun?"

Daphne shrugged. "When I have a special project, it is," she said. "And now I do. Revenge on my grandmother."

That made Anastasia nervous. "Don't do anything to your grandmother because of *me*, Daphne. I did mash the silver thing, after all. I do owe her the money."

"But she's making you be a *maid*, for heaven's sake. Don't you hate her for that?"

"Well, yes, I guess I do."

"So. I happen to hate her for another reason, at the moment."

"What's that?"

For a moment Daphne didn't want to tell. She looked very angry. Then she whispered, "She gave me a *doll* for my birthday."

"Oh," said Anastasia, feeling sympathetic. "*Oh*."

"You see? Revenge is definitely in order. Listen, we'd better get back. But I'll call you tonight. I'll get your phone number from Grandmother. And we'll plot something fiendish. Really sinister. I'm very good at that."

Anastasia had no doubt of that. But she liked Daphne. "Okay," she said, and grinned.

"Now," whispered Daphne, as she opened the door, "be careful when you pass stuff at lunch. Stand up *straight*, or your bosom will fall in again, and I don't know if I can rescue you a second time. You're on your own kid."

"Thanks," said Anastasia, and she headed for the kitchen, where Mrs Fox was waiting.

5

Daphne called that very evening. By then, Anastasia was back to her normal appearance. She had ridden home, put her bike into the garage very quietly, watched from the back garden until she was certain her mother wasn't in the kitchen, and then crept as stealthily as a spy through the back door and up the back stairs to her third-floor room.

"Hi!" she had called from her room, after she had taken off her mother's bra, thrown the pantyhose into her waste-paper basket, wiped off the eye make-up and brushed the powder out of her hair. "I'm home!"

"Hi there!" Her mother's voice came from the second floor. "How did it go?"

"Better today," Anastasia called back. "And I worked five hours, so I'm twelve-fifty less in debt!"

"Can I come up?" asked Sam's little voice from the foot of Anastasia's stairs.

"Sure. How was your visit to nursery school?"

Thu-dump, thu-dump, thu-dump. Sam's trainers came up the stairs carefully, and he appeared in Anastasia's room, grinning. He was still holding volume one of the Encyclopaedia.

"I can read." Sam beamed.

"Liar," said Anastasia.

"Look," said Sam. He put the book on her bed and turned to the section that he loved, the section with the aeroplane pictures.

Meticulously he inched his chubby finger along the lines of print until he came to the word "aeroplane".

"Aeroplane," he said solemnly. "That says 'aeroplane'."

"Right. It does."

"Now look." His finger went along the lines again until he found the same word a second time. "Aeroplane."

"Right," said Anastasia.

"Everywhere it says "aeroplane", I can read it." Sam turned the page and his finger searched the lines. "Aeroplane," he pointed out triumphantly. "The lady at the school showed me."

So he hadn't been humiliated. Anastasia was glad. Two and a half was too young to be humiliated, actually.

Sam closed the book happily. "When nursery school starts, I'll take volume two. Then I can learn to read 'boat'. Volume two had boat pictures in it."

"Don't they have things to play with at the nursery school? Blocks? Swings? Toy trucks? Didn't they show you those things?"

Sam thought, with his thumb in his mouth. "Yeah," he said after removing his wet thumb. "But those are for the babies. I'm only going to do books."

Anastasia groaned. Sam was such a weird brother. Probably he would be admitted to Harvard when he was nine. Probably he would still be wearing Pampers.

Later, at dinner, he wanted to bring volume one to the table. He wanted to read "aeroplane" while he ate.

"No," said his mother. "Absolutely not. You can't read the Encyclopaedia with food on your fingers. It's against the rules of this house."

Sam's face puckered up, and he began to whimper.

"I have an idea," said his father. "Here, we'll set your highchair aside and put you on a real chair. And you can sit on volume one to make you high enough."

Sam thought about that. "Okay," he said. He pushed another chair to the table and put his Encyclopaedia volume on it.

"Hold it," said his mother. "Your pants aren't wet, are they? No wet nappies allowed on the Encyclopaedia."

"Against the rules of the house?" asked Sam.

"Right. Against the rules of the house."

Sam felt his overalls. "No," he said triumphantly. "Not wet."

He sat on top of the thick volume, with his legs dangling. "Now I can read 'aeroplane'," he said. "But when I can read 'boat' I'll sit on two books. When I can read all the words, I'll be up to the ceiling."

"If you ever *ever* wet your pants on those books," said his mother, "I won't forgive you."

"I won't," promised Sam, swinging his legs cheerfully.

"I met a girl today," said Anastasia, "whose parents forgive absolutely everything. Probably if she burned their house down, they would forgive her."

"No kidding," said her father. He was carving a chicken.

"Even if she melted her father's Billie Holiday records, he would forgive her," said Anastasia pointedly.

"He sounds like a very strange sort of person," said her father as he passed her a plate of chicken. "Certain things are unforgivable in my book."

"My book," murmured Sam happily, and stroked volume one.

"He's not strange," said Anastasia. "He's the minister of the Congregational Church. That's why he forgives everything."

Her mother passed the mashed potatoes. "The Congregational Church? That's right in the next street. It's that pretty brick church on the corner, Anastasia. The rectory's next door."

"No kidding! Hey, that's neat. I have a new friend who lives in the next street!"

"I'm not sure," said her father, "that I'd be in favour of a friend who would melt her father's Billie Holiday records."

"*Dad*, I didn't say she had. Or that she was going to. I just said that *if* she did, he would be very forgiving. Unlike other people's fathers."

"Well," said her father, "I may not be a minister, but I hold some things sacred. Original recordings by Billie Holiday are one."

Anastasia sighed. She was sorry she had brought up Billie Holiday. She hadn't meant to melt the records, anyway. She had simply stacked them on the radiator.

"What does it mean, hold things sacred?" asked Sam, with his mouth full of chicken.

"That you love them dearly," said his mother.

"That you respect them enormously," said his father, who seemed to be sulking a little bit, remembering his Billie Holiday records.

"That you wouldn't ever do anything to harm them," said Anastasia, reaching for a little piece of chicken skin. "Unless, of course, it was an absolutely unavoidable accident," she said meaningfully, looking at her father, "and then, of course, you shouldn't be held responsible."

Sam sucked his thumb dreamily for a moment. "I hold my aeroplane book sacred," he said.

When the phone rang, after dinner, Daphne

Bellingham didn't even say hello when Anastasia answered. She said instead, "'Vengeance is mine, saith the Lord'," in a sinister voice.

"What?"

"It's a quotation from the Bible," Daphne explained, giggling. "I know lots of Bible stuff because I've gone to Sunday school every Sunday since I was born, practically."

"Oh. I don't go to Sunday school. My parents said when I grow up I can choose whatever religion I want. I'm thinking of becoming a Buddhist."

"I think you have to be a vegetarian if you're a Buddhist," said Daphne. Then she giggled again. "But that would be okay. I notice you like devilled eggs."

"*Daphne.*"

"Sorry. I won't ever mention it again, honest. Anyway, I've been thinking about vengeance. I'm making a list of possible revenges on my grandmother. Can you come over? Where do you live?"

Anastasia told her.

"We're practically neighbours! Come on over. It'll take you about two minutes to get here. We're the brick house right next door to the church. There's a Nazi swastika mowed into the front lawn. I did it when I was supposed to cut the grass yesterday. My father forgave me, of course. But I have to mow it out tomorrow."

Anastasia promised her parents she'd be home by

nine, and she went upstairs to change her clothes. She had already changed her clothes when she came home from work, but she didn't think ordinary jeans and shirt would be appropriate for visiting crazy Daphne Bellingham. She thought she should wear something outrageous.

Trouble was, she realized when she poked through her wardrobe, she didn't own anything outrageous. Once she had wanted to buy a tee shirt that said BOOGIE TILL YOU PUKE. But her mother had said no. Actually, what her mother had said was no, absolutely not, not under any circumstances, over my dead body, that is final, the answer is No.

It had sounded fairly definite, so Anastasia had given up on the tee shirt. But now she wished she had it.

"Mum!" she called down the back stairs. "I don't have any clothes at *all*!"

"That's odd," her mother called back. "I didn't notice that you were nude at dinner."

Typical. It was tough to get sympathy from a mother. Anastasia finally pulled on her Mona-Lisa-with-a-moustache sweatshirt, some old jeans with paint on the knees, and a pair of trainers.

"See you at nine," she told her parents, and grabbed a peach to eat on the way. "Night-night, Sam. I'm glad you learned to read 'aeroplane'." Sam was sitting on the kitchen floor in his pyjamas, reading his Encyclopaedia again. He blew her a kiss.

Daphne's house looked quite ordinary from the outside.

Brick and square, with shutters. Anastasia liked her own house better, with its odd porches and unexpected shapes, and the tower bedroom, which was hers. The only thing unusual about Daphne's house was the swastika in the lawn, and even that was barely noticeable, and also very crooked.

"Look!" cried Daphne, when she opened the front door. "How do you like them?"

"Like *what*?" asked Anastasia. Daphne was wearing bright red lipstick. It went way outside her own lips, like a clown's mouth.

"My Joan Crawford lips, of course," said Daphne. "And my Joan Crawford shoulders."

Anastasia looked more closely. She had been so startled by the lips that she hadn't noticed the shoulders. Daphne had put something inside her sweatshirt shoulders so that she looked like a football player.

"What do you think? If I can find some platform shoes, will I look just like Joan Crawford, or not? The shoulder pads are made of my father's ski socks."

"I guess it's okay. The mouth looks kind of like a clown, though."

"Yeah, I was afraid of that. I tried to make a crimson gash. Well, win some, lose some. Come on up, and I'll wipe it off. I'm bored with it already, anyway."

Inside, Anastasia could see that the house was very proper, very pretty. Furniture that matched, and no dust. Her own house was not as pretty but much more interesting, and messier.

But Daphne's room was different. The walls were

painted black, and there was a huge obscene poster of two dogs pinned up between the windows. There were clothes all over the floor; Anastasia recognized the yellow and white dress that Daphne had worn to her grandmother's luncheon lying in a pile with sweaters and jeans and underwear. On the unmade bed was a brand new, expensive doll, with its clothes removed, staring with blue glass eyes at the ceiling. A kitchen paring knife had been plunged into its chest.

"I murdered the doll," said Daphne, grinning as she wiped off her Joan Crawford mouth and dropped the Kleenex on the floor.

"Did your parents *let* you paint the room black?" asked Anastasia.

"Of course. They let me do anything I want, provided it doesn't harm anyone. They're very big on not harming anyone."

Anastasia picked up the striped dress and hung it over the back of a chair, on top of a pair of shorts. "I like this dress," she said.

"Keep it. You can have it," said Daphne.

"Thanks," said Anastasia, a little embarrassed, "but my parents wouldn't let me. They'd kill me if I gave my clothes away."

"'Faith, Hope and Charity'," said Daphne, "'and the greatest of these is Charity.' Bible again."

"They'd *really* kill me if I accepted charity. Even a dress from" – she looked at the label – "Saks Fifth Avenue."

"Big deal. My grandmother gave it to me. I'm

going to cut off the bottom and make it into a tee shirt, if you don't want it. My parents won't mind."

"Where are your parents, Daphne?" Anastasia realized suddenly that the house was very quiet. "And don't you have any brothers or sisters?"

"They're at a meeting. Or choir practice or something. They'll be home later. And no, no brothers or sisters. That's why I'm spoiled rotten."

"I have a stupid little brother," said Anastasia. "So I'm not spoiled rotten." In a way, she envied Daphne. But the black walls of the bedroom bothered her. They made her feel claustrophobic and depressed.

"Yeah, I guess it is. Here. Here's my list I've been making, of revenges. Some of them are just crazy, like putting poison in her iced tea. Some others are okay, like planting poison ivy in the rose garden, but I think it's too complicated. It probably wouldn't grow till next summer. What do you think about releasing a whole jar full of bees in her bathroom or something?"

"No. She might be allergic to bee stings. Anyway, we don't want to hurt her. You've already said you weren't into hurting people."

"What exactly do we want to do to her?" asked Daphne, chewing on her pencil rubber.

"Well, there's all sorts of practical-joke stuff. Like once my brother, Sam, put my goldfish into my mother's cup of tea."

"I don't have a goldfish," said Daphne.

"I do, but you can't use him. He's been through enough. He's come so close to a nervous breakdown that now I'm seeing to it he leads a very quiet sort of life," said Anastasia.

"Anyway," she went on, "I don't think we want just a simple practical joke. She humiliated me by making me be a maid. Did she humiliate you by giving you a doll?"

"Yeah. *Really.*"

"So. We have to humiliate her somehow."

"You know," said Daphne thoughtfully, "for someone to be humiliated, something has to happen in front of other people. Like all those people were there today, *looking*, when she gave me that doll. And you have to be a maid in front of everyone."

"Yeah, that's right. There have to be other people," said Anastasia, remembering what her mother and father had described about their humiliations. Other people. Other people *laughing*.

"Anastasia," said Daphne slowly, beginning to smile, "I am getting an idea. The perfect idea. The absolutely perfect humiliation for my grandmother. It's brilliant. It's so brilliant you won't believe it. It's—"

Anastasia interrupted her. "I'll believe it, Daphne. But hold on a minute. Could we go out into the garden or something? Frankly, these black walls are driving me crazy. If you want to know the truth, Daphne, I think your room is kind of sick."

"Yeah, you're probably right. I only did it to bug my parents. And now it's boring to have a black room. Maybe I'll paint it yellow next week. Come on down on the veranda, and I'll get some lemonade. Hey, I know where my father keeps the vodka. Do you—"

"*No*, Daphne."

"Just asking." Daphne shrugged and grinned.

They sat on the screened back veranda and sipped lemonade. Outside it had got dark. Somehow the dark of the night sky wasn't the same as the awful black walls of Daphne's room. It felt cooler here, healthier, and much more sane, Anastasia thought.

"Okay," said Daphne, when they were settled in the veranda chairs, "here it is. The absolutely brilliant, absolutely foolproof, Krupnik and Bellingham Revenge and Humiliation Plot. Ready?"

"Ready," said Anastasia. "Atcher Service," she added.

"Okay. My grandmother is giving a big party next week."

"Oh, *no*," Anastasia said. "Probably she'll ask me to help serve." She groaned, thinking of herself in a maid's apron again.

"Well, it's a really big deal. It's to raise money for some charity. People have to donate a hundred dollars to some orphanage or hospital or something – I forget what – in order to get an invitation to this party. So a whole bunch of rich people are coming. And there'll be society reporters from the papers there. And an orchestra. And it's formal. Black tie."

"What does black tie mean?"

"Formal, stupid. Tuxedos."

"Gross. My father would never wear a tuxedo for a million dollars."

"Well, snobs like to wear tuxedos. And this party will be all snobs. Except . . ." Daphne started to giggle.

"Except what?"

"Well, the invitations have all been sent. But there was a batch left over. I guess my grandmother couldn't think of enough rich snobs to send them to. And I know where the leftover invitations are!"

"So?"

"So, I'm going to steal some. Maybe about twenty. And I'm going to send them to some other people."

"Like who?"

Daphne was roaring with laughter. "You haven't lived around here long enough. But I know all the so-called undesirable people in this town! There's an old drunk who sleeps on the pavement near the barber shop . . ."

"I've seen him! He's *awful*!"

"Right. Then there's a nutty lady who walks around over by the town park all the time, carrying a bag full of dog food. She wears about three pairs of stockings on top of each other. Grey, so her legs look like Babar the Elephant's."

Anastasia was giggling. She was beginning to get the picture.

"Then, let's see, there's all that low-income housing on the other side of town. I'll distribute a few over there. And there's a group home for deinstitutionalized psychotics, on Haverford Street."

"Group home for *what*?"

"Deinstitutionalized psychotics. Mad people, but they're not dangerous, so they don't have to be in an institution any more. I'll give them some."

"Daphne," said Anastasia slowly, "you know, we're really not being fair. All of those people have problems. But it isn't fair to call them undesirable."

"*I* don't call them undesirable. I *like* them. I think they're the most interesting people in town. I even like that grubby old drunk. But my grandmother will think they're undesirable. And she's the one we want to humiliate, right?"

"Right." Actually, it was beginning to shape up as a terrific plan.

"There are a couple of guys who hang out in the park and smoke dope all the time. One of them was in jail once, I think, for selling drugs. I'll invite them."

Inside the house, the telephone rang. It rang a second time.

"Daphne, aren't you going to answer the phone?"

Daphne shook her head. "It'll just be for my parents. Let it ring."

"You're weird, Daphne. You're really weird," said Anastasia. She got up to go and answer the telephone. But by the time she found it, after the fifth ring, there was no one at the other end.

"It's almost nine. I have to go home, Daphne," she said when she went back to the veranda.

"Listen, don't worry about a thing. I'll get the

invitations and I'll distribute them. They won't even have your fingerprints on them."

"Daphne, is this against the *law*? Could we get arrested?"

But Daphne just laughed. "Thou shalt not sweat it," she said.

Something was wrong at home. Anastasia could tell when she turned the corner. All the downstairs lights were on, and if something wasn't wrong, all the downstairs lights wouldn't be on. Her father was always yelling about the electricity bill.

Then her heart sank. There was a police car in the driveway.

How could the police know *already* about the revenge she and Daphne were plotting?

I'll deny everything, she thought. Even if they put lighted matches under my fingernails. I'll say I've never met Daphne Bellingham in my life.

They have to read me my rights, she thought. I'm entitled to a lawyer. I won't say anything that can be used against me.

It was an *accident* that I dropped the thing down the waste disposal. And I've already paid back $17.50 of it.

Anastasia tried to think of every bad thing she had ever done. Surely her mother wouldn't have noticed yet that one pair of pantyhose was missing. Anyway, her mother wouldn't call the police about one lousy pair of pantyhose.

And the Billie Holiday records were two whole years ago. She shouldn't have reminded her father about them. But still, even though it had made him sulk at dinner, thinking about the Billie Holiday records, he wouldn't have called the *police*.

Terrified, she opened the back door.

"Anastasia!" said Mrs Stein, their next-door neighbour. What on earth was Mrs Stein doing in their kitchen at nine P.M.? Mrs Stein never went out at night. She had all her favourite TV shows to watch. She even liked the summer re-runs.

"Sweetheart," said her mother, coming into the kitchen. "I tried to call you at Daphne's, but no one answered. You must have been outside. But I knew you'd be home in a few minutes. Thank God you're here."

Her mother's eyes were red. Anastasia could tell that she had been crying.

"What's wrong?" asked Anastasia in a small voice. Her stomach felt funny. She would confess, she knew. They wouldn't have to put the matches under her fingernails. She would tell everything: the plot, the pantyhose, even all the way back to the little iced cake she had stolen when she was nine. If only her mother wouldn't cry.

"There's been an accident," said her mother, and put her arms around Anastasia.

"WHERE'S DAD?" asked Anastasia. "WHAT'S HAPPENED TO DAD?"

"Dad's okay," said her mother. "It's Sam. Dad's at

the hospital with Sam. The police are going to take us there."

Later, Anastasia could barely remember the ride to the hospital. It seemed like a blur, or a dream. But she remembered her mother holding her hand and telling her what had happened.

They had put Sam to bed, with his ragged security blanket, which he always took to bed, and with his Encyclopaedia volume. He hadn't even wanted a bedtime story. He just wanted to read "aeroplane" to them once more, and then he kissed them goodnight, and they turned off his light and went downstairs.

Later – much later – her parents were in the living room, reading, when they heard a crash.

"Sam fell out of bed, right, Mum?" asked Anastasia, holding tightly to her mother's hand. "Stupid old Sam. He was fooling around with his cot, and he fell out of bed. He probably broke his arm or something, didn't he, Mum?" Funny, how when you wanted someone to laugh and say "Yes, that's right", you talked on and on, not giving them a chance to say it because secretly you were scared they wouldn't say it, but would say something else that you didn't want to hear.

And finally her mother squeezed her hand back and said no. Sam had apparently got out of his cot and had taken his aeroplane book over to the window – they didn't know why, but they thought maybe he had wanted to look into the sky for aeroplanes – and when he leaned against the screen it had broken, and Sam had fallen from the window.

Anastasia's stomach felt sick. The *window*. That was practically like the Empire State Building. Sam's window was very high. If they had only never moved from the flat where they used to live – their first-floor flat in Cambridge – if they had never moved to this enormous house – if only . . .

"Did it hurt?" she asked in a small voice. "Did he cry?"

"Sweetie," said her mother, "he was unconscious. We think his head hit that tree stump, where the dead elm tree had been taken down."

There was something else Anastasia wanted to ask, but she couldn't make her voice say the words. The police car was pulling up to the hospital entrance. Anastasia was still holding her mother's hand, and someone guided them in and put them in a lift, and doors closed and doors opened, and suddenly she saw her father, sitting in an ugly green plastic chair, with his head down, looking at the floor. He looked up when he heard them, but he didn't smile; he just stood up, with his face sad and puzzled, and he reached out his arm.

Anastasia ran to him, and she began to cry. She made her voice say the words, and she asked the question, but it was the most terrible question she had ever asked.

"Daddy," she sobbed, "is our Sam going to die?"

6

No, they told her, but she didn't believe them. Sam is not going to die, her father told her, but she didn't believe him, even though he had never lied to her, not ever.

She cried and cried, and she didn't care that her face was red and her hair was messy and her glasses were falling off because tears made them slippery.

Then a nurse said it too, that Sam wasn't going to die, but she didn't believe the nurse, because nurses always said stuff like penicillin shots don't hurt, which was one of the most blatant lies in the world.

She cried because they had called her at Daphne Bellingham's, and Daphne hadn't answered the phone. She cried because she had called him old stupid Sam, and it wasn't true: he was smart, and he was young, and he was the only brother she had, and she loved him more than anything, and now she was sure they were all lying and he was going to die.

Once – more than once: *often* – she had hidden his blanky just to make him cross, just to tease him. She cried because she kept remembering that.

They all kept saying it to her, and she kept not believing them. But finally a doctor came through a doorway, wearing the same kind of operating room clothes that doctors on soap operas wear, and he said it, too, that Sam wasn't going to die, and when he said it, her parents began to smile. And then she believed it, because of the smiles.

Then she was able to stop crying, at last. The nurse gave her a little grey cardboard box of hospital tissues, and Anastasia blew her nose about a thousand times, and cleaned her glasses, and then she was able to listen to what the doctor was saying, because the inside of her head had stopped making crying noises.

"Your boy had a depressed skull fracture," the doctor said to Anastasia's parents, and he pointed to his own head to show them exactly where it was on Sam's, "and that's why we had to take him to surgery. But he's going to be just fine. At his age he'll heal in no time. You'll have him back home, oh, probably in a week or less."

"Can we see him?" asked her mother.

"Well, he'll be sound asleep for a good while. You folks may as well all go home and get some sleep yourselves. But if you want to wait twenty more minutes or so, you can peek at him while they wheel him to the recovery room. They'll be bringing him right along through here."

"Can we give him this?" asked Anastasia's father, and he held up Sam's ragged yellow blanky.

The doctor looked startled. "What *is* it?" he asked.

"His security blanket."

The doctor grinned. "Sure. Put it on the stretcher with him when they bring him out. Then he'll have it when he wakes up."

The doctor turned to leave. "Sometimes," he said, "I could use one of those myself," and he chuckled at Sam's blanky, nodded his head in response to their thank yous, and went back through the door.

Anastasia, her mother, and her father, all sat down on the ugly green plastic chairs. Her father took his pipe out of his pocket and began to fill it with tobacco.

"I suppose they'll hand me a pamphlet about smoking if I light this in here," he said guiltily.

But there were ashtrays overflowing with the remains of other people's cigarettes. The Krupniks were the only ones in the waiting room. But Anastasia could tell that a lot of people had been there, worrying, that day. She wondered who they had been, and if they had all leafed through the same wrinkled *People* magazines on the table, and she hoped that they had all been as lucky as her family, and as lucky as Sam. She wondered if some of them had cried, and if the nurses had given them tissues.

Sometimes, when they had to kill time, like in a dentist's waiting room, or on a boring drive somewhere, she and her mother played a game they had invented. Her father would never play; he said it was demented. The game was called Choices. "If you had a choice", it always began. They tried to think of the most terrible choices they could for each other, and it was against the rules not to choose. The worst one was one that her mother had given her: if you had a choice, would you eat liver at every meal for the rest of your life, and you would live to be ninety-seven, or would you stand naked in Lord & Taylor's main window for two hours on a Saturday afternoon?

She had tried, when her mother asked her that one, to narrow it down a little. To make it easier. Would the liver be *raw*? No, her mother said; it could be cooked. Could you wear a ski mask over your face in Lord & Taylor's window so that no one knew who you were? Well, said her mother, okay. You could wear a ski mask.

Even then, it was an impossible choice.

Now she began to pass the time, while they waited to see Sam, by asking herself: if you had a choice. But all of the choices centred on Sam.

If you had a choice, she said to herself, would you have leprosy, and your nose would have to be amputated, or would you let Sam die?

Leprosy, she told herself instantly. Nose and all.

Well, she said to herself: if you had a choice, would you marry that jerk Robert Giannini, and also never wash your hair for the rest of your life, and also join the Ku Klux Klan – or would you let Sam die?

I would do all that, she told herself, so that Sam wouldn't die.

I would *even*, she realized suddenly, eat liver *raw* three meals a day, and also stand in Lord & Taylor's window naked, *without* a ski mask, before I would let Sam die.

But he isn't going to, she thought happily.

Then, suddenly, there he was, being wheeled past by two nurses, who stopped briefly so that they could all look down at him. He was sound asleep; and his head was bandaged; and there was a needle in one of his arms, going to a tube that went up to a bottle hanging on a rack. But none of that mattered. He was still Sam, still old stupid Sam, and he was okay. Her father gave the blanky to the nurse, who tucked it in under Sam's limp little hand, and then they wheeled him away.

In the car, going home, Anastasia leaned against her mother. She was exhausted.

"Mum," she said sleepily, "I was thinking, at the hospital, and I decided that if I had a choice, I would eat liver raw . . ."

"Shhhh," said her mother, stroking her hair.

"And," she murmured, "I would marry Robert Giannini, and I would have my nose amputated, and join the Ku Klux Klan . . ."

"Mmmmm," said her mother.

"I forget the rest, but I would do it all, just for old Sam."

"Me too."

"Even the Lord and Taylor's window. I'd even do that, without a ski mask."

Her mother chuckled. "Of course you would. We all would. But we don't even have to think about that. Old Sam is going to be okay."

"You know what *I* was thinking, in there, while we waited to see Sam?" asked her father suddenly.

"What?"

"I was thinking what a weird injury he has. A depressed skull fracture. Can you imagine a *cheerful* skull fracture?"

They couldn't. But thinking about it made them smile, and they decided they would tell Sam about it. When he woke up. When he was okay. Tomorrow.

"Anastasia," said her mother, after she hung up the phone the next morning, "the doctor says Sam is awake and doing just fine. And we can go to see him. But they have a rule about visitors. No one under fourteen." Anastasia slammed down the dish towel that she was using to dry the breakfast dishes. "That's crummy! That's absolutely *crummy*! Everyone in the whole world is conspiring to get me! It's the one day I don't have to work, because Mrs Bellingham is having people come to clean all the rugs and she's afraid I'll get in their way – which is idiotic – but I had the whole day free, and I was going to go and read to Sam, for Pete's sake. I was going to go to the library and get books about aeroplanes and take them to the hospital to read them to old Sam. And now they say I can't do that unless I'm fourteen? My own, my *only* brother, and some jerk has made a rule that I can't even read to him when he has a depressed skull fracture? That's not fair! It's crummy!"

She picked up the dish towel and slammed it down again. It wasn't very satisfying to slam a dish towel. A dish would have been better. But the dishes they had used for breakfast were her favourites – yellow, with white flowers on them.

Her mother looked angry, too. "You're right, Anastasia. Sam would *want* to see you. Probably if you didn't come he would start to cry, and run a fever . . ."

"And get a stomach ache. It would be terrible for his health."

"Absolutely. It would be detrimental to Sam's entire recovery if you couldn't visit him. That is the *stupidest* rule!"

Dr Krupnik appeared at the door to the kitchen. "What on earth is going on in here? You people are shouting and slamming and stamping your feet. You made the needle jump on the stereo."

Anastasia and her mother explained the hospital's rule.

"For heaven's sake," said Anastasia's father, "a rule like that is so stupid, it deserves to be broken. You're tall for your age, Anastasia. We'll just pretend you're fourteen. If they question us at the door I will swear a solemn oath, on pain of death, that you are fourteen years old."

"But Dad," said Anastasia, startled, "it would be a lie. Your whole philosophy of life is always to be honest."

"What's the date?" asked her father.

"August the nineteenth."

Her father stood in front of the refrigerator, very straight and tall, with his hands at his sides. "On this date," he announced, in a loud, speech-making voice, "August the nineteenth, Myron David Krupnik, PhD, honours graduate of several distinguished institutions of higher learning, member of the Authors' Guild, Incorporated, vice-chairman of the English Department at Harvard University, noted author of several milestone volumes of poetry, contributor to the Civil Liberties Union and the Museum of Fine Arts, and general nifty person, declares that he has changed his entire philosophy of life. Drum roll, please."

Anastasia grabbed the frying pan that she had just dried, and beat on it solemnly with a wooden spoon. Her mother made some trumpet noises into the plastic funnel top of the coffee pot.

"Thank you," said Dr Krupnik, and they stopped. "My *new* philosophy of life," he announced, "allows for the occasional posing of a five-foot, seven-inch, twelve-year-old girl as a fourteen-year-old girl, for the emergency purpose of cheering up her little brother, in the face of an idiotic bureaucratic rule."

He bowed. Anastasia and her mother applauded. Dr Krupnik left the kitchen.

Maybe, thought Anastasia, it would help if I borrowed a bra again, and took some pantyhose, and . . .

No, she thought. Absolutely not. Her own philosophy of life, she decided suddenly, was never, under any circumstances, ever, to go anywhere again wearing a pantyhose bosom. You just could never predict when someone might ask you to pass a tray of devilled eggs.

When they stopped at the library on the way to the hospital, Anastasia found all sorts of aeroplane books. *All About Aeroplanes. Conquering the Sky. Flight Through the Ages*, which opened with a picture of Icarus and his wax wings, melting when he flew too close to the sun.

She looked through it because it had some wonderful photographs of jets at the end, but the picture of Icarus made her feel funny, because it made her think of Sam, falling. For a minute she wished that Sam had taken up submarines? Probably he would have drowned. What if he had become interested in animal training? Somewhere he would have found a wild rhinoceros and been eaten up.

She shuddered. Well, her father had spent the whole morning fixing the screens on all the upstairs windows. At least Sam would never fall from his window again. And from now on, she told herself, she would keep a very careful eye on her brother *all the time* so that he wouldn't have any more accidents, ever. She planned to be the very best sister in the whole world.

And she would start by being a wonderful hospital visitor. She planned to sit by Sam's bed and say soothing things to him, wiping his forehead with a damp cloth now and then, reading to him in a soft voice, and saying, "There, there", now and then when he whimpered with pain.

Maybe, in fact, she would go to nursing school, or even medical school, when she grew up. If only they wouldn't make her wear those white stockings. She really hated the white stockings that nurses wore.

But Anastasia's image of Sam the Invalid faded even before she saw him. She could *hear* him when they were still outside in the hall approaching his room. Not because he was whimpering feebly with pain. He was singing, in his loudest voice, "The monkey he got drunk, and sat on the elephant's trunk . . ."

He stopped singing when he saw his family. He grinned, waved, and said, "Hi! Did you bring me anything?"

The nurse who was in his room grinned also, and said, "Hi, there. You have quite a boy here. His repertoire of songs beats anything I ever heard at a fraternity party!"

Sam's mother went to the bed and kissed Sam's little face where it poked out beneath the turban of bandages. So did his father. Sam wiggled and made a face. He didn't like being kissed.

Anastasia thought about kissing him, but she just squeezed his feet through the covers, and said, "Hello, old Sam."

"It's okay to squeeze my feet," said Sam. "But don't squeeze my arm, because I have ivy on my arm."

Good grief, thought Anastasia. His brain has been damaged.

"You have *what*, Sam?" asked her mother.

"Ivy," said Sam. He pointed with one finger to the needle in the back of his other hand. A tube ran from the needle up to a bottle hanging on a metal stand.

"Oh." Mrs Krupnik laughed. "An IV."

"That's how they feed you, Sam, until you get a little better," his father explained.

"Yep. They feed me poison. It's my poison ivy machine."

Anastasia groaned. Sometimes Sam was impossible.

Later, back at home, the telephone rang.

"Anastasia? Willa Bellingham here. I've tried to reach you several times today."

"Well, I wasn't home, Mrs Bellingham, because my little brother had a very serious acci—"

But Mrs Bellingham interrupted her. "The rug cleaners have just left, and I am completely dissatisfied with the job they did. It is simply impossible to find conscientious workers these days."

"I try to be conscientious, Mrs Bellingham," said

Anastasia pointedly, and as politely as she could. But it was hard to be polite. She was furious. Mrs Bellingham had interrupted her in the middle of telling about Sam's accident. Mrs Bellingham was an insensitive creep. She didn't have the slightest interest in anyone else's problems. All she cared about were her stupid Oriental rugs.

"Yes," said Mrs Bellingham. "Of course you do. Now I would like you here tomorrow at ten, promptly. I'm giving a large party next week and there's a great deal to be done. I won't be home because I have my volunteer work to do. Mrs Fox will give you your instructions."

Good grief, thought Anastasia. Probably the silver all needs to be polished again. She groaned silently, and calculated quickly in her head. She would have paid back her debt to Mrs Bellingham in just seven more hours. Then she could leave.

But in a million years she didn't want to miss that party next week. She wanted to *be* there when Mrs Bellingham was humiliated. She decided she wouldn't leave until after the party. School would be starting the week after that, anyway.

"All right, Mrs Bellingham," she said.

"You'll be here *promptly* at ten?"

Anastasia sighed. "Atcher service," she said.

7

Rachel and Gloria were washing all the slipcovers in the house. There seemed to be about three million slipcovers. But Rachel and Gloria didn't seem to mind. They trudged back and forth to the washing machine and dryer and the ironing board, and they were quite cheerful. They called "Hi!" to Anastasia when she arrived. Anastasia had been a little worried that they might comment about her bosom, but they didn't seem to notice that it had disappeared.

Neither did Mrs Fox, who was very busy making lists. She sat at the kitchen table, writing long lists of foods for the party, and she had ball-point pen marks on her lips, because she kept chewing on her ball-point pen.

Please don't ask me to polish silver, thought Anastasia. Please.

And it worked.

"Books," said Mrs Fox, when Anastasia asked her what she could do. "In the library. Dust all the books." Then she nibbled at the ball-point pen again. Her lips were turning quite blue, like a creature in a horror movie. It was a rather interesting effect, and Anastasia thought briefly that maybe if she became a writer some day she would write a novel about a fat housekeeper who secretly became a werewolf at times, and maybe ate raw liver out of the refrigerator. Thinking about it made her stomach feel queasy.

But working in the library was fun. It was a medium-sized room that opened off the front hall, and all four walls were lined with bookcases. In the centre there was a large mahogany desk. Probably Mrs Bellingham sat at that desk and counted her money.

Probably she sat there and wrote her will.

Probably, thought Anastasia uncomfortably, she would disinherit her granddaughter if she knew what Daphne was up to.

There was a photograph of Daphne in the study, a colour photograph of Daphne looking happy and windblown, wearing a blue sweater, somewhere with ocean in the background. It was in a silver frame.

The smiling Daphne in the photograph didn't look like the sort of person who would hate her own grandmother.

In fact, until she had met Daphne, Anastasia had never known anybody who had hated her own grandmother. There had been times when Anastasia had become cross with her grandmother, but that wasn't the same. She had always loved her. Now that her grandmother was dead, she had her grandmother's wedding ring, which she kept in a small leather box. Sometimes she wore it to bed, because she thought that it might make her dream about the person she would marry. It hadn't worked yet, but it might, sometime.

Jenny MacCauley always went to her grandmother's house for Thanksgiving and Christmas, and her grandmother always made a miniature pumpkin pie just for Jenny.

Craig Robishaw had told her once that his grandmother had taken a ride on his trail bike, without even wearing a helmet.

Steve Harvey's grandmother lived in England, and when he had gone to visit her there, she hadn't made him go to museums or anything, but had got him a ticket to a rock concert.

Why was Mrs Bellingham such a crummy grandmother?

Or – thought Anastasia suddenly – why was Daphne such a crummy granddaughter?

Anastasia took a rag from the bundle Mrs Fox had given her and began to dust books. The books in Mrs Bellingham's study weren't your ordinary Literary Guild Alternate Selection, bestseller sorts. And no trashy novels. These books were all leather-bound, deep blues and reds, with gold printing on the covers.

Classics, thought Anastasia. First editions. The kinds of books her father would love.

Her father had once said that he would kill for a first edition of something by Joyce James. Or maybe it was James Joyce; she couldn't remember.

Probably the book her father would kill for was right here in Mrs Bellingham's study. She knew he was exaggerating, though. Her father would never kill anything. Maybe a cockroach. Nothing else.

Probably Mrs Bellingham never even read any of these books. Some of their pages were stuck together, proof that they'd never been opened.

Her father would read every one, she thought sadly. Life just wasn't fair. She had never really wished before that her family was rich. Now she wished it for a minute, just so that her father could have these books.

She had dusted a complete set of novels by Henry James. Anastasia didn't know who Henry James was, but she had heard her father speak about him. Her father taught a course in Henry James at Harvard. She had once wondered how someone could spend an entire term just teaching about one author. If she ever had to take a whole course in, say, Nancy Drew, she would be so bored by the second week that she would probably drop out of college and become a waitress.

Now she could see that Henry James, whoever he was, had written more books than the author of Nancy Drew. Now *that* was an accomplishment. Poor Henry James. He had to spend all his time writing in order to write so many books. He probably never went out for pizza or anything. He couldn't possibly have any social life; there wouldn't be time. She wondered if Henry James had ever been to a movie or a disco. Probably he was *old* by now and had never had any fun in his whole life. He must have been sitting at a typewriter for fifty years.

Probably he was Mrs Bellingham's age.

Probably he would enjoy meeting Mrs Bellingham, since she had bought all of his books. He wouldn't have to know she'd never read them.

I could get my father, thought Anastasia, to tell Mrs Bellingham the plots of the books. Then she could pretend she'd read them. A lot of kids at school did book reports just by reading the inside flaps of the covers and maybe the chapter headings. My father could fill old Bellingham in on the plots; then we could invite Henry James to dinner, and Mrs Bellingham, and it might be the start of a big romance. She could say stuff like, "Henry, I loved that last book of yours" – Anastasia glanced at a title – "*The Turn of the Screw.*" Then old Henry could twirl his moustache, if he had one, and say, "Thank you, Willa. May I take you to the movies on Friday?"

But then Anastasia made a face. It would never work. With a title like *The Turn of the Screw*, old Henry's novel was going to be about hardware. Hardware or sex. She was quite certain Mrs Bellingham wasn't interested in either subject.

Anyway, why should she drum up a romance for

Mrs Bellingham, who had never done anything for her except humiliate her?

She had another idea. There was a fountain pen on the desk. What if she wrote, inside the cover of *The Turn of the Screw*. "To my dear Willa, with fond memories of the passionate night we spent together. Henry James"?

She could do it in *lots* of books.

"Willa, dearest: I will never forget the week in the hotel room in Paris. Fondly, Scott Fitzgerald."

Or: "Willa, my love, you are the inspiration for all of my work. Charles Dickens."

Anastasia giggled, thinking about it. But she didn't do it. Not that she cared anything about Willa Bellingham's reputation. But she cared about the books.

Carefully, she dusted the last of the Henry James and set it back on the shelf. She started on the complete set of Virginia Woolf.

Suddenly the door to the study flew open, and there was Daphne, grinning.

"Greetings from the Cat Burglar!" Daphne said. Then she whispered, "I'm here to steal the invitations. They're in her desk, and I knew she wasn't home today. She spends half her time out doing stupid charity work. Giving her money to poor people or something."

Daphne opened a desk drawer, took out a handful of thick, engraved cards, and stuck them into her knapsack. "There, that'll do it. I'll make the deliveries over the weekend."

"Let me know how it goes," said Anastasia.

"I will. I'll call you. Where were you yesterday? I kept ringing, and no one was home."

Anastasia explained briefly about Sam's accident. Daphne's blonde eyebrows furrowed, and she looked concerned.

"Gee, that's awful. Is he going to be okay?"

"Yeah. He's doing fine."

"You really love him, don't you, Anastasia? I can tell from the way you talk about him."

"Love Sam? Of course I love Sam. He's my *brother*, for Pete's sake!"

"I wish I had a little brother," said Daphne wistfully. Anastasia was startled. It was the first time that she had seen Daphne being anything other than flippant, funny, or sarcastic.

Then Daphne's mood changed. "Hey," she said, "I have to go. I told Mrs Fox I'd come over to pick up a sweater I left here. *Voila*! The missing sweater!" She laughed, and took a sweater out of her knapsack.

"I'll phone you!" she said, and left the study.

Anastasia picked up a volume of Virginia Woolf and began to rub the soft leather with her dustcloth.

That was weird, she thought, when Daphne said she'd like a little brother. Daphne hates her whole family. Why would she want one more person to hate?

She doesn't, Anastasia thought suddenly. Daphne wants someone to love.

It seemed lonely at the dinner table, with just the

three of them and no Sam. Anastasia's mother had spent the afternoon with him at the hospital.

"Tell us everything," said Anastasia. "How he looks, and what the doctor said, and everything."

"How soon can he come home?" asked her father. He had had to teach a class that afternoon. "I really miss him. I even miss changing his nappies."

"Well," said Mrs Krupnik, "I guess it falls into the category of Good News, Puzzling News, and Terrible News."

"Start with the Good," said Anastasia. "And if the Terrible is really terrible, I don't want to hear it."

"Good News: he can come home on Monday. He's recovering just fine. The nurses say they've never seen anybody bounce back as quickly as Sam has. He's sitting up, doing puzzles, looking at his books – he really loves those aeroplane books you brought him, Anastasia."

"Good! I'll go over tomorrow afternoon and read to him, if I get out of work in time."

"You said there was *puzzling* news?" asked her father.

"Yes. When I got there, he was having lunch. They've taken out his IV and started him on regular food. So he was sitting there with a tray of food in front of him. They'd given him soft-boiled eggs."

Anastasia burst out laughing. "Oh, gross! The one thing Sam hates more than anything else in the world! Soft-boiled eggs! He always makes fake throwing-up noises when he even *sees* a soft-boiled egg!"

"Well," said her mother, "that's part of the puzzling thing. There he sat, with a nurse's aide helping him, and he was eating his soft-boiled egg. I didn't want to create any problems, but I was so startled that after he was all finished, I said casually, "Gee, Sam, I sort of remembered that you didn't much care for soft-boiled eggs.'"

"Understatement of the world," Anastasia pointed out. "What did he say?"

"He said, "Mrs Flypaper told me to eat everything so that I'd get well quick.'"

"Who's Mrs Flypaper? The nurse's aide?"

"Well, that's what I thought. So I said, 'Are you Mrs Flypaper?' to her, but she said no, her name was Miss Cameron. Then I asked Sam who Mrs Flypaper was, and he just grinned and said, 'She's my friend'."

"What kind of friend could ever get Sam to eat a soft-boiled egg?"

"I don't know. I asked all the nurses, but none of them knew of anyone named Mrs Flypaper or anything that even sounded like Mrs Flypaper. When the doctor came in, I asked *him*, but he didn't know who it could be."

"It doesn't sound terribly important, Katherine," said Anastasia's father.

"Well, it wouldn't be. But I started thinking, what would make a child eat something that he never in his entire life has eaten voluntarily? Even when he was an *infant* he'd spit soft-boiled eggs out all over his high-chair tray! And on top of that, what would make a child say that someone who apparently doesn't even *exist* had convinced him to eat soft-boiled eggs? Especially if that child had had a serious head injury?"

"Good grief," said Anastasia. "Brain damage."

"Right," said her mother. "That's exactly what I started thinking. And I suggested it to the doctor. But he said they've done all sorts of tests, and Sam's brain is functioning just fine. In fact, Sam is the brightest two-and-a-half-year-old they've ever seen in the paediatric ward."

"Of course he is," said Anastasia's father smugly.

"But then the doctor and the nurses and I were all starting to wonder about the mysterious Mrs Flypaper and the soft-boiled eggs. So they called in a child psychiatrist."

"A junior shrink!" said Anastasia.

"Right. So the psychiatrist came in – a woman named Dr Cunningham – and she talked to Sam for a long time."

"What did she decide?"

"She said he's the brightest two-and-a-half-year-old they've ever had in the paediatric ward."

"Big deal," said Anastasia. "We already knew that. What about Mrs Flypaper?"

"She said Sam has invented an imaginary friend."

"A *what*?"

"Well, she said Sam has been through a very stressful situation . . ."

"Big deal," said Anastasia a second time. "He fell

about a million feet from a window, landed on his head, had an operation, and woke up in a hospital bed with ivy in his arm. *I* could have told you he's been through a stressful situation, and I never went to psychiatrists' school!"

"Let me finish. She said that very often, particularly with very bright children, they will invent an imaginary companion to help them get through the fear and loneliness and pain of hospitalization. So Sam invented an imaginary friend named Mrs Flypaper."

"You'd think he would have chosen a better name," said Anastasia. "*Mrs Flypaper.* That's so stupid."

"Well, stupid or not, Sam invented her, or him, or it, and she convinced him to eat soft-boiled eggs."

"That's weird."

"Well, I told you it was puzzling."

"Katherine," said Anastasia's father, "you've given us the Good News and the Puzzling News, but—"

"I don't want to hear the Terrible News," said Anastasia firmly. "May I be excused? I'm full."

"No, stay here, Anastasia. You've got to hear the Terrible News, especially if you're going to visit Sam tomorrow. You may as well be prepared."

"My stomach hurts. My stomach hurts already, and I haven't even heard the news yet."

"They've taken the bandages off Sam's head," said her mother. "The doctor said the incision will heal faster if it's exposed to air."

"I hate that word, *incision*. Does it look awful?"

"No, actually it doesn't look all that bad. It's very neat, with little even stitches."

Anastasia's father said, "I'm surprised that you can even *see* the incision, with all of Sam's curly hair."

Her mother looked miserable and didn't say anything.

"His hair!" said Anastasia suddenly. "It's his *hair*, isn't it? His curls. What have they done to Sam's curls?"

But she knew, even as she asked. It *was* Terrible News.

"They shaved his head," said her mother in a sad voice.

Her father sighed, and then started to laugh. "Good grief," he said. "That's not the end of the world. It'll grow back!"

But Anastasia knew how her mother felt. She felt the same way. "Dad," she said unhappily, "you don't understand."

She asked her mother fearfully, "How does he *look*?"

Her mother's eyes were filled with tears. But she was biting her lip, too, and Anastasia could tell that she didn't know whether to laugh or to cry. So she did both. The tears ran down her cheeks. But she was chuckling when she answered the question.

"He looks like Kojak," she said.

8

It was true. A miniature Kojak, wearing seersucker pyjamas printed with pictures of Mickey Mouse.

Anastasia flinched when she saw Sam. But she didn't say a word about his shaved head. She had decided, while riding her bike to the hospital, that she wouldn't, no matter how gross it looked.

She remembered how terrible she had felt one morning, back when they lived in Cambridge, when her best friend, Jenny, had greeted her with "Hi, Anastasia! That's an awful mosquito bite on your forehead. It looks just like advanced acne."

It really was only a mosquito bite. But after Jenny said that, Anastasia was self-conscious all day. She tried to comb her hair over her forehead. She sat with her hand over her forehead as much as possible, until her class 7 teacher asked whether she had a headache, and when she said no, told her that she looked like Balboa discovering the Pacific Ocean. And showed her a picture of Balboa, with his hand over his forehead, discovering the Pacific.

Hah. Probably old Balboa had advanced acne.

So Anastasia was always very careful not to point out anyone's physical flaws, because she knew from experience how awful it made them feel.

So she said, "Hi there, Sam!" just as if he didn't look like Kojak at all.

But to her surprise, Sam said, "Hi! You can call me Baldy!"

Stupid old Sam. He wasn't old enough to be self-conscious yet.

"Well," she said uncomfortably, "I guess I'll just call you Sam, the way I always do."

Sam shrugged happily. "Okay. But Mrs Flypaper calls me Baldy. Mrs Flypaper says I look like Bald Eagle the Indian chief."

Imaginary Mrs Flypaper. Anastasia was still puzzled by that. What good was an imaginary companion who said you looked like Bald Eagle the Indian chief?

Well, obviously it made Sam feel okay about the way he looked. What if, when she had had the mosquito bite on her forehead, and Jenny had made that obnoxious remark, Anastasia had had an imaginary companion – a Mrs Flypaper – who had said, "Don't worry about it. It just looks like a mosquito bite. No big deal"?

No. It wouldn't have worked for her. She needed a *real* friend to say that, not a made-up one.

But if it worked for Sam, okay.

"I'll bring you a feather next time I come, Sam, and we can make an Indian headdress for you."

"Okay," said Sam cheerfully.

"We really miss you at home."

"Yeah," said Sam.

"Last night when Mum was setting the table, she forgot and set four places. One for you."

Sam giggled. "I eat on a tray. Sometimes Mrs Flypaper comes when I'm eating."

And makes you eat soft-boiled eggs, thought Anastasia. Weird.

"Where does Mrs Flypaper come *from*, Sam?"

Sam looked puzzled. "I don't know."

"When you come home on Monday, will Mrs Flypaper come with you?"

Sam looked startled. "No," he said. "Mrs Flypaper lives *here*."

Well, that made sense. Sam needed his imaginary companion only while he was in the hospital. Just like the shrink said.

"Would you like me to read to you?"

"Yeah. About aeroplanes."

So Anastasia climbed up on the high hospital bed and read to Sam from one of the library books she had brought him. She skipped the Icarus section. She had a feeling that it would be dangerous to read it to him. Old stupid Sam, he might start trying to build a set of wings.

After a while, Sam snuggled down in his pillow and fell asleep. Anastasia kissed the top of his bald Kojak head, whispered, "See you tomorrow, Bald Eagle", and tiptoed out of his room.

She didn't have to be home for supper for another hour, so Anastasia rode her bike to Daphne's house. Funny, she thought as she rode, how quickly this town had begun to feel like home. She rang her bicycle bell as she rode past the library, and waved in case Mr Mason, the librarian, was looking out of the window. He and she had become good friends, even though she thought he was overly strict about the number of books you could take out at a time.

She rang her bell again, and waved again, as she passed the Senior Citizens' Centre. Sometimes when she was bored at home, she stopped in there and played draughts or gin rummy with the senior citizens. They didn't seem to mind that she wasn't a senior citizen herself.

She waved to Mr Mastrolucci at the Gulf station where her father got petrol. Then she waved to Gladys at the Clip 'n' Curl Beauty Salon. For a while she had been cross with Gladys, because Gladys had refused to bleach Anastasia's hair platinum blonde. But then she had realized that Gladys was right. Anastasia didn't really have a platinum blonde face. Or figure. Maybe she would when she got older, especially if she got contact lenses and stopped being so skinny.

She also waved at a lady she didn't even know, a lady who was walking a stupid-looking dog with droopy ears. The lady looked surprised. The dog didn't.

Then she turned into Daphne's driveway, and there was Daphne, sitting on the front steps with a cat on her lap.

"Hi, Daph! You said you'd call me, and you didn't! What are you doing?"

"Picking fleas off the cat." She let go of the big grey cat, who looked relieved, jumped off Daphne's lap, and ran away into a thick clump of bushes. "I *did* call you. I called you this morning, and your mother said you were at work. And I called you this afternoon, and your father said you were at the hospital. Boy, your parents really keep track of you, Anastasia, like a couple of jailers."

"No, they don't. They just like to know where I am. I like to know where they are, too. If you don't keep your eye on people, they fall out of windows and stuff."

"How's your brother?"

"He's okay. I read him a couple of books." Anastasia decided not to tell Daphne that Sam was bald all of a sudden. It seemed too personal. And Daphne might laugh.

"Guess what? I did it," said Daphne.

"Did what?"

"Delivered the you-know-whats."

"No kidding! How many?"

"Twelve. That was all I took. My grandmother didn't notice they were gone, did she?"

"She wasn't home this morning. She was out doing charity again, I suppose. But Mrs Fox didn't say anything. Anyway, they're all so busy cleaning the house and the dishes and the furniture and everything, they're not even thinking about the invitations. Who did you give them to?"

"Everybody I told you I would."

"The drunk who sleeps by the barber shop?"

"Yep. He was sitting there on the pavement nodding over a bottle of Gallo's rosé. I gave him one."

"What did he do?"

"He read it. Then he stood up, bowed, and said, 'My dear, I am decidedly honoured'." Daphne did a pretty good imitation of a staggery bow. Anastasia giggled.

"How about the lady who carries the dog food around?"

"Yeah. I found her sitting on a bench near the police station, mumbling to herself. I gave her the invitation, and she stuffed it into her bag and went on mumbling."

"Probably she won't even read it."

"Of course she will. I said to her, 'Aren't you even going to read it?' And she got all cross and yelled at me that of course she was going to read it, she always reads everything, she's read the complete works of Proust fourteen times, and when there's nothing else to read she reads the telephone book. Then she started mumbling again."

"Who else?"

"The potheads in the park. I gave them two. And two to the deinstitutionalized psychotics."

Anastasia counted. "That's six. Who got the other six?"

"Well, then I walked over to the low-income housing. You know what my grandmother calls that housing project?"

"What?"

Daphne stood up, stuck her nose in the air, pinched her lips tight together, squinted her eyes, until she looked amazingly like Willa Bellingham, and said, in a throaty voice, "The Habitation of the Great Unwashed."

"Daphne!" Anastasia was shocked. "That's terrible! Being low income doesn't mean being unwashed!"

"It does to my grandmother. Unless you wash with imported lilac soap from England, you're unwashed. She says that every time we drive past that project: the Habitation of the Great Unwashed." She did her Willa Bellingham imitation again. Anastasia was impressed.

"You know, Daph, you'd be a really good actress. I can't think of any professional actress who could do that imitation as well as you."

"Bull. Jane Fonda could. Vanessa Redgrave could. Maybe Bo Derek couldn't, though."

"Is there a Dramatic Club at school?"

Daphne shrugged. "I suppose so. I'm only going into class 8, the same as you, so I don't know much about the junior high. But there was a Dramatic Club where I went to class 7."

"I bet you got the lead in all the plays, didn't you?"

Daphne made a face.

"*Didn't* you?" asked Anastasia again.

"No," said Daphne finally. "I didn't belong to the Dramatic Club."

"Why *not*?"

Daphne didn't say anything. She looked around, into the bushes where the cat had hidden. "Here, Scooter!" she called.

"*Daphne*. Listen to me. You *have* to join the Dramatic Club in junior high, because you'll get the lead in everything. Then after you finish high school you can go to New York, to the Academy of Dramatic Arts or something, and then Hollywood will find you, and you'll be a star. You'll win Oscars, and write your autobiography, and all that. I can tell you have a lot of talent. I bet not even Lily Tomlin could do that imitation of your grandmother. Honest. Now tell me *why* you wouldn't join the Dramatic Club!"

Daphne stood up again, and looked down her nose at Anastasia. "Because it met after school," she said in a haughty voice. "And I was not available after school."

"Why not?"

Daphne's shoulders sagged, and she spoke in her

own voice, but it sounded sad and angry. "I told you, Anastasia. I am a *troublemaker*. I was always in detention after school."

She turned and went up the steps to her house. "It doesn't leave much time for extra-curricular activities," she said sarcastically. Then she went inside and slammed the door.

Boy, thought Anastasia, as she rode her bike home. I thought I was worried about Sam. But all he has is a depressed skull fracture. Daphne is really the one to worry about. Daphne has a depressed *brain* or something.

9

Anastasia was making pancakes. She often made pancakes for the family on Saturday mornings. But this Saturday it wasn't much fun, without Sam there. Sam liked pancakes shaped like rabbits or snowmen. Her parents didn't.

"You want a snowman, Mum?" she asked, raising the bowl to pour the batter into the pan.

"No, thanks. Just round will be fine."

So Anastasia made a boring round pancake and served it to her mother.

"Dad?" she asked. "How about a rabbit? I can really make good ears when the pan's nice and hot."

But he made a face. "Frankly, your pancake rabbits make me cringe. They make me think I'm slicing the Easter bunny. Just do me a round one like the one you did for your mother."

"I could put raisins in it," Anastasia suggested.

But he made an even more hideous face. "Spare me the raisins. A round, plain, unadorned pancake, please."

Adults were so boring about food. Anastasia wished for the millionth time that Sam were home. Sam even let her put food colouring in his milk.

She served her father an enormous round pancake, made herself a half-hearted snowman, and sat down to eat.

Boring, boring, boring Saturday morning. I bet breakfast isn't boring at Daphne's house, because Daphne can do those great imitations, Anastasia thought. If Daphne were here, my parents would be holding their sides from laughing, instead of just reading the newspaper.

Anastasia decided to try doing an imitation. She decided to do a waitress routine, since she was making pancakes anyway.

She chewed a wad of imaginary gum, and said, "Pancakes are on special today. Only a dollar sixty-nine. Can I give you folks another order of pancakes?"

"No, thank you," said her mother, and folded the newspaper into quarters so that she could begin the crossword puzzle. "You could pour me some more coffee, though."

"Me too," said her father without looking up from the paper, and pushed his cup over.

Anastasia glowered and poured both of her parents some coffee.

She chewed harder on the imaginary gum, scraped the frying pan noisily with the spatula, and said, in her waitress voice, "Tips sure are lousy in this here diner."

Her father cleaned his glasses with a paper napkin. "Katherine," he said, "do you have page thirty-six? I need the rest of this article on the defence budget."

"It's on the chair," said her mother, and pointed to the section that contained page thirty-six.

Rats. It hadn't been a *great* waitress routine, but surely it had deserved some polite applause, at least.

She decided to borrow Daphne's imitation of her grandmother. She *knew* that was funny.

"Have you guys ever noticed," Anastasia asked casually, "that over on the other side of town there's a low-income housing project?"

"Mmmmm," said her mother, filling in a word in the crossword puzzle. She looked at the word, frowned, and rubbed it out.

"Yes," said her father, as he turned a page of the paper. "I drive past it when I go to work. I've forgotten what it's called. Hazelnut Estates, or something."

"No," said Anastasia's mother, looking up. "It's Hazelwood. Hazelwood Acres, I think, Myron."

Perfect, thought Anastasia. If she had been writing dialogue for a play, she couldn't have written it any better, to lead up to her great line.

"Actually," she said, "what it's called is" – and she drew up her shoulders very stiffly, pinched her mouth into a sour expression, and looked down her nose – "the Habitation of the Great Unwashed."

But no one laughed. Both of her parents were looking at her. And there was an ominous silence.

Her father, in the terrible voice he reserved for the most awful occasions, broke the silence by saying, "Did I just hear you say what I *think* I heard you say?"

"Repeat that, please," said her mother, staring at her. "I want to be certain I heard you correctly, Anastasia."

Good grief, thought Anastasia. *Big* trouble. She looked at her plate, where one bite of a pancake snowman still lay soggily in some syrup.

"Thehabitationof thegreatunwashed," she finally repeated, mumbling miserably. "I was only—"

"That," interrupted her father angrily, "is the stupidest, most uneducated, mindless, bigoted remark I have ever heard you say!"

"But—" began Anastasia.

"*Snobbish*," said her mother. "I can't believe it. You of *all* people, turning into a *snob*!"

"What I mean was—"

"What you *said* was 'unwashed'. Is that correct? Did I hear you correctly?" asked her father.

"Yes." Anastasia sighed. "You heard me right. Unwashed. But I was only—"

"Do you have any understanding of what low income means?" her father demanded.

Anastasia looked him in the eye. Now *she* was

cross. "Dad," she said, "I myself am low income. So far this week, at work, I earned forty dollars, out of which I had to pay thirty-five for a bockle, so that my take-home pay was five dollars. Plus the extremely low-income allowance that you give me. Don't talk to *me* about understanding poverty, for Pete's sake. I *live* it."

"And do you consider yourself 'unwashed'?" Her father said the word with distaste.

"No. My jeans are unwashed, but—"

"And do you consider *poor* to be synonymous with *unclean*?"

Anastasia could see that she was doomed to lose a war she hadn't intended to start. "No," she said.

"Or the underprivileged to be lacking in human dignity?"

"No. Definitely not."

Her mother had gone back to the crossword puzzle. "It was just a thoughtless remark, Myron," she said.

Unfortunately her father didn't have a crossword puzzle, and he had apparently finished the article about the defence budget. He set the newspaper aside.

"You haven't ever seen where I grew up, have you, Anastasia?"

"You grew up in Boston," Anastasia said.

"I grew up in Boston. I also grew up in *poverty*. My mother, my father, my four brothers and I all lived in a four-roomed flat." Her father stood up and took his plate and coffee cup to the sink.

Anastasia poked unhappily at the last bit of her soggy pancake. She didn't want it. But she didn't want to hear a lecture, either, about the millions of underprivileged people who aren't fortunate enough to have pancakes for breakfast. She gulped down the last bite.

"The bathroom was down the corridor," her father said. "We shared it with two other families." He rinsed his plate. Back at the table, her mother sighed and rubbed out another mistake in the crossword puzzle.

Anastasia carried her own plate to the sink and held it under the running water. Her father watched her, meaningfully.

"We didn't have hot water," her father said. "My mother heated water on the stove."

Ho-hum, thought Anastasia. But she nodded politely.

"BUT WE WERE NOT UNWASHED!" said her father. "Can you get that through your head?"

Not if you yell at me, thought Anastasia. All I get through my head if you yell at me is an aspirin headache.

But she nodded again. "Yessir," she said.

Dr Krupnik stroked his beard. He looked more cheerful all of a sudden. "You know what?" he said. "It's Saturday. And it's a beautiful day. Let's go for a ride, Anastasia. I'll show you where I lived when I was a kid."

Anastasia stifled a groan. There was nothing she

wanted to do *less* on a Saturday than take a trip down Memory Lane with her father. But she smiled sweetly, and said, "Sure, Dad."

I brought it on myself, she thought, and went to brush her teeth.

"Mum," said Anastasia, as her father got the car out of the garage, "up in my room, on my desk, is a big feather. Would you take it to Sam when you go to the hospital? I promised him."

"Yes."

Out of the driveway, her father honked the horn. Anastasia sighed. "He really knows how to ruin someone's Saturday," she said.

Her mother picked up the crossroad puzzle again. "Good for you, Anastasia! *Ruin*! Four down. The clue was 'to devastate'."

"Right. That's what I meant. He's completely devastated my Saturday." She went glumly out to the car.

"My father never had a car," announced Dr Krupnik as he pulled into a Boston parking garage. "Never in his whole life did my father own a car. If he *had* owned a car, he would never have been able to afford six dollars for parking in a garage. Six dollars would have fed our whole family for a week, back in 1935."

Anastasia tried to look interested. Actually, she was bored stiff. Though she had never seen her father's childhood home before, she had heard all his dull poverty stories. Every twelve-year-old kid had, she was quite sure. Every twelve-year-old kid in the entire world had to listen to things like "When I was your age I walked five miles to school in my bare feet." Or, "When I was your age I had to milk twenty-three cows by hand before the sun came up, in the middle of winter." Or, "When I was a kid, all we got for Christmas was an orange and a pair of mittens." Probably even Rockefeller kids had to listen to things like that.

Anastasia vowed that when she had children she would never ever tell them what a deprived childhood she had had. That she had had to work as a maid when she was only twelve. That she had lived in a house with an old refrigerator that couldn't make reliable ice cubes. That she had never in her entire childhood been taken to Disneyland.

She looked around as they left the garage.

"Dad!" Anastasia said. "This is Quincy Market, for Pete's sake! I've been here before! I *hate* Quincy Market! It's all tourists! Did you live here when you were a kid? Did your father run a boutique or something?"

Her father looked at her in surprise. Then he looked around at Quincy Market: at the restaurants, art galleries, gift shops, pubs and clothing stores. He began to laugh.

A middle-aged couple, each carrying a camera, glanced at Anastasia and her father, and frowned. Nearby, a young man with a scraggly moustache tuned his violin and began to play; someone tossed a coin into his violin case, which was open on the brick pavement.

"Of course I didn't live here. This wasn't even here when I was a kid. I mean, the *buildings* were here – you can see that the buildings are very old – but in those days, when I was a boy, this whole area was . . ." He stopped talking, scrunched his nose, moved aside to let a throng of tourists pass, and tried to think of the right word.

"The pits?" asked Anastasia, beginning to get the picture.

Her father grinned. "Yes. It was definitely the pits. Anyway, where I lived was over this way. Come on."

He guided her across a street, under an underpass – she could hear the cars zooming overhead – and onto the pavement in front of an Italian meat market. A burly dark-haired man wearing a white apron called to them from the doorway. "You want chicken? We got lotsa chicken parts on special today! Eight-nine cents a pound!"

"No, thanks," her father called back. "Not today."

"Lamb chops?" the butcher called. "Loin lamb chops?"

But they were already around the corner. Anastasia's father was guiding her as he looked for street signs.

"Salem Street," he said, almost to himself. "If we go down Salem Street, and then turn right, I think . . ."

She trotted beside him, dodging the people.

Children darted here and there, calling to each other. From upper windows women leaned, calling to the children. In shop-front doorways, men stood, calling to the women at the windows.

One of the men called to Anastasia, "Hey, Blondie, you and your papa wanta pizza?"

Actually, Anastasia would have loved a pizza, as long as it didn't have anchovies. Anchovies always made her think of her goldfish. She had always suspected that unsold goldfish ended up as pizza anchovies.

But her father was striding ahead of her, looking down side streets. She said, "No, thank you," politely to the pizza man and ran to catch up. "Maybe later," she called back, over her shoulder, but the pizza man was already calling to someone else.

From an open window above her somewhere she could hear familiar music. Anastasia looked up. A woman was reaching from the window, hanging nappies on a clothesline that stretched across to the next building. The music was coming from behind the woman.

"Dad," she said, pulling at his sleeve. "Listen. Someone's playing that opera that you always play."

He stopped walking, listened for a moment, and then looked up at the woman, who was snapping nappies straight as she pinned them to the line.

"Puccini, eh?" her father called. Ordinarily, Anastasia was grossed out when her father spoke to total strangers in public. But somehow it seemed okay here. The woman grinned down from her window and called something back to Dr Krupnik, in another language.

He smiled, waved, and called, "*Ciao*!"

"Chow?" said Anastasia. "That sounds like a good idea. All these restaurants smell terrific."

"No: *ciao*. That's Italian. It's just a greeting."

Two little boys ran past, chasing each other, almost knocking over a woman pushing a pushchair, and disappeared into a sweet shop. The woman with the baby called after them angrily and then turned to jounce her baby back to sleep. Anastasia couldn't understand what she was saying.

"Dad," Anastasia said, "*everybody's* speaking Italian!"

"It's their native language," her father explained. "They know how to speak English. If they were talking to us, they'd speak English. But to each other they speak Italian. Here: I think we want to turn down that next street. It's been so long since I've been back here."

They turned to the right, down a twisted, crooked street so narrow that she didn't see how a car could possibly get through. One had, though, and had parked, and it had a ticket that said VIOLATION, in big letters, on the windshield. Shabby buildings rose on either side and shadowed the street. Old women sat knitting, in lawn chairs, right on the pavement. Two men played draughts at a card table set up in a doorway; a dog by their feet yawned and scratched at a flea. Children scampered and giggled and chased each other. Babies cried; mothers scolded; a cat slept, unconcerned, at a window.

Even the graffiti spray-painted on the side of a building were in Italian.

"There it is!" said her father triumphantly, and he pointed to an undistinguished brick building on the corner. "Third floor rear!"

They climbed the three cement steps that led to the doorway, and peered inside. A row of metal letter boxes was attached to the wall. Anastasia read the names aloud: "Castelucci, De Luca, Ronzoni, Di Benedetto.

"It sounds like the cast of a Fellini movie," she said.

Then she looked around again, at the tiny street throbbing with life, at the children, the grand-mothers, the cats and dogs. She listened to the noises: doors slamming, radios playing, the shouting, arguing, laughing, singing. "As a matter of fact," she said, "being here is like being in a Fellini movie."

Her father grinned. "I love it," he said.

"I love it, too," Anastasia admitted. "I thought it would be boring, coming here, but it isn't. But there's something I can't work out, Dad. Were you *Italian* when you were a kid?"

He laughed. "Anastasia, do I *look* Italian?"

She studied his face carefully. A little chubby. Head bald on top; remaining hair red and curly, with some streaks of grey on the sides. Pink nose, with dents in it because his glasses had slid down a bit, the same way hers did when it was hot and her face got slippery. Curly beard.

"No," she said finally. "You don't."

"My parents came here from Czechoslovakia. This whole area, when I was young, was a place where immigrants from many different countries settled. My father came here first. Then, after he'd saved enough money, he sent for my mother."

"What about you? What about your brothers? Did she come alone, and leave you behind in Czech – in Czech – I can't say it."

"Czechoslovakia. No, no. We were all born right here. Third floor rear."

"Not in a *hospital*?"

"Hospitals were too expensive. I told you, Anastasia, my family was *poor*."

She cringed, waiting, but he didn't say anything about unwashed.

He was wrinkling his forehead, looking around, remembering. "My father was a tailor. At first he worked for someone else. But I don't know where that was. It was before I was born. By the time I came along, he had his own shop; it was around the corner and down about half a block."

He looked around the corner and down. But there was nothing except an Italian restaurant, a dry cleaner and a pastry shop.

"Well," he said finally, "it's gone now, of course. But in the summer, when I wasn't at school, I used to carry his lunch down to the shop every day."

"Were there other people around from Czech – from Czech – *Rats*, Dad; I *still* can't say it."

"Czechoslovakia. Sure there were. Lots. A whole community. Some of them were even old friends from the same village back in the old country."

"Where did they all go? Why aren't they here now?"

"Let's walk, and we'll find a place to have some lunch." He put his arm around her shoulders, and they turned onto another street, walking slowly. "Where did they go? Different places, I suppose. They all worked hard, and saved, and looked for good places to raise their children. I think they looked for places that reminded them of the old country. My mother and father eventually bought a little house farther out, where they could have more space and my mother could have a garden."

"But he never ever had a car," Anastasia mused. "I thought everybody in the suburbs had to have a car."

"Nope. He could never afford a car. But he sent all five sons to college," her father said proudly.

"And then two of them died," Anastasia prompted him. "I remember you told me that."

"Right. My brothers Joe and Ben. Both of them killed in the war."

"That is *so* sad," said Anastasia. "When I thought *my* brother was going to die, I couldn't stand it."

"But there's still my brother George, in California."

"Uncle George. He and Aunt Rose always send me

terrific stuff on my birthday. An Indian necklace once, remember?"

Her father nodded. "And then, of course, there's Irving."

Anastasia groaned. "The doctor. He is so boring, Dad."

"Anastasia!"

"I'm sorry. But he is."

"I suppose you're right. Irving was always boring, even when he was a kid."

"But you liked him anyway, didn't you, Dad?"

"Sure I did. I still do. He's my brother."

"Like me and Sam. Even when Sam is boring, I still like him," said Anastasia.

Her father began to laugh. "Anastasia, Sam is *never* boring!"

"True," she acknowledged. Then she said, "You know what, Dad? I know someone who hates her whole family."

"Extraordinary," said her father. "Extra-absolutely-ordinary. Unless her whole family are axe murderers or something."

"No. They're just your basic family types. They do some stupid things, though."

"We all do. I remember just last week I blew up at you because you used all the ice cubes and didn't put the ice trays back. That was a pretty stupid thing."

"Which was? Not putting the trays back? Or blowing up about it?"

"Both, in fact. But we didn't hate each other

because of it. I think your friend must be just *pretending* to hate her family."

"Why would she do that?"

"Beats me. Hey, you hungry yet? Want some chow?"

"*Ciao*!" said Anastasia.

"*Ciao* to you, too!" said her father.

Two nuns walking past looked at them curiously, nudged each other, giggled, and walked on.

"In here okay?" asked her father. Anastasia nodded, and they entered a small Italian restaurant.

"I'm glad the Italians didn't scrimp and save and move away, like the Whatchamacallits," said Anastasia, after two mouthfuls of spaghetti. "I'm glad they stayed here."

"Well," said her father as he ate his antipasto. "Lots of Italians moved away to the suburbs, too. But some of them chose to stay here even after they could afford to move."

"They stayed because they liked it, I bet."

"Sure. They made it into something like a part of Italy. A little bit of Naples or Florence. It felt like home."

Anastasia slurped a long piece of spaghetti when she thought no one in the restaurant was looking.

"Dad," she said slowly, "I was really cross with you this morning."

He poked in his antipasto with his fork. "You want an anchovy?"

"Yuck," said Anastasia. "Blecchhh."

"A simple 'No, thank you' would be sufficient," her father said, and ate the anchovy himself. "I was pretty cross with you, too."

"I know you were. But the reason I was cross was that you didn't even give me a chance to explain."

"There isn't any explanation for bigotry," he said. "Not ever."

"I know that. I really do. But I wasn't even thinking about *what* I was saying. It was the way I was saying it. I was imitating Mrs Bellingham. Mrs Bellingham is so *awful*."

"You know," said her father, "I agree that Mrs Bellingham did a pretty thoughtless thing when you applied for one job and she sort of tricked you into another. But on the other hand, Anastasia, I've decided that she's not such a bad person after all."

"Dad! She made me be a *maid*!"

"You didn't let me finish. I read in the local paper that she's giving a party next week. Did you know about that?"

"Did I *know* about that? Who do you think is going to be a maid at the party?"

He poked at the last bits of lettuce in his salad. "Oh. I see. Well, let's try looking at it in a different way, Anastasia."

Now Anastasia was getting cross. "There isn't any other way. No matter how you look at it, a maid is a maid is a maid is a maid."

"Not always. How about being a maid for a very worthy cause?"

Anastasia made a face. She couldn't think of a single cause worthy enough to justify Anastasia Krupnik's being a servant. A scullery maid. A slave.

"The paper said that it's a benefit. People are paying enormous amounts of money to go to that party," her father said.

"I know. A hundred dollars a piece," said Anastasia, almost smiling as she thought of the wonderful disaster that she and Daphne were going to cause.

"And all of that money," her father went on, "probably twenty thousand dollars, is going to go to the paediatric section of the hospital. The same place that saved Sam's life."

Oh, no. Oh, *no*. Anastasia's heart sank. Her heart sank and her stomach churned. A whole plateful of spaghetti began to *move* inside her stomach. She felt first hot and then cold. Her hands began to sweat.

"Holy Moley," she said under her breath. "Excuse me, Dad."

She ran to the ladies room. Four dollars and ninety-five cents' worth of spaghetti with sausages and mushrooms. Right down the drain.

10

It was too late. It was just too late, and Anastasia knew it, but she called Daphne anyway, on Sunday afternoon, after she had recovered from being sick.

She had thrown up four times on Saturday. Her parents blamed it on the sausage in the spaghetti. You could never tell, her mother said, what people put into sausage. She had heard rumours about dead cats and ground-up tennis shoes. Anastasia's father threatened to call the Board of Health, but he couldn't remember the name of the restaurant.

Anastasia knew it wasn't the sausage anyway. The sickness had started in her brain and her heart – and in her conscience – and had worked its way down, very quickly, to the sausage, which was an innocent bystander.

By Sunday afternoon her stomach felt okay. But her conscience was terminally ill.

"Jeez," said Daphne on the phone, after Anastasia had explained, "there's nothing we can do now. I don't even know the names of any of the people I gave invitations to. The only thing I can think of is to phone in a bomb threat so the party will be cancelled."

"No good. I think that's a federal offence. If we get caught, we'd go to prison. I'm already nervous enough about making friends in class 8. Imagine what prison would be like. I can't think of one single thing to say to a bank robber or an axe murderer."

"Anyway," Daphne pointed out, "we don't want the party cancelled. Then the hospital wouldn't get the twenty thousand dollars."

"Right," said Anastasia. "The party has to be held. But we'll have to try to keep it from being a disaster. Forget about humiliating your grandmother."

"Yeah. We'll just keep an eye on all the weird guests. Keep them from making awful scenes. If the drunk guy starts getting drunk . . ."

"Or the dope dealer starts trying to sell drugs . . ."

"Or if that crazy lady comes with her bag full of dog food . . ."

"We'll just ask them to leave," said Anastasia.

"Politely," said Daphne.

"But firmly," said Anastasia.

"And quietly," said Daphne, "so my grandmother never knows what's going on."

"Then the party will be a success," said Anastasia, beginning to feel relieved.

"And the hospital will get its money," said Daphne, "and we won't get into trouble."

"Daphne," said Anastasia, "I really wish we hadn't dreamed up this idea in the first place."

"I know the feeling," said Daphne. "I feel that way about most of my crazy ideas. Usually by then it's too late."

Sam's homecoming on Monday was something of a disappointment to Anastasia. She had expected to meet the car when her mother drove in, to help carry Sam up to his bed, to sit there with him and read him stories, to feed him custard – maybe even soft-boiled eggs – and say soothing words. But she should have known better. Sam had been driving the nurses crazy for two days now with his high spirits, good health and energy. Ever since his mother brought him the feather, he had worn it Scotch taped to his bald head and had pulled Bald Eagle commando raids in the corridors of the paediatric ward. There had even been, the nurses told Anastasia's mother, a terrible collision involving a bedpan.

They all adored Sam, they said at the hospital. But they were awfully glad he was well enough to go home.

Now he climbed exuberantly out of the car, wearing his little blue jeans, with a baseball cap on his head, and carrying an armful of aeroplane books. So much for Anastasia's fantasy about having an invalid for a brother. The invalid came noisily through the back door, dropped his books on the kitchen floor, and demanded a SpaghettiOs sandwich for lunch.

Anastasia had seen too much of spaghetti in various stages of digestion lately. She didn't think she could survive watching a SpaghettiOs sandwich being eaten.

"Welcome home, Sam," she said. "I cleaned up your room for you."

"Did you mess up my stuff?" he asked.

"Nope." She had left a pile of blocks and a half-constructed castle on the floor, some mysterious Tinker Toy objects that might have been aeroplanes on his little table, and a long line of Matchbox cars running from one side of the room to the other. "I should have, though," she said. "You've messed up *my* stuff often enough."

Rats, thought Anastasia, and felt guilty. She had made a solemn vow that if Sam got well, she would never be cross with him again. Now he hadn't been home five minutes, and she had already made a grouchy remark. In her entire life, she thought, she had probably made at least four hundred solemn vows, and she had never been able to keep a single one of them.

I am definitely Lacking in Character, thought Anastasia.

Then and there she made a solemn vow that she would keep Mrs Bellingham's party from turning into a disaster so that the hospital where Sam had been fixed up would get its twenty thousand dollars. Never before had she made a solemn vow involving so much money. This solemn vow she would keep, she thought, and the size of it would make up for the four hundred others.

Still, she was not about to watch Sam eat a SpaghettiOs sandwich. It was almost time to go to work, anyway.

"See you later, guys," she said to her mother and to Sam. "I'm off to wax the Bellingham antiques."

By seven P.M. on Wednesday, the antiques were waxed, the rugs were shampooed, the books were dusted, the silver was polished, the caterers were busy in the kitchen with the food and the orchestra was tuning its instruments on the terrace. Anastasia had been picked up at home by the chauffeur, because she wasn't allowed to ride her bike at night. Daphne was there, wearing a blue silk dress. There were no devilled eggs. Chinese lanterns were hanging outside, lighting the terrace and the gardens. A photographer from the newspaper was loading his camera with film, and in the study a bartender had set up a bar with so many bottles that it looked like the Ritz.

Mrs Bellingham came down the staircase dressed in a flowing gown sewn with tiny pearls, and her hair piled on top of her head.

"Anastasia," she said. "You—"

"I know, Mrs Bellingham," Anastasia interrupted. "I'm to pass the *hors d'oeuvres*, and ask people if they would like another drink, and pick up empty plates and glasses and take them to the kitchen. Mrs Fox has already told me."

Mrs Bellingham smiled. "I'm sure she did. And I know you'll do everything perfectly, because you've been very conscientious about every job you've been given, ever since you began work. I'll miss you, after this evening."

Tonight was to be Anastasia's last night of work. School would begin next week.

"Could you come over tomorrow, Anastasia, to be paid? Things will be so hectic this evening," Mrs Bellingham went on.

Anastasia nodded.

"As it happens, dear, you interrupted me," said Mrs Bellingham. "I wasn't going to tell you what to do tonight. I was going to tell you that you look beautiful. Very grown up."

"Oh," said Anastasia, startled. "Thank you." She was wearing her very best dress, new shoes, and tiny silver earrings. She had *felt* beautiful, at home, when she got dressed. Her mother and father had said that she looked beautiful. But it was kind of nice to hear Mrs Bellingham say it. Parents always said stuff like that even when it wasn't true, so you couldn't entirely trust them. She smiled after Mrs Bellingham, who had gone on into the living room to rearrange the cushions for the millionth time, and made the solemn vow again that she would keep the party from being a failure.

Two hours later, the party was not yet a disaster. But

Anastasia's nerves were. Things weren't going the way she had expected them to.

First of all, she hadn't been able to recognize any of the special guests that she and Daphne had invited. She had thought that they would be very visible because of their clothes. The invitation had said "black tie". She knew that, because Daphne had told her. That meant that the official guests – the rich guests – would be wearing tuxedos, at least the men would, and the women would be wearing evening gowns.

She had thought that it would be very easy to recognize the town drunk, in his stained and rumpled clothes. And the dog-food lady in her many layers of unmatched dresses and stockings. And the drug dealer in his ragged jeans.

But there was only one man wearing anything like jeans, and that was a tall, slender man in a denim jumpsuit with sequins decorating the pockets. Anastasia had thought for a minute that he must be the drug dealer, wearing his dressiest outfit, and that she should go over and (politely, firmly, quietly) ask him to leave, before he tried to peddle some marijuana, maybe to the mayor or something.

She had made her way over to where he was standing, pretending that she was going to offer him some mushrooms stuffed with crabmeat. But just as she approached, a grey-haired woman in a black satin dress swooped down on the man.

"Lester!" she had cried. "I've caught you at last! I have a potential client I want you to meet!" She took his hand and pulled him over to another woman, who was sipping champagne.

Good grief, thought Anastasia. He's going to make a sale right here, practically publicly, right in front of a twelve-year-old maid. If my parents hear about this, I'll be killed.

"Darling," the woman in black was saying to the other woman, "this is Lester, the *best* decorator in Boston!"

"And the most expensive," said Lester haughtily as he shook hands.

Anastasia had leaned against the wall, unnerved. What if she had asked the best decorator – and the most expensive – in Boston, politely, firmly and quietly, to leave? She felt sick to her stomach just thinking about it.

She had realized, then, that she must make her moves very, very carefully. She must be completely certain that she was kicking out the right people. But it was so hard to tell. Not all of the men were wearing tuxedos; some were in ordinary suits. The women were in all kinds of outfits, not just evening gowns; some wore strange pants – one was even in chiffon knickers – and some were wearing plain short dresses. Almost any one of them could have come from the low-income housing project. There was no way to tell.

And they were all ages. She had thought that she would recognize the guys who hung out in the park smoking pot – even if they weren't wearing their ragged jeans – because they were young. But there were many young people here. The most humiliating moment of the evening so far had been when a young man – college-student age – had politely asked Anastasia if she would like to dance.

In her entire life no one (except Robert Giannini, at a square dance once, and that didn't count. Robert Giannini, of all people. At a *square* dance, for Pete's sake) had ever asked Anastasia to dance. Now it was actually happening. And the guy was as handsome as a movie star. The orchestra was playing something romantic, and there was an almost full moon. It was the worst moment of Anastasia's entire existence.

"I can't," she mumbled.

"You mean you don't know how? Come on, it's easy," he said, smiling at her.

"No," she said, agonized. "I mean I'm the maid." And she ran away.

Anastasia kept passing the endless trays of mushrooms, chicken livers and cheeses, wondering what she should do. Suddenly she spotted, standing against the wall, someone who looked vaguely familiar. He was standing alone, wearing a very ordinary suit, apparently half asleep, drinking a drink.

She watched him. As she watched, he gulped down that last of his drink, set the glass on a table, and went to the bar for another. He came back to his place against the wall and stood there, drinking sleepily again. Anastasia was quite certain that she recognized him. But she had never seen him dressed in a suit and tie before.

He has to be the drunk who sleeps on the pavement near the barber shop, she thought. And if I don't kick him out, he's going to slump to the floor, sound asleep and *drunk*, and ruin Mrs Bellingham's party.

I will be polite, she said to herself. And firm. And quiet. I will say, I'm sorry, sir, but you're going to have to leave now.

She rehearsed it in her mind. I'm sorry, sir, but you're going to have to leave now. I'm sorry, sir, but you're going to have to leave now.

But when she walked over to him, she didn't say it. Instead, she said politely, "Hello."

He stared at her for a moment, and then smiled. "You look familiar," he said. "I'm sorry, but I can't remember your name."

That was weird. She shouldn't look familiar to him. It was supposed to be the other way around. She recognized him because she'd seen him sprawled on the pavement. But he had never seen her. He'd always been asleep.

"My name is Anastasia Krupnik," she said, "and you look familiar to me, too." And she said to herself once more: I'm sorry, sir, but you'll have to leave now. But she couldn't make herself say it aloud.

"Krupnik," he said suddenly. "Of course. I should have remembered. You're Sam's big sister. How's he doing?"

Anastasia was stunned. How on earth did the town drunk know Sam?

"He's fine," she said, puzzled. "He has a scar on his head, but when his hair grows back you won't even be able to see it."

"Of course not," the man said, smiling. "I stitched it very carefully."

Then she knew. The man wasn't the town drunk at all. He was the surgeon who had operated on Sam.

She wanted to sink through the floor and disappear. What if she had actually said to him, I'm sorry, sir, but you'll have to leave now? What if she had taken his arm (firmly, quietly) and tried to propel him to the door.

"Excuse me," Anastasia said. "I have to pass food. I'm the maid."

Then she went to the bathroom to recover. Daphne was just coming out. They looked at each other.

"Big trouble," said Daphne. "I've just thrown up."

"Why? Have you been drinking champagne or something?"

"No," said Daphne, but she looked stricken. "I've just blown the whole thing. Ruined the party."

"I *almost* did, myself," said Anastasia miserably. "What did you do?"

"I've spent the whole last hour trying to work out who is who. I couldn't even recognize the people I gave the invitations to."

"I know. I've been doing the same thing."

"And *finally* I thought I recognized one."

"Me too. But I was wrong."

"I bet you weren't as wrong as I was," said Daphne.

"I bet I was," said Anastasia. Sam's surgeon. Good grief. It made her cringe to think of it.

"I saw this man, and he looked familiar . . ."

"Yeah. I know."

"So I watched him for a while. And he was talking and talking, telling some long dull story with no point to it. Everyone around him was trying to be polite, but you could tell they were all bored and wished they could get away from him. And I *knew* I'd seen him before."

"Yeah," said Anastasia sympathetically. "I know the feeling."

"Then I noticed that his suit jacket was buttoned wrongly. You know, he had the wrong button in the wrong buttonhole, so it was all bunched up down the front. And there were other clues, too. He was wearing a Red Sox button in his lapel. Nobody in his right mind would wear a Red Sox button to a black-tie party, right?"

Anastasia groaned. "Right. So what did you do?"

"I went up to him and said very politely, the way we practised, 'I'm sorry, sir, but you'll have to leave now'."

"What did he do?"

"He just looked at me for a minute. *Everybody* looked at me. There was a hideous silence. Then he said" – Daphne drew herself up, tucked her chin against her neck, and imitated a deep, pompous voice – "'Young lady, who do you think I am?'"

Anastasia groaned again. "What did you say?"

"Well, he *asked*. So I told him the truth, about what I thought. I said, politely and firmly . . ."

"And quietly?"

"Not quietly enough. Everybody heard me. I said, 'I think you're a deinstitutionalized psychotic'."

"And he wasn't," said Anastasia. But she already knew that he wasn't.

"No," said Daphne, "he definitely wasn't."

"Who was he?"

Daphne took a deep breath. "He was the mayor," she said.

11

Anastasia woke up the next morning with the sense that she had had a bad dream. Then she remembered. It hadn't been a bad dream at all. It had been real.

The mayor had sputtered and glowered and sought out Mrs Bellingham to ask *who* this obnoxious child was. And it was Daphne.

Mrs Bellingham had demanded an explanation from Daphne, who had excused herself and run to the bathroom to throw up. That was when Anastasia discovered her there and heard what had happened.

They had talked briefly about the possibility of running away together, maybe joining a circus or something. Hitchhiking to Hollywood, perhaps, where Daphne could achieve stardom with her dramatic talents, and Anastasia could be her manager.

But none of it seemed very practical, and besides, there was Mrs Bellingham, suddenly standing over them.

"Anastasia," she said, "you can go on back to the party and continue your duties. I have something to discuss with Daphne."

It was her chance to flee. But she couldn't.

"Mrs Bellingham," she said, "you may as well discuss it with me, too. Because I was just as involved as Daphne."

"It was my idea, though," Daphne pointed out.

"*What* was?" asked her grandmother. "What *is* going on? You two girls come with me right now into the study and explain this to me."

So they did. They had no choice.

Funny, though, that it wasn't too hard explaining what they had done. Daphne even got into being dramatic about it, imitating the lady with the bag of dog food and the drunk on the pavement receiving their invitations to the black-tie party. Mrs Bellingham's lips twitched, as if she wanted to laugh.

The hard part – the *impossible* part – was explaining *why* they had done it.

"I was cross," said Daphne hesitantly, "because you gave me a doll for my birthday."

Mrs Bellingham looked puzzled. "But it was a beautiful doll, Daphne," she said. "I bought it at—"

"Grandmother," Daphne interrupted angrily, "I'm *thirteen* years old."

"Mrs Bellingham," Anastasia said so that Daphne

wouldn't have to take all the blame, "I was cross too. Because when I was looking for a job, I wanted to be a *Companion*, and you made me into a *maid* without even asking me."

"I see," said Mrs Bellingham, and Anastasia could tell that she was *trying* to see. But also that she didn't, really.

There was a silence. Then Mrs Bellingham said slowly, "Why didn't you tell me? Both of you. Daphne, why didn't you explain to me about the doll? And Anastasia, why didn't you come to me and explain your dissatisfaction? You were always so courteous and hard-working that I had no idea you were angry."

Anastasia thought for a minute. Then she said, "Because I was scared of you, Mrs Bellingham."

And Daphne said, "Me too, Grandmother. I was scared of you."

Mrs Bellingham looked startled.

Anastasia suddenly felt very, very sorry about the whole thing. Not because she had been caught. And not because the party had been ruined. But because Mrs Bellingham looked so surprised and so sad.

"Well," said Mrs Bellingham, "I think I'll have the chauffeur run both of you girls home. Anastasia, don't forget to come over tomorrow for your money."

"Mrs Bellingham, I don't think I deserve to be paid," said Anastasia. And she meant it. But it felt terrible, saying it. All of those hours of work for no pay.

"Nonsense. You worked hard, and you did a good job, even tonight. Come over about ten tomorrow morning."

"Grandmother," said Daphne, "I don't mind being sent home. In fact, I *want* to go home, because my stomach hurts. But what about the party?"

"What do you mean, what about the party? The mayor seems to have simmered down. The party will continue without your presence, Daphne."

"But Grandmother," Daphne said meekly, "all of the people whom we invited are still out there somewhere. The dog-food lady, and the drunk, and the psychotics, and the low-income people, and . . ."

Her grandmother sighed. "Daphne," she said, "surely it is apparent by now that those people, whatever their problems, know how to behave at a party. Which is more than I can say for you at the moment."

Then she led both girls through the back hall to the kitchen door and instructed the chauffeur to take them home.

Anastasia lay in her bed and remembered it all. She felt awful. Even her goldfish wouldn't look at her. He swam with his tail turned towards her.

"Well, the hospital got its money, anyway," she said belligerently to Frank, the goldfish. But he only twitched his tail. He wouldn't turn around.

How humiliating, to be snubbed by your own goldfish.

After a while she sighed, got up, pulled on some old clothes, and went downstairs. Her parents were drinking coffee in the kitchen, and Sam was running a toy truck around the floor.

"Hi!" said her mother. "How was the party? You went to bed so fast last night that I didn't have a chance to ask you. You must have been exhausted."

"I was." Anastasia poured some milk over a bowl of cornflakes and began to eat. "The party was okay."

Some day she would have to tell them the truth about it. Not now, though. Maybe when she was thirty or something.

"I have to go over to Mrs Bellingham's pretty soon and collect my pay."

Sam looked up from his truck. "Can I come?"

"No," said Anastasia. But then she began to think. Maybe it would help, having Sam along. Maybe Mrs Bellingham wouldn't say too much if Sam was there.

"Well, maybe," she said. "Mum, may I take Sam with me? Did the doctor say Sam could go out?"

Her mother hesitated. "He can go out. But not on the back of your bike, Anastasia. It's too risky. We're supposed to keep him from bumping his head."

"*Mum*, I haven't had a wreck on my bike since I was *nine*."

"I know. But still, it's just too dangerous."

"Well, I'll walk. It's only a mile or so. I'll take Sam in his pushchair, okay?"

"Yeah," said Sam. "In my pushchair! Can I go? Can I?"

"Well," said his mother. "Okay. If you're careful."

"I will be," said Sam. "I'll be careful. I told Mrs Flypaper I'd be careful."

Anastasia, her mother and her father all groaned. They were sick of hearing about Sam's imaginary friend.

Sam just grinned and went off to find his Indian feather.

As they approached the gate to Bellmeadow Farm, Anastasia detached the feather from Sam's head.

"You can't wear that here, Sam," she said, "because I want the lady to think we're very respectable. I won't be able to explain to her about Bald Eagle. She wouldn't understand."

"Okay," said Sam agreeably.

"Now, when I introduce you to her, I want you to shake her hand. Okay?"

"Okay," said Sam.

"And say 'How do you do, Mrs Bellingham'. Can you say that?"

Sam giggled. "How do you do, Mrs Bellybutton," he said.

"SAM! Don't you dare! I'll clobber you if you say that! Now say it right."

"How do you do, Mrs Bellingham," Sam said dutifully.

Anastasia pushed the pushchair to the back door, lifted Sam out, and rang the doorbell. "Now, don't forget," she whispered to her brother.

Mrs Bellingham came to the door herself.

"Good morning, Anastasia," she said.

"Good morning. This is my brother, Sam. Sam, this is Mrs Bellingham." She watched Sam carefully to be sure he behaved properly.

"How do you do," said Sam, and held out his little hand. Then he looked up and stared at Mrs Bellingham. His eyes widened. Anastasia nudged him. "How do you do, *Mrs Bellingham*," she reminded him in a whisper.

But he wasn't listening. He was grinning at Mrs Bellingham. And she was grinning back at him.

"It's brave Bald Eagle!" she exclaimed, and reached down to pick Sam up. "Where's your feather, Chief?"

"Mrs Flypaper!" cried Sam happily, and threw his arms around her neck.

Good grief, thought Anastasia. This is what I thought it would be like, being Mrs Bellingham's Companion. Here I am, sitting in her study, like a real human being instead of a maid, drinking iced tea brought in on a tray by Mrs Fox. And there's Sam, drinking orange juice out of a silver cup, which I won't have to polish.

And there was Mrs Bellingham, stirring sugar into her tea with something that looked very like a bockle, and smiling like a real human being, too.

"You see, Anastasia," she was explaining, "I work as a volunteer in the paediatric ward of the hospital. I never know the children's last names, because I don't read their charts. That's why I didn't know Sam was your brother.

"All the volunteers wear pink smocks," she went on. "I wear a name tag on mine, but of course a lot of the youngsters aren't old enought to read . . ."

"*I* am," said Sam smugly. "I can read 'areoplane'."

"So some of the little ones just call me Pinky. It's easier to remember than Mrs Bellingham."

"Mrs Bellybutton." Sam giggled.

"*Sam*!" hissed Anatasia.

But Mrs Bellingham was laughing. "Good old Sam," she said. "He doesn't like to do what everyone else does. When I suggested that he call me Pinky, he made a face . . ."

Sam scrunched up his nose and eyebrows. He stuck out his tongue. It was one of his standard yuck-I-don't-want-to-do-that faces.

"Right," Mrs Bellingham laughed, watching him. "It was that face exactly. Then he said that he would call me Mrs Flypaper. Don't ask me why."

"Because you made one for me," Sam explained. "You zoomed it across the room."

For a moment Mrs Bellingham looked puzzled. Then she brightened. "The paper aeroplane! I made him a paper aeroplane!"

"Yep," said Sam. "A flypaper. I zoomed it right into your behind, remember?"

Mrs Bellingham blushed. "I believe it was my *hip* you hit, Sam, not my – ah, my behind."

She looked at Anastasia, who had been watching the two of them in amazement. "*Sam* isn't afraid of me," she said. "Are you Sam?"

Sam was busy folding an envelope he had found on Mrs Bellingham's desk. "Nope," he said. "Because I love you."

"Mrs Bellingham," said Anastasia, "Daphne loves you, too. I know she does. It's just that she's growing up. And it isn't *easy* to grow up. Life gets very complicated when you're thirteen."

"Yes," said Daphne's grandmother thoughtfully, "I suppose that's true. Daphne and I will have to work things out. We'll have to talk.

"Anastasia," she added, "I haven't told your parents about last night. I had to tell Daphne's, I'm afraid. But I'll leave it to you to tell your own."

"I will," said Anastasia. When I'm thirty, she thought.

"Look!" said Sam suddenly. "I made a flypaper all by myself!" He launched the folded envelope and it sailed across the room, coming to rest on top of the set of Henry James.

"Anastasia," said Mrs Bellingham, "that was your pay that just zoomed by your nose."

Later that afternoon, while Sam was taking his nap, Daphne called.

"Anastasia," she said dramatically, "this is the last time you'll hear my voice until school starts next week."

"Why?"

"Because I'm practically in solitary confinement. I got permission to make one phone call – even criminals are allowed to make one phone call before they go to prison.

"But after this I'm restricted to the house. And no phone calls. No nothing, until school."

"Because of last night?"

"Of *course* because of last night. I practically ruined my grandmother's reputation and everything."

"But, Daphne," said Anastasia, "you told me that your parents were very forgiving. They let you do anything!"

"Yeah, that used to be true. But my father really blew his stack over this. They almost sent me off to reform school."

"*Reform school*?"

"Well, boarding school. Same thing. But I cried so much they changed their minds. And I said I was sorry, and promised to do well in school this year, and everything."

"Were you acting when you said it?" asked Anastasia.

Daphne hesitated, as if she was thinking. "Actually, no," she said finally. "I really was sorry. And I really do want to do well in school for a change. Trouble is, I'm not sure I remember how. I'm used to making trouble."

"What happens if you get into more trouble?"

"Boarding school for sure." Daphne moaned. "Probably one with bars on the windows."

"Well, Daph," said Anastasia, "I'll tell you what. I'll be your watchdog when school starts. I'll keep reminding you all the time to stay out of trouble."

"You will? Promise?"

"Sure. And I'll pester you to join the Dramatic Club and to try out for plays, okay?"

"Okay. And, Anastasia . . ."

"What?"

"If I start thinking up sinister schemes or anything, *stop me.* Will you do that?"

Anastasia laughed. "Atcher service," she said.

Anastasia at This Address

Anastasia was going to write to SWM, 28, boyish charm, inherited wealth, looking for tall young woman, nonsmoker, to share Caribbean vacations, re-runs of *Casablanca*, and romance.

Anastasia was only thirteen, but fifteen years didn't seem too much of an age difference, she was sure she would be on the same wavelength as SWM, and she was *definitely* ready for romance.

But Anastasia has to prepare herself for a humiliating meeting when SWM unexpectedly decides to pay a visit...

£3.50

Order Form

To order direct from the publishers, just make a list of the titles you want and fill in the form below:

Name ....
Address ....
....
....
....

Send to: Dept 6, HarperCollins Publishers Ltd, Westerhill Road, Bishopbriggs, Glasgow G64 2QT.

Please enclose a cheque or postal order to the value of the cover price, plus:

UK & BFPO: Add £1.00 for the first book, and 25p per copy for each additional book ordered.

Overseas and Eire: Add £2.95 service charge. Books will be sent by surface mail but quotes for airmail despatch will be given on request.

A 24-hour telephone ordering service is available to Visa and Access card holders: 041-772 2281